1928

YANKEE STADIUM

World's Championship Games

Important | **GAME**

Read notice and warning on reverse side of this ticket.

1

DO NOT DETACH
this coupon from

RAIN CHECK

WORLD'S NATIONAL LEAGUE

READ the notice printed on reverse side of attached coupon.

WORLD'S 1928 SERIES

Ihret Kurpert
President

M.B. BROWN PTG & BDG CO. N.Y.

BALL GAME

TODAY

— AT THE —

YANKEE STADIUM

BKLYN. 00000000 000
YANKS 00010100 250
9/25/08
Happy Birthday
Jeremy! The
Big 15! Enjoy
the book we have great
memories here.
Love, mom

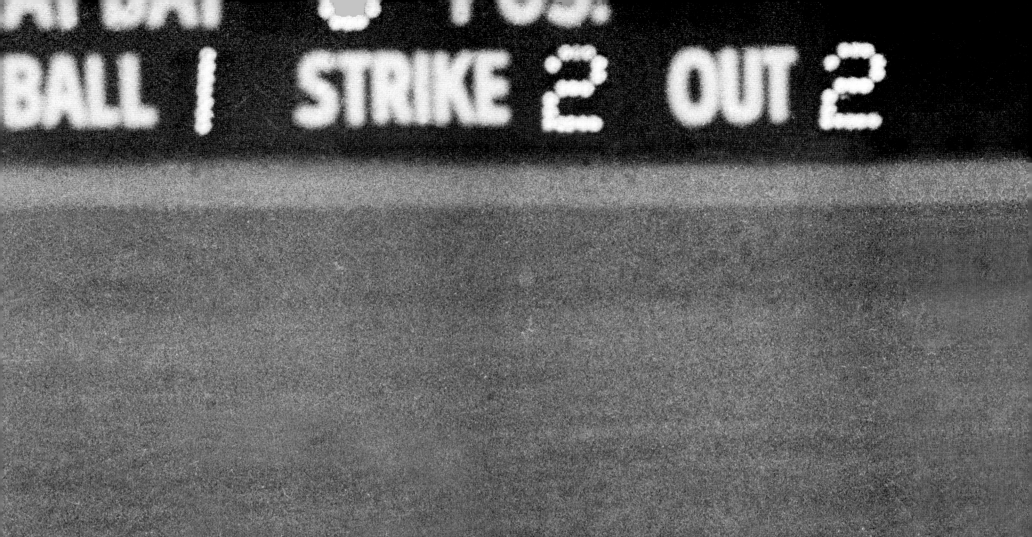

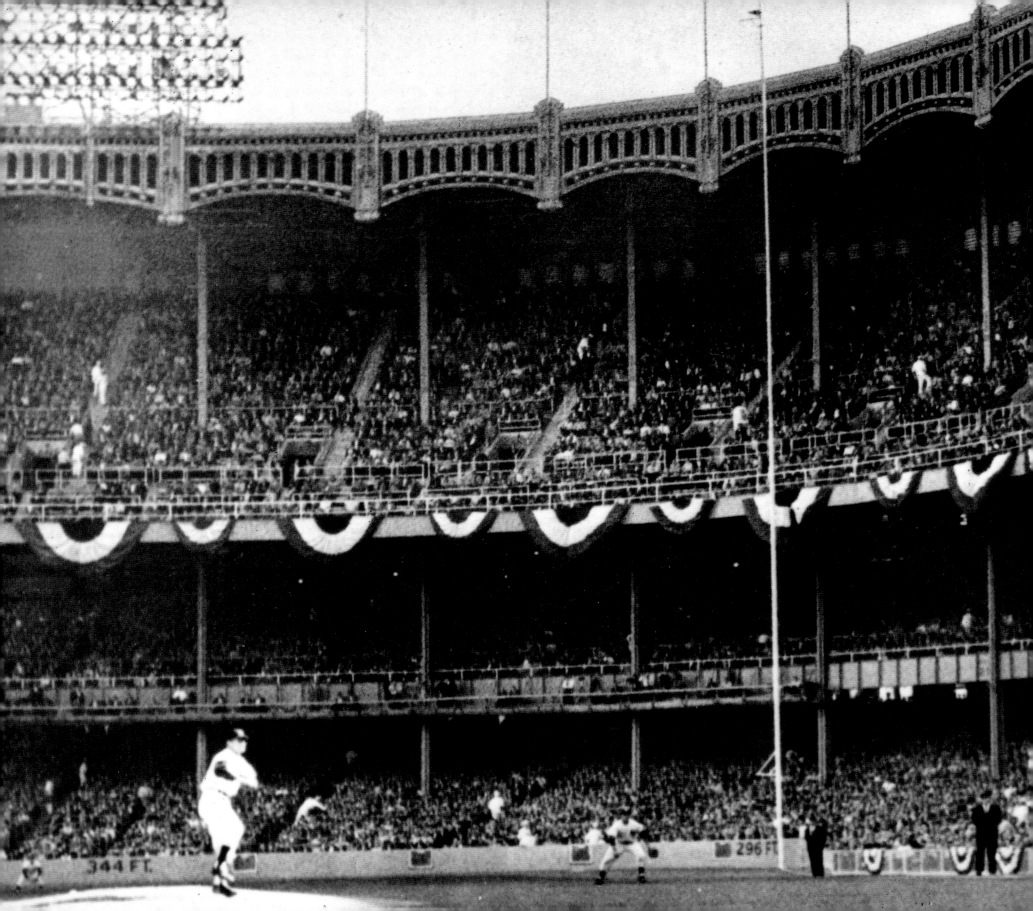

REMEMBERING YANKEE STADIUM

— *AN ORAL AND NARRATIVE HISTORY OF* —

THE HOUSE THAT RUTH BUILT

HARVEY FROMMER

STEWART, TABORI & CHANG | NEW YORK

DESIGNED BY THINK STUDIO, NYC

Published in 2008 by Stewart, Tabori & Chang
An imprint of Harry N. Abrams, Inc.

Library of Congress Cataloging-in-Publication Data

Frommer, Harvey.
 Remembering Yankee Stadium : an oral and narrative history of "the house that Ruth built"
/ by Harvey Frommer.
 p. cm.
 ISBN 978-1-58479-716-6
 1. Yankee Stadium (New York, N.Y.)--History. 2. Sports--New York (State)--New York--History. I. Title.

GV416.N48F76 2008
796.357068747'1--dc22
 2007045888

Editor: Kristen Latta
Designer: Think Studio, NYC
Production Manager: Jacquie Poirier

Printed and bound in China.
10 9 8 7 6 5 4 3 2 1

harry n. abrams, inc.
a subsidiary of La Martinière Groupe

115 West 18th Street
New York, NY 10011
www.hnabooks.com

What visions burn, what dreams possess him, seeker of the night.
The packed stands of the stadium,
the bleachers sweltering with their unshaded hordes,
the faultless velvet of the diamond.
The mounting roar of 80,000 voices and Gehrig coming to bat.

—THOMAS WOLFE

FOREWORD
BY BOB SHEPPARD

"Good afternoon, ladies and gentlemen. Welcome to Yankee Stadium." It's hard to believe that almost 60 years have passed since I first delivered this greeting to Stadium fans. When I joined the Yankees, I never imagined that I would be the public address announcer for thousands of games of baseball played on these hallowed grounds. How many have I done? "Is it 4,000? 5,000?" I have been asked. "Do you remember?" I can't.

While I wasn't a part of the Yankees during the Ruth-Huggins-Gehrig era, I've been privileged to announce the names of almost all of the great baseball stars of the past half century. Considering that my public address announcing career has been an avocation, an accompaniment to my career as professor of public speech, I find this most remarkable. Not a small accomplishment for one who arrived at Yankee Stadium as a New York Giants baseball fan!

From the old days when Bronx cheers bounced off the Stadium's copper facade to recent times when the Stadium's visage is DiamondVision and the sounds of "We Will Rock You" are part of the scene, Yankee Stadium has been the citadel of sport. Where in one place could so many baseball icons display their rare talents with such regularity? Where else could I have viewed the transformation of Yankee fans from the jacket-and-tie cognoscenti of the 1950s to today's bleacher creatures?

The public address announcer's chair has afforded me a virtual front-row seat to 23 World Series and dozens of playoff contests; to Mickey Mantle's and Reggie Jackson's towering home runs; the brilliance of Joe DiMaggio's final year; the magic of Don Larsen's and David Cone's perfect games; Roger Maris' 61st homer clouted under tremendous pressure from both press and fans; the nimble play of Phil Rizzuto, Bobby Richardson, Elston Howard, Willie Randolph, Graig Nettles, and Scott Brosius; the crackling sliders of Whitey Ford and Sparky Lyle; the dazzling sinkers of Mel Stottlemyre; the sublime fastballs of Ron Guidry, Rich Gossage, and Mariano Rivera; the perseverance of Yogi Berra, Gil McDougald, Lou Piniella, Paul O'Neill, and Bernie Williams; the steady leadership of Thurman Munson and Don Mattingly; and the sheer pleasure of watching Derek Jeter blossom from raw rookie into classic Yankee champion.

From what better perch could I have observed the strategic and individual brilliance of Casey Stengel, George Weiss, Ralph Houk, Lee MacPhail, Gabe Paul, Billy Martin, Gene Michael, and Joe Torre?

Sitting in my catbird seats, first in the loge along the third-base line and now from the press box behind home plate, I've witnessed the Stadium go from brown and green to white and blue. This grand cathedral of baseball has given me treasured memories, not the least of which is seeing several generations of Yankee fans.

As author Harvey Frommer, in these pages, brings the story of Yankee Stadium's past to us in its full and vivid glory, I'll reflect upon my own privileged past with this extraordinary organization and the hope that I will be remembered as an announcer who carried the dignity and the style of the Yankee organization and the tradition of this magnificent Stadium through clear, concise, correct spoken words.

I'm not the guy who says: "Time to rumble." Rather than a barker, a rooter, a screamer, or a cheerleader, I have always aspired to be in harmony with the Yankee gestalt.

My greatest wish is that the new Yankee Stadium brings yet another four score and five years of cherished and exciting memories to new generations of Yankee fans.

THE
VOICES

SPARKY ANDERSON, Baseball Hall of Famer, is the only manager to lead a team from each league (the Cincinnati Reds and the Detroit Tigers) to a world championship. He played for the Philadelphia Phillies in 1959.

DENNIS R. ARFA, owner of Artist Group International Talent Agency, is a fervent and longtime Yankee fan.

ELI S. BELI, research and marketing director for Scholastic, *Playboy*, and *Bon Appetit*, is a well-known figure in New Jersey politics and a longtime Yankee fan.

JOHNNY BLANCHARD, Yankee catcher and outfielder in the late fifties and sixties, was a potent backup throughout his career.

MICHAEL BOLTON, a famed songwriter and entertainer, has performed at Yankee Stadium.

STEPHEN BORELLI is an editor on the baseball desk at *USA Today* and the author of *How About That!: The Life of Mel Allen*.

JIM BOUTON was a Yankee pitcher from 1962 to 1968 and a sports anchor for the New York station WABC-TV. He is the author of *Ball Four*.

BOBBY BROWN, American League president from 1984 to 1994, played in 548 regular-season games and four World Series as an infielder for the New York Yankees.

ROD CAREW, Baseball Hall of Famer, was a longtime Minnesota Twin and later a California Angel. Rookie of the Year and an All-Star virtually all the seasons of his career, he grew up near Yankee Stadium.

ANDY CAREY, New York Yankee third baseman from 1952 to 1960, was signed as a "bonus baby" and became a key performer.

DON CARNEY, a Major League Baseball producer-director, was on the scene of New York Yankee baseball for more than three decades, beginning in the early years of television with WPIX-TV.

JOE CARRIERI was a Yankee batboy from 1949 to 1955. He is an attorney with the New York firm Carrieri and Carrieri and the author of *Searching for Heroes: The Quest of a Yankee Batboy* and *The Promise*.

CHRIS CARTER is a longtime Yankee fan and host of the Los Angeles–area radio show *Breakfast with the Beatles*.

BILL CHUCK of B. Czar Productions, Inc., and Billy-Ball of Billy-Ball.com, is the author of *Walk-offs, Last Licks, and Final Outs: Baseball's Grand (and Not So Grand) Finales*.

FRED CLAIRE, former executive vice president and general manager of the Los Angeles Dodgers, authored *My 30 Years in Dodger Blue*.

RUSS COHEN is a writer and lifelong fan of the New York Mets. He is part-owner and director of communications of www.sportsology.net.

JERRY COLEMAN, Baseball Hall of Famer, Ford C. Frick Honoree, and broadcaster for the San Diego Padres, was a Yankee infielder from 1949 to 1957.

GENE CONLEY had an 11-year career as a major league pitcher with the Boston Red Sox and other teams; he also played for the Boston Celtics.

JOEY COOPERMAN is a longtime Yankees fan and photographer.

DON CRONSON, a sports agent for 33 years and Yankee zealot, is currently in financial management.

MARIO CUOMO, longtime Yankee fan, was the governor of New York State for three terms and a minor league outfielder in the Pittsburgh Pirates organization in 1952.

PHILLIP DEMERSKY, the service manager of BMW Manhattan, is a longtime Yankee fan.

BARRY DEUTSCH is a banking consultant and longtime Yankee fan.

PAUL DOHERTY is partner at CESD: Cunningham· Escott·Slevin·Doherty Talent Agency in Los Angeles and New York. He is the world's number one Bob Sheppard fan and has been a devout Yankee fanatic since August 10, 1972.

MICHAEL DUKAKIS, governor of Massachusetts for two terms and Democratic presidential candidate in 1988, is a longtime Red Sox fan and Yankee-watcher.

SAL DURANTE was a truck driver from Brooklyn when he caught the ball that Roger Maris hit for his 61st home run. He lives in Staten Island.

DENNIS ECKERSLEY, Baseball Hall of Famer, pitched in the major leagues for 24 years as a starter and a reliever. He is studio analyst on NESN for the Red Sox.

ROB EDELMAN, author of *Great Baseball Films*, teaches film history at the State University of New York at Albany.

JONATHAN EIG, author of *The Luckiest Man* and *Opening Day*, writes for the *Wall Street Journal*.

DWIGHT EVANS played all but one of his 20 major league seasons with the Red Sox.

TONY FERRARO was a New York Yankee batting-practice pitcher for many years.

DAVE "BOO" FERRISS was a pitcher for the Red Sox from 1945 to 1950, a pitching coach for the Red Sox from 1955 to 1959, and a pitching coach for Delta State University until his retirement in 1988.

ROLLIE FINGERS, Baseball Hall of Famer, was one of the great relief pitchers in baseball history. In his 17-year career in the majors, he pitched for Oakland, San Diego, and Milwaukee.

RED FOLEY was a *New York Daily News* sportswriter and Yankee Stadium press-box fixture for many years.

WHITEY FORD, Baseball Hall of Famer, was a standout Yankee pitcher for 16 seasons as well as a coach and broadcaster.

BILL GALLO, famed cartoonist for the *New York Daily News*, is a longtime sporting-scene observer.

RUDY GIULIANI was mayor of New York City and is a longtime Yankee fan.

DICK GROAT, five-time All-Star infielder in the fifties and sixties, played primarily for the Pittsburgh Pirates and appeared in two World Series at Yankee Stadium.

RALPH HOUK was a Yankee player, manager, and executive. He also managed the Tigers and the Red Sox.

FRANK HOWARD was a power hitter for four major league teams and a talent evaluator for the Yankees.

JEFF IDELSON is president of the National Baseball Hall of Fame and Museum and a former public relations director for the Yankees.

MONTE IRVIN, Baseball Hall of Famer, was a great star in the Negro League and played for the New York Giants in the fifties.

ROGER KAHN, renowned author of the classic *The Boys of Summer* and other notable reads, is a longtime astute observer of the sporting scene.

BOB KEANEY is the baseball historian for the North Shore Spirit team of Lynn, Massachusetts, an avid Red Sox fan, and an involved observer of the Yankees.

GEORGE KELL, Baseball Hall of Famer, was a third baseman for 15 seasons for several clubs but primarily the Tigers, and enjoyed a long tenure as a radio play-by-play announcer for the team.

MIKE KILKENNY was a Yankee Stadium vendor.

JACK LANG was a New York City baseball writer for many years.

DON LARSEN was a major league pitcher whose greatest career accomplishment was pitching a perfect game for the Yankees in the 1956 World Series.

EDDIE LAYTON was the Yankee Stadium organist from 1967 to 1970, and from 1978 until his retirement in 2003.

BILL LEE was a major league pitcher primarily in the 1970s for the Red Sox. He is the author of four books, including *The Wrong Stuff*.

GARY LEFKOWITZ is a genuine Yankee fan who has attended many games at the Stadium.

EDDIE LOPAT pitched in the major leagues for a dozen seasons, mainly with the Yankees, and managed the Kansas City Royals for the 1963 and 1964 seasons.

PATRICK MACKIN is a Yankee fan currently at work on a biography of Snuffy Stirnweiss.

RICH MARAZZI is the author of *Baseball Players of the 1950s*, an ESPN radio personality, and a longtime Yankee fan.

DAN MARENGO is a lifelong Yankee fan from the Bronx.

DICK McAULIFFE was a standout Tiger infielder.

BOBBY MURCER, a major league outfielder from 1965 to 1983, mainly with the Yankees, is a longtime broadcaster for the team.

DAN McCOURT is a longtime Yankee fan who has seen many games at Yankee Stadium.

SAM MELE was a Red Sox outfielder, part of the legendary trio that also included Dom DiMaggio and Ted Williams, and manager of the Minnesota Twins.

JON MILLER is an acclaimed and long-tenured ESPN baseball announcer and San Francisco Giants broadcaster.

PAUL MOLITOR, Baseball Hall of Famer, was a major league infielder and designated hitter for 21 seasons, mainly with the Milwaukee Brewers.

LEIGH MONTVILLE was a columnist at the *Boston Globe* and is a senior writer at *Sports Illustrated*. He is the author of *Ted Williams* and *The Big Bam*.

TRACY NIEPORENT, marketing director for the Myriad Restaurant Group, is a highly astute follower of the New York sports scene and an avid Mets fan.

BILL NOWLIN is the author of some 20 books on the Red Sox and is vice president of the Society for American Baseball Research.

BERT PADELL was a Yankee batboy in 1949 and 1950 and is currently a financial consultant.

MEL PARNELL, star hurler for the Red Sox in the forties and fifties, is a longtime participant in the Yankee–Red Sox rivalry.

CHRIS PAVIA, a loyal Yankee fan, has long been fascinated by Stadium audio, especially Eddie Layton's organ music and Bob Sheppard's announcements.

MARVIN POLANSKY, a retired New York City assistant principal, grew up in Brooklyn but has vivid memories of his times at Yankee Stadium.

FRANK PRUDENTI was a Yankee batboy from 1956 to 1961. He is the author of *Memories of a Yankee Batboy*.

PEDRO RAMOS was a pitcher for the Yankees and other major league teams.

JIM REISLER is the author of *Babe Ruth: Launching the Legend*, *The Best Game Ever*, and other baseball books.

BOBBY RICHARDSON starred as a Yankee infielder and is currently a national leader in the Fellowship of Christian Athletes.

ARTHUR RICHMAN, formerly a New York City sportswriter, has been a longtime vice president of public relations for the Yankees.

PHIL RIZZUTO, Baseball Hall of Famer, was a Yankee shortstop in the forties and fifties. He subsequently enjoyed a long career as broadcaster for the team.

BROOKS ROBINSON, Baseball Hall of Famer, was a third baseman for the Baltimore Orioles.

HERB ROGOFF, illustrator for magazines, books, album covers, TV, and films, is editor and publisher of the monthly baseball magazine *One More Inning*.

FRANK RUSSO wrote *Bury My Heart at Cooperstown*. He is a longtime, ardent Yankee fan.

JAY SCHWALL owns Invirex, the Long Island–based construction company that did demolition work on Yankee Stadium in late 1973 and early 1974.

BOB SHEPPARD has been the cultured and informed "Voice of Yankee Stadium" since 1951.

PAUL SHEPPARD is the son of Bob Sheppard and a longtime Yankee fan. He is first vice president—investments at Smith Barney in Bethesda, Maryland.

DUKE SIMS was a catcher in the majors for 11 seasons with five teams. As a member of the Yankees, he hit the last home run before the Stadium closed for renovation in 1973.

PHIL SPERANZA, has been a genuine Yankee fan for many years and is the creator of BehindtheBombers.com.

BOB SULLIVAN is executive editor of *Life* magazine and editorial director of Life Books.

SETH SWIRSKY is a hit songwriter, a recording artist, author of the best sellers *Baseball Letters* and *Every Pitcher Tells a Story*, and a renowned baseball memorabilia collector. His web site is Seth.com.

STEVE SWIRSKY is a lifelong Yankee fan and a Long Island–area businessman.

RON SWOBODA, a major leaguer for nine years, played parts of his last three seasons with the Yankees. He is a baseball broadcaster in New Orleans.

SUSAN TUCKER was a vice president at Citicorp. She is a devout Yankee Fan.

BRAD TURNOW is an elementary school teacher and webmaster of UltimateYankees.com.

BILL VIRDON, a longtime major league center fielder, was Yankee manager in 1974 and 1975.

BILL WERBER played for the Yankees and other major league teams in an 11-year career that spanned the forties and fifties. He is the author of *Memories of a Ballplayer*.

MICHAEL WISE is a columnist for the *Washington Post* and was formerly a *New York Times* sportswriter.

BOB WOLFF, Baseball Hall of Famer and Ford C. Frick Honoree, is a longtime broadcaster.

CHAPTER

TWENTIES

Jacob Ruppert always insisted, "Yankee Stadium was a mistake—not mine, but the Giants'." And in truth, had it not been for the Giants, there might never have been a Yankee Stadium. Beginning life as the Baltimore Orioles in 1901, the franchise moved to Manhattan in 1903 at the prodding of league president Ban Johnson, who was determined to have American League representation in New York City.

	YEAR	POSITION	WON	LOST	PCT.	MANAGER	ATTENDANCE
	1920	THIRD	95	59	.617	MILLER HUGGINS	1,289,422
	1921	FIRST	98	55	.641	MILLER HUGGINS	1,230,096
	1922	FIRST	94	60	.610	MILLER HUGGINS	1,026,134
	1923*	FIRST	98	54	.645	MILLER HUGGINS	1,007,066
	1924	SECOND	89	63	.586	MILLER HUGGINS	1,053,533
	1925	SEVENTH	69	85	.448	MILLER HUGGINS	697,267
	1926	FIRST	91	63	.591	MILLER HUGGINS	1,027,675
	1927*	FIRST	110	44	.714	MILLER HUGGINS	1,164,015
	1928*	FIRST	101	53	.656	MILLER HUGGINS	1,072,132
	1929	SECOND	88	66	.571	HUGGINS/ART FLETCHER	960,148

YANKEES YEAR BY YEAR 1920 – 1929

*WORLD CHAMPIONS

The relocated club, named the Highlanders, played at Hilltop Park in Washington Heights for a decade. In 1913, now known as the Yankees, the team became tenants of the New York Giants at the Polo Grounds. It was a very unsatisfactory arrangement. The landlord Giants and the tenant Yankees never got along.

On January 11, 1915, Colonel Jacob Ruppert and Colonel Tillinghast L'Hommedieu Huston paid $460,000 to purchase the Yankees. They had wanted to acquire the Giants, but the Giants were not for sale. The Yankees, on the other hand, mismanaged for years by co-owners professional gambler Frank Farrell and ex-police commissioner Bill Devery, were on the block.

"It was an orphan club," Ruppert said, "without a home of its own, without players of outstanding ability, without prestige." In truth it was a team whose average annual attendance was 345,000 and whose dozen-year record was a mediocre 861 wins and 937 defeats. But Jake Ruppert, the man they

would later call "master builder in baseball," would change all that.

On January 3, 1920, in a move that changed baseball history, Babe Ruth, a month short of 25, was purchased from the Red Sox. In his first season as an everyday player in 1919 with Boston he established a single-season home run record with 19. In 1920 he shattered that record, blasting 54 homers for the third-place Yankees.

In 1921 the Yanks won their first American League pennant. In 1922, they would win it again.

Fans, in Babe Ruth's word, were coming out in "droves." Yankee manager Miller Huggins explained: "They all flock to Babe Ruth because the American fan likes the fellow who carries the wallop." Ruth's Yankees were a magnet, drawing more than a million each season from 1920 to 1922. Never had the Giants drawn a million fans. Angered and annoyed at the gate success of Babe Ruth and company, the Giants told the Yankees to look around for other baseball lodgings.

Ruppert and Huston suggested that the Polo Grounds be demolished and replaced by a 100,000-seat stadium to be used by both teams as well as for other sporting events. Nothing came of the suggestion.

So the duo set about to create a new ballpark. Shaped along the lines of the Roman Colosseum, it would be the greatest and grandest edifice of its time. Many sites and ideas were considered. One idea was to build atop railroad tracks along the

West Side, near 32nd Street. The site of the Hebrew Orphan Asylum, at Amsterdam Avenue and 137th Street, was a serious contender. Long Island City in Queens also was given consideration.

Finally, on February 6, 1921, a little more than a year after the Yankees had acquired Ruth from the Red Sox, a Yankees press release announced that 10 acres in the western Bronx, City Plot 2106, Lot 100, land from the estate of William Waldorf Astor, had been acquired for $675,000 (just under $8 million in 2007 dollars). The site sat directly across the Harlem River, less than a mile from and within walking distance of the home of the New York Giants, at the mouth of a small body of water called Crowell's Creek.

Some noted that the site was strewn with boulders and garbage. Others criticized the choice as being too far away from the center of New York City. Some dubbed the plan "Ruppert's Folly," believing that fans would never venture to a Bronx-based ballpark.

"They are going up to Goatville," snapped John J. McGraw, manager of the Giants. "And before long they will be lost sight of. A New York team should be based on Manhattan Island."

Ruppert never publicly responded to McGraw's criticism. But he did request newspapers to print the address of Yankee Stadium in all stories. And for the first game at his new baseball palace, he included on each ticket stub: "Yankee Stadium, 161st Street and River Avenue."

Design responsibilities for the new "yard" were handed over to the Osborn Engineering Company of Cleveland, Ohio. The White Construction Company of New York was awarded the construction job, which Huston oversaw. Ever demanding

and meticulous, Ruppert mandated that the massive project be completed "at a definite price" of $2.5 million (about $29 million in 2007 dollars) and by Opening Day 1923.

Ground was broken on May 5, 1922. Sixteen days later, Ruppert bought out Huston's share of the Yankees for $1.5 million. "The Prince of Beer" was now sole owner, a driven and driving force behind the vision of the new home.

A millionaire many times over, Ruppert enjoyed giving orders and having them followed to the letter. He lived at 1120 Fifth Avenue in Manhattan, in a 15-room town house. He also had a castle on the Hudson.

Some thought his new baseball park should be named "Ruth Field." Ruppert, however, was adamant that it be known as "Yankee Stadium." It would be the first ballpark to be referred to as a stadium.

Original architectural plans called for a triple-decked park roofed all the way around. An early press release explained that the new ballpark would be shaped like the Yale Bowl, enclosed with towering embattlements, making all events inside "impenetrable to all human eyes, save those of aviators." Those without tickets would be unable to catch even a glimpse of the action.

However, that initial lofty design was quickly scaled down. It was thought that those plans would create a foreboding sports facility, too much a tower and not a place to play baseball, a place where the sun would shine only when overhead. Instead, the triple deck would stop at the foul poles.

And Jacob Ruppert notwithstanding, action on the field of play would be visible from the elevated trains that passed by the outfield, from the 161st Street station platform as well as from roofs and higher floors of River Avenue apartment houses that would be built.

Fortunately, a purely decorative element survived the project's early downsizing. A 15-foot-deep copper frieze would adorn the front of the roof that

covered much of the Stadium's third deck. It would become the park's signature feature.

The new stadium's field, virtually double the size of almost any existing ball park, favored left-handed power: the right-field foul pole was only 295 feet from home plate (though it would shoot out to 368 by right center). The left- and right-field corners were only 281 feet and 295 feet, respectively, but left field sloped out dramatically, to 460 feet. Center field was a monstrous 490 feet away.

A quarter-mile running track made of red cinders that doubled as a warning track for outfielders surrounded the field. Under second base, a 15-foot-deep brick-lined vault containing electrical, telephone, and telegraph connections was put in place for boxing events.

Three concrete decks extended from behind home plate to each outfield corner. There was a single deck in left center and wooden bleachers around the rest of the outfield. The new stadium had the feel of a gigantic horseshoe. The 10,712 upper-grandstand seats and 14,543 lower-grandstand seats were fixed in place by 135,000 individual steel castings on which 400,000 pieces of maple lumber were fastened by more than 1 million screws. Total seating capacity was 58,000, enormous for that time.

The Yankee bullpen was in left center. The Yankee dark green dugout was on the third-base side. Bats were lined up at the top of the dugout stairs. There was a record eight toilet rooms for men and as many for women.

On Wednesday, April 18, 1923, "The House That Ruth Built" opened for business. It had been constructed on almost the same spot where baseball had begun in the Bronx, a place where the Unions of Morrisania had played and close to where the old Melrose Station of the Harlem Railroad was located. The original street address was 800 Ruppert Place.

"Governors, general colonels, politicians, and baseball officials," the *New York Times* reported, "gathered solemnly yesterday to dedicate the biggest stadium in baseball."

True to Jake Ruppert's mandate and vision, "The Yankee Stadium," as it was first called, had been constructed at a cost of $2.5 million in just 185 working days.

The reaction to the newest playing field in the major leagues was over the top. A Philadelphia newsman declared: "It is a thrilling thought that perhaps 2,500 years from now archaeologists, spading up the ruins of Harlem and the lower Bronx, will find arenas that outsize anything that the ancient Romans and Greeks built."

Opening Day was, appropriately, Red Sox versus Yankees. A massive crowd assembled for the most exciting moment in the history of the Bronx. The day was chilly. Many in the huge assemblage were bundled up with heavy sweaters, coats, fedoras, and derbies, although some, in the spirit of the moment, wore dinner jackets.

The announced attendance was 74,217, later scaled back to 60,000. The Fire Department ordered the gates closed, and 25,000 were denied entrance. Those unable to get inside soldiered up outside against the cold, listening to the noise of the crowd and the martial beat of the Seventh Regiment Band, directed by the famed John Philip Sousa.

Red Sox owner Harry Frazee walked on the field side by side with Jake Ruppert, who always claimed that his idea of a great day at the ballpark was when "the Yankees scored eight runs in the first inning and then slowly pulled away." The Yankees and the Red Sox were escorted by the band to the flagpole in deep center field, where the home team's 1922 pennant and the American flag were raised.

Ruppert then took a seat in the celebrity box, where baseball commissioner Kenesaw Mountain Landis, New York State governor Al Smith, and New York City mayor John Hylan were waiting for the game to begin.

At 3:25 Babe Ruth was presented with an oversized bat handsomely laid out in a glass case.

At 3:30 Governor Al Smith tossed out the first ball to Yankee catcher Wally Schang.

At 3:35 home plate umpire Tommy Connolly shouted "Play ball!"

The temperature was a brisk 49 degrees. Wind blew dust from the dirt road leading to the Stadium and whipped away at pennants and hats.

ABOVE: The 1923 Yankees, the first team to play in Yankee Staadium

In the third inning, with Whitey Witt and Joe Dugan on base, George Herman "Babe" Ruth stepped into the batter's box. He had said "I'd give a year of my life if I can hit a home run in the first game in this new park." Boston pitcher Howard Ehmke threw a slow pitch. Bam! Ruth slugged the ball on a line into the right-field bleachers—the first home run in Yankee Stadium history.

The *New York Times* called it a "savage home run that was the real baptism of Yankee Stadium."

Sportswriter Heywood Broun remarked "It would have been a home run in the Sahara Desert."

Crossing home plate, removing his cap and extending it, Ruth waved to the standing, screaming crowd.

LEIGH MONTVILLE: Babe Ruth always said that of all the home runs he hit, his favorite home run was the one he hit the day they opened Yankee Stadium, the ballpark that was kind of built for him.

The game moved on. Yankee stalwart "Sailor" Bob Shawkey, a red sweatshirt under his jersey, fanned five, walked two, allowed just three hits, and pitched the Yankees to a 4–1 victory.

On April 22 the first Sunday game at Yankee Stadium was played, before a crowd of 60,000. The Yankees lost to the Washington Senators and Walter Johnson, 4–3. Two days later President Warren G. Harding attended the Yankee-Senator game, where Babe Ruth's homer paced the 4–0 New York win in the first shutout at the Stadium.

That first season at their new stadium, the Yankees drew 1,007,066—tops in the American League. Posting a 98–54 record, they finished 16 games in front and won their third straight pennant.

For the third year in a row the World Series competition for the Yankees was their old landlords, the Giants of John J. McGraw. The Yanks had been winless

in their last nine World Series games against the Giants, having lost eight and tying in the other.

McGraw announced that he would follow his usual practice of calling all the pitches thrown to Ruth. "Ballplayers can do a more workmanlike job when they feel someone else is taking the responsibility," he said.

The pugnacious pilot of the New York National League team would not permit his team to use the Yankee Stadium visitors' clubhouse. Instead, all Giant players dressed in their Polo Grounds clubhouse in Manhattan and then, in full uniform, took cabs across the Harlem River over the Central Bridge to Yankee Stadium.

Games alternated between Yankee Stadium and the Polo Grounds with the first, third, and fifth taking place at "The House That Ruth Built." They featured the initial and primitive World Series broadcast on a nationwide radio network, with Graham McNamee and baseball writers taking turns describing the action.

Yankee Stadium's first World Series game was played on October 10, 1923. Autumn's afternoon sun created odd mosaic designs on the grass in center field, interfering with the vision of outfielders. The umpires for that Series were Billy Evans (AL), Hank O'Day (NL), Dick Nallin (AL), and Bob Hart (NL).

The Yankees jumped out to a 3–0 lead, but Heinie Groh tripled in a couple of runs, capping a four-run third for the National Leaguers. In the top of the ninth, salty Casey Stengel hit a changeup thrown by Joe Bush for the first Yankee Stadium World Series homer, an inside-the-park shot.

"His arms flying back and forth like those of a man swimming with a crawl stroke," Damon Runyon wrote in the *New York American,* "his flanks heaving, his breath whistling, his head far back. Yankee infielders...say Casey was muttering to himself, adjuring himself to greater speed as a jockey mutters to his horse, saying, 'Go on Casey, go on.'

"The warped old legs, twisted and bent by many a year of baseball campaigning, just barely held out under Casey until he reached the plate, running his home run home. Then they collapsed."

The 33-year-old Stengel's homer gave the Giants a 5–4 victory, enabling John McGraw's team to draw first blood. The Yankees had now lost eight consecutive Series games to the Giants.

In game two, at the Polo Grounds, Ruth was the difference for the Yankees. Going deep in the fourth (over the right-field roof) and in the fifth, he gave Herb Pennock all the offense he needed. The Yanks won 4–2.

Like two fighters in close proximity and intense competition, the teams moved back and forth from their home ballparks. The third game of the World Series was at Yankee Stadium. Art Nehf bested Sad Sam Jones in a nail-biter, 1–0, to put the Giants up, two games to one. After taking game four at the home field of the Giants, 8–4, the Yankees scored eight runs in game five, at Yankee Stadium. They were within one win of becoming world champs.

Game six was played at the Polo Grounds on October 15, before 34,172. It was Herb Pennock for the Yankees against Art Nehf for the Giants. Nifty Nehf led 4–1 after seven innings. The Yankees, however, broke the game open in the top of the eighth, helped by three walks and a two-run single by Bob Meusel. The five runs scored that inning put the game away for the Yanks. Sad Sam Jones in relief allowed but one hit and no runs, shutting down the Giants.

It was the first world championship for the Yankees. It was also the first World Series million-dollar gate ($1,063,815). The three games played at Yankee Stadium drew 55,307, 62,430, and 62,817. The Yankees took home a winner's share of $6,160.46; the Giants, $4,112.81—big change for that time.

The star of stars of that 1923 fall classic was the Sultan of Swat. Homering three times in 19 times at bat, he also tripled, doubled, singled twice, and batted .368. John J. McGraw had his pitchers walk the Babe eight times, intentionally or unintentionally.

With the first year of Yankee Stadium now in the books, with the Yankees atop the world of baseball, property values all over the area of "The House That Ruth Built" skyrocketed. New parking lots, a small theater, restaurants, and bars opened. Drugstores installed lunch counters. The nearby Concourse Plaza Hotel, dedicated that October, thrived as home to visiting players and Yankees, who were often seen in the lobby. The *Bronx in Tabloid* newspaper noted that the new hotel would "enable the social life of the borough to assemble amid luxurious surroundings, in keeping with its prestige as the sixth greatest city in the country."

The dirt roads on Walton and Girard Avenues would be paved, and apartment houses with big foyers and elevators would line these wide avenues. And those who lived along Girard Avenue would bring chairs to the roofs of their building and watch games.

From the start Yankee Stadium attracted pigeons who took up residence in the rafters and beams and swiftly became fat and wobbly from peanuts and popcorn.

Billboards also were always part of the scene: "Ever-Ready Sterilized Shaving Brushes" at the base of the bleachers in left center, "Gem Razors" in right center. Advertising signs stood atop the bleachers.

A grass slope rose up to the outfield walls from foul pole to foul pole. Babe Ruth in right field and other outfielders, as a matter of course, backed up the small hill going after fly balls. There was a single manually operated, wooden scoreboard above the bleachers in right-center field that gave the scores for games of all major league teams for up to 12 innings. Other new and improved boards would come and go through the years, but that was the first at the Stadium, and fans marveled at it.

They also marveled at Jack Lenz, Yankee Stadium's first public address announcer, who made known the starting lineups and the goings-on of note. He was aided by a big cheerleader's megaphone and a very loud voice.

An asymmetrical "bloody angle" between the bleachers and the right-field foul line caused crazy bounces during the 1923 season. In 1924 it was eliminated when home plate was moved forward 13 feet and the deepest left-center corner was reduced from 500 to 490 feet.

May 24, 1924, was Babe Ruth Day, and he received his American League Most Valuable Player award for his splendid work the previous season, when he hit .393 with a league-leading 41 home runs and 131 RBIs. The St. Louis Browns ruined the show, trashing the Yanks, 11–1, and holding the Big Bam to a single.

It seemed on August 29th that many of the 30,000 fans at the Stadium were rooting against the home team. They seemed to be rooting on the Senators and their ace, Walter Johnson. He shut out the Yanks for seven innings and was taken out in the eighth inning when a liner grazed his pitching hand. Washington notched a 5–1 win.

No one really took note of it, but on June 1, 1925, a young lad pinch-hit for Pee Wee Wanninger at Yankee Stadium. The next day first baseman Wally Pipp groused about a headache, and as the story goes, was told by Miller Huggins to take a couple of aspirins. The youngster replaced Pipp at first base. But it was his pinch-hitting the day before that began the monumental 2,130 consecutive-games-played streak for Lou Gehrig.

In 1926, three-year-old Yankee Stadium was the site of game one of the fourth World Series appearance for the Yankees in six years. Their opponents, the Cardinals of St. Louis, were in the fall classic for the first time. A crowd announced at 61,658 clogged the aisles. Thousands more followed the game in downtown Manhattan on two giant scoreboards. Behind Herb Pennock's three-hit pitching, the Yankees clipped the Cardinals, 2–1.

St. Louis won the next game at the Stadium. Then the Series jockeyed back and forth, setting up a seventh-game showdown on an overcast October 10 at Yankee Stadium. Only 38,093 were in the stands. In the seventh inning, the Yankees loaded the bases. St. Louis clung to a 3–2 lead. With two out, Cardinal player-manager Rogers Hornsby called for veteran Grover Cleveland Alexander to face rookie Tony Lazzeri, who had gone hitless against the 39-year-old hurler the day before.

Reports were that after pitching complete-game victories in games two and six, Alexander was recuperating from too much partying.

"The bullpen in Yankee Stadium," Alexander explained, "was under the bleachers then, and when you're down there you can't tell what's going on out in the field only for the yells of the fans overhead. There was a telephone in the only real fancy, modern bullpen in baseball. Well, I was sitting around down there not doing much throwing. The phone rang and an excited voice said 'Send in Alexander.'

"So I come out from under the bleachers. I see the bases full and two out and Lazzeri standing at the box. Tony is up there all alone with everyone in that Sunday crowd watching him. So I just said to myself, 'Take your time, Lazzeri isn't feeling any too good up there and let him stew.'"

The first pitch—a curve. Lazzeri swung and missed. The next pitch—a curve. Lazzeri swung and hit a line drive into the left-field seats—foul ball. Then an overanxious Lazzeri swung and

MEZZANINE &
UPPER STAND
ADMISSION UNRESERVED

Number 5006
Ticket $3.00
Tax .30
Total $3.30

YANKEE STADIUM 1923
World's CHAMPIONSHIP Games
American League vs Nat'l League

GAME 3
RAIN CHECK
Retain this Coupon
In event of postponement account of RAIN it will be good for one admission whenever this game is played.
Jacob Ruppert
President

M. B. Brown Ptg. & Bdg. Co. N Y

WORLD'S CHAMPIONSHIP 1923 GAMES 1923 at YANKEE STADIUM
GAME 3
Important Read notice and warning on reverse side of this ticket.
DO NOT detach this coupon from RAIN CHECK.
Jacob Ruppert President

missed—strike three. Alexander breezed through the eighth.

In the ninth inning he got the first two outs, walked Babe Ruth, and watched as the dangerous Bob Meusel came up.

"If Meusel got hold a one it could be two runs and the Series," Alexander said. "So I forgot all about Ruth and got ready to work on Meusel. On my first pitch, the Babe broke for second. I caught the blur of Ruth starting for second as I pitched, and then came the whistle of the ball as catcher Bob O'Farrell rifled it to second. I wheeled around and there was one of the grandest sights of my life: Hornsby, his foot anchored on the bag and his gloved hand outstretched, waiting for Ruth to come in. There was the Series."

Through the seasons there was always some tinkering and tweaking of the Stadium. The seating capacity at Yankee Stadium was 62,000 in 1927, when Jake Ruppert reduced the price of the 22,000 bleachers seats from 75 to 50 cents. Dimensions that year were 281 feet to the left-field line, 415 feet to deeper left, 490 feet to left center, 487 feet to center, 429 feet to right center, 344 feet to deeper right, and 295 feet down the right-field line. Behind home plate there were 82 feet.

"The big parade toward Yankee Stadium started before noon yesterday," was the way Peter Vischer described Opening Day 1927 in the *New York World*. "Subways brought ever-increasing crowds into the Bronx. Taxicabs arrived by the hundreds. Buses came jammed to the doors. The parade never stopped."

BOB SHEPPARD: I went a bit in my early teens to Yankee Stadium with a group of fellows from my neighborhood in Queens. And believe it or not, the one player who played first base for the St. Louis Browns caught my eye—his name

LEFT: World Series time and fans are jammed into the big ballpark

was George Sisler. Left-handed, graceful, and a phenomenal hitter. And since I was a first baseman myself, I thought "That's my idol: George Sisler."

The man who would become an idol of Japanese baseball fans, Babe Ruth gave some of their navy officers a thrill in the spring of 1927. Their ships were docked in New York Harbor and some of the officers were invited to the Bronx as guests of the Yankees. Babe Ruth popped two homers, one a bases-loaded job. The officers were much taken with the huge slugger; they had never seen anyone before hit a baseball the way the Babe did.

Seven years later, in 1934, when the Sultan of Swat tooled about in Japan, he was a superhero. Some called him the "Father of Japanese Baseball." Other called him "Baby Roos!" And it all started at Yankee Stadium.

It all started for Bill Werber at Yankee Stadium, too.

BILL WERBER: The great Yankee scout Paul Krichell gave me a good deal to become a member of the Yankees after my freshman year at Duke in 1927. I had a uniform and a locker by myself. I stayed downtown at the Colonial Hotel with a coach by the name of O'Leary. I took the train uptown and got off across from the Stadium at the 161st Street stop. It was maybe a half an hour ride.

Yankee Stadium was enormous. It was immaculate. I was somewhat awed. I was told by Paul Krichell to stay as close to the manager, Miller Huggins, as I could. Sometimes I was very close. He was really hands on. He didn't miss a trick.

The clubhouse didn't have any food, and there wasn't anything to drink other than water. The secretary, Mark Roth, used to come in and place an envelope on the seat in front of every player's locker. One of the players would usually get Ruth's envelope, slit it open, and paste the check, which was for about $7,500 on the mirror where the fellows combed their hair. The Babe was usually the last player to arrive for a game, and he would take the check off the mirror and put it in his pocket and take it out onto the field with him.

I was a stranger in their territory. They were rough, a hard-nosed, tobacco-chewing crew. If I got in at shortstop to field a ball in batting practice they would run me out. Some player would say, "Get out of here, kid." When I would go to the outfield, some player would yell: "Get out of here kid." And I never had a chance to get into the batting cage.

The whole experience in 1927 was not that much of a thrill for me. After I was there for about a month, I told Mr. Barrow, the general manager, that I had made a bad decision and I was leaving the Yankees. One that I felt bad about leaving was Pete Sheehy; he was a good fellow, not much older than me, maybe younger.

RON SWOBODA: Pete Sheehy had started in the clubhouse as a boy working with the 1927 Yankees. He told me how Babe Ruth would come in and say: "Petey, give me a bi [bicarbonate of soda]."

A Yankee culture created by manager Miller Huggins was always in place. The little pilot was like a schoolteacher, training each member of the team. Players had to report for games at 10:00 A.M. at the Stadium—to sign in, not to practice, a move designed to reduce late-night ribaldry. Backslapping was frowned upon, as were flamboyant displays, noisemaking, and razzing of opponents.

The 1927 Yankees were a symbol of their time: power and dash. But a rival to their throne was Charles Lindbergh, the daring aviator who had flown solo round-trip across the Atlantic.

On June 16th he was scheduled to be an honored guest at the Stadium. Three field boxes were painted and primed for him and other dignitaries. Extra police patrolled the aisles all over the park. But as game time approached, there was no "Lucky Lindy."

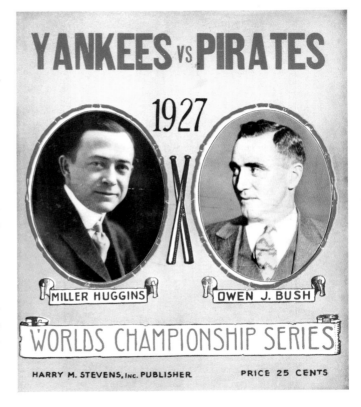

Fifteen thousand fans who'd come to see the game with the St. Louis Browns were antsy. Umpire George Hildebrand held up the first pitch for almost half an hour. Finally, at 3:55 P.M., he decided he could wait no more and yelled, "Play ball!"

"I feel a homer coming on," Babe Ruth said. "My left ear itches. That's a sure sign. I had been saving that homer for Lindbergh, and then he doesn't show up. I guess he thinks this is a twilight league."

In his first at-bat of the game, the Babe hit his 22nd homer, halfway up in the bleachers in left-center field. It came off 31-year-old southpaw Tom Zachary. The Bambino would hit a much more significant shot late in the season off that same Zachary.

The Yankees romped, 8–1, over the sad-sack Browns.

The next day's headline in the *New York Times* declared: "Lindbergh Got to Paris on Time but Was More Than an Hour Late to See Babe Ruth Hit a Home Run Yesterday."

Yankee manager Miller Huggins was fond of saying "We'd beat you in the late innings if not before."

Waite Hoyt, in G. H. Fleming's *Murderers' Row,* recalled, "Almost every day whether we were behind or in front, before our time at bat in the eighth, Earle [Combs] came trotting in from center field yelling, 'C'mon, gang. Five o'clock lightning, five o'clock lightning!'"

OPPOSITE: The Iron Horse, Lou Gehrig, hitting away

The colorful phrase referred to the eruption of Yankee power in the late innings to put games away. But it also referred to the five-o'clock blowing of a factory whistle close by Yankee Stadium, signaling the workday's conclusion.

At workday's conclusion, Lou Gehrig would dress quickly and leave. But Babe Ruth would hang around, shooting the breeze with reporters and other players. The way the two Yankee superstars kept their lockers, which were just a few feet apart, said a lot about them. Gehrig's was orderly, Ruth's disorderly. Telegrams, letters, powders, salves, and toiletries, as well as phonograph records of "Babe and You" overflowed the Sultan of Swat's locker.

On the Fourth of July 1927, a hot and humid day, the largest crowd in baseball history, 72,641, showed up for a Yankee doubleheader against the Washington Senators. There were 1,500 "deadheads," nonpaying types, on hand, too. Before the game, thousands had gathered outside the park seeking to buy standing-room-only tickets. Very few got the chance.

"The crowd ringed itself four and five deep at the back of the stand," wrote James R. Harrison in the *New York Times,* "intent on seeing the Yankees in action. Spectators overflowed into runways and aisles, forsaking comfort and safety, squishing themselves into 'The House That Ruth Built.'"

Yankee fans got what they came for: Yankee hitting power on display. The home team ripped Washington, 12–1 in the first game, and 21–1 in the nightcap. Lou Gehrig was ablaze. He smashed two homers in the first game and was not retired until his ninth and final at-bat of the doubleheader. Babe Ruth and Joe Dugan stroked five hits.

Washington may have been dumped that Fourth of July by the Yankees; however, St. Louis had been ravaged all season long, failing to win a single game in 21 attempts against the New York bashers. The hapless Brownies came into the Stadium on September 11 for their final meeting of the season, aching for a

win. They got the win, 6–2, and for the team's fans it was like they had won the World Series. For Ruth it was just another home-run day—number 50, the third time he had reached that mark. No other player had ever reached 50.

He ripped number 54 on September 18th at his home yard. A 10-year-old got the ball. He ran onto the field to have the Babe sign it. Always a soft touch for a kid, The Bambino obliged.

Obliging kids and pounding homers was the way of Ruth all through his Yankee Stadium years, but especially in 1927. On September 29 at Yankee Stadium he ripped numbers 58 and 59 off two different Washington pitchers, Hod Lisenbee and Paul Hopkins, respectively, both into "Ruthville," the right-field bleachers.

"The bullpen in Yankee Stadium was perched deep in left field and you couldn't even see how the game was going," hurler Paul Hopkins recalled. "Well, the call came down that they wanted me to relieve, and I could see that the Yankees had three men on base. I guess I would have been nervous if I knew who the next batter was. It was Babe Ruth with the bases loaded. The rest is history. I threw him a series of curveballs and he finally hit one into right field at least five rows in.

"The ball landed halfway up the right-field bleachers, and though there were only 7,500 eyewitnesses, the roar they sent up could hardly have been drowned out had the spacious stands been packed to capacity," John Drebinger wired the *New York Times.* "The crowd fairly rent the air with shrieks and whistles as the bulky monarch jogged majestically around the bases, doffed his hat, and shook hands with Lou Gehrig."

Hopkins had given up number 59. Hod Lisenbee was touched up for number 58. Game over, the home run ball he gave up in hand and dressed in street clothes, Lisenbee entered the Yankee clubhouse, wanting Ruth to sign it. The Babe did, even though he didn't even know who Lisenbee was.

On September 30 Tom Zachary, who had been homered against that season by the Babe, took the mound for the Senators. "I had made up my mind that I wasn't going to give him a good pitch to hit," he said.

Home run number 59 had been bashed with "Black Betsy." Now the reddish "Beautiful Bella" was in Ruth's hands as he stepped into the batter's box in the bottom of the eighth inning, score tied 2–2, one out. Mark Koenig had tripled and was on third. Ruth had singled twice in the game.

On a one-and-one count, the Babe reached for the ball and pulled it fair by about 10 feet into the first row of the stands near the right-field foul pole. Number 60!

"I don't say it was the best curve I ever threw, but it was as good as any I ever threw," Zachary said later. "I gave Ruth a curve, low and outside. It was my best pitch. The ball just hooked into the right-field seats, and I instinctively cried 'foul!' But I guess I was the only guy who saw it that way. If I'da known it was gonna be a famous record, I'da stuck it in his ear."

"Sixty!" Babe Ruth screamed in the clubhouse when the game was over. "Let's see some son of a bitch try to top that one!"

The talented Pittsburgh Pirates had the misfortune of being World Series competition for the 1927 Yankees, aka "Murderers' Row," the greatest

In the Yankee clubhouse, the atmosphere was atypical. Generally, the team was controlled. Now players shouted and danced.

"Well, friends," W. O. MacGeehan wrote in the *New York Herald Tribune,* "I hope you don't expect too much of a story out of me in regards to yesterday's game as I was too sleepy to watch what was going on."

Saturday, October 8th was a damp and dreary day. It had rained that morning. The Yankees and Pirates were tied, 3–3, in the bottom of the ninth. Pirate reliever John Miljas walked Earle Combs. Mark Koenig managed a bunt single. Up came

BABE RUTH — 60 HOME RUNS IN 1927

#	DATE	PITCHER	#	DATE	PITCHER	#	DATE	PITCHER	#	DATE	PITCHER
1	APRIL 15	HOWARD EHMKE	18	JUNE 7	TOMMY THOMAS	35	AUGUST 5	GEORGE SMITH	52	SEPTEMBER 13	JOE SHAUTE
2	APRIL 23	RUBE WALBERG	19	JUNE 11	GARLAND BUCKEYE	36	AUGUST 10	TOM ZACHARY	53	SEPTEMBER 16	TED BLANKENSHIP
3	APRIL 24	SLOPPY THURSTON	20	JUNE 11	GARLAND BUCKEYE	37	AUGUST 16	TOMMY THOMAS	54	SEPTEMBER 18	TED LYONS
4	APRIL 29	SLIM HARRISS	21	JUNE 12	GEORGE UHLE	38	AUGUST 17	SARGE CONNALLY	55	SEPTEMBER 21	SAM GIBSON
5	MAY 1	JACK QUINN	22	JUNE 16	TOM ZACHARY	39	AUGUST 20	JAKE MILLER	56	SEPTEMBER 22	KEN HOLLOWAY
6	MAY 1	RUBE WALBERG	23	JUNE 22	HAL WILTSE	40	AUGUST 22	JOE SHAUTE	57	SEPTEMBER 27	LEFTY GROVE
7	MAY 10	MILT GASTON	24	JUNE 22	HAL WILTSE	41	AUGUST 27	ERNIE NEVERS	58	SEPTEMBER 29	HOD LISENBEE
8	MAY 11	ERNIE NEVERS	25	JUNE 30	SLIM HARRISS	42	AUGUST 28	ERNIE WINGARD	59	SEPTEMBER 29	PAUL HOPKINS
9	MAY 17	RIP COLLINS	26	JULY 3	HOD LISENBEE	43	AUGUST 31	TONY WELZER	60	SEPTEMBER 30	TOM ZACHARY
10	MAY 22	BENN KARR	27	JULY 8	DON HANKINS	44	SEPTEMBER 2	RUBE WALBERG			
11	MAY 23	SLOPPY THURSTON	28	JULY 9	KEN HOLLOWAY	45	SEPTEMBER 6	TONY WELZER			
12	MAY 28	SLOPPY THURSTON	29	JULY 9	KEN HOLLOWAY	46	SEPTEMBER 6	TONY WELZER			
13	MAY 29	DANNY MACFAYDEN	30	JULY 12	JOE SHAUTE	47	SEPTEMBER 6	JACK RUSSELL			
14	MAY 30	RUBE WALBERG	31	JULY 24	TOMMY THOMAS	48	SEPTEMBER 7	DANNY MACFAYDEN			
15	MAY 31	JACK QUINN	32	JULY 26	MILT GASTON	49	SEPTEMBER 7	SLIM HARRISS			
16	MAY 31	HOWARD EHMKE	33	JULY 27	MILT GASTON	50	SEPTEMBER 11	MILT GASTON			
17	JUNE 5	EARL WHITEHILL	34	JULY 28	LEFTY STEWART	51	SEPTEMBER 13	WILLIS HUDLIN			

Babe Ruth trotted out the historic homer, touching each base carefully, doffing his cap several times to the 8,000 cheering fans. A double line of Yankees waited as he crossed home plate. Back on defense in the top of the ninth in "Ruthville," he got a kick out of the cheers and applause and handkerchief waving of his loyalists.

LEFT: Babe Ruth wallops his record 60th home run in 1927

OVERLEAF: What a difference a year makes . . . roster turns over from 1926 to 1927. Yankees go from runners-up to greatest team of all time.

baseball club ever, winners of 110 games and the pennant by 19 games.

The Yankees swept the first two games, in Pittsburgh. In the Bronx on Friday, October 7, lines for bleacher seats were already active at 5:00 A.M. That was five hours before the Stadium was to open.

There were 60,695 present, and they generated the largest gate to that point in time for a World Series game: $209,665.

The Yanks ripped the Bucs, 8–1, behind southpaw Herb Pennock, who pitched a perfect game into the eighth inning, finishing with a three-hitter.

Ruth. A wild pitch moved up the runners. Ruth was intentionally walked. Miljas bore down, fanning Gehrig and Meusel. Tony Lazzeri was next. Again, a wild pitch. Combs charged in from third base. The Yankees won 4–3, and had their World Series sweep.

The 1928 season was another powerhouse one for the Yankees. On September 9 a total of 85,265 were wedged into the Stadium as the Yankees swept a doubleheader from the Philadelphia A's. The Bombers went on to win the pennant and sweep the Cardinals in the World Series.

LEFT: Ruth crosses the plate in a 1927 World Series game
ABOVE: Earle Combs singles in a 1928 game

Poor weather postponed two Opening Day starting dates in 1929. On April 18 the Yankees finally opened against the Red Sox. Before the game, baseball commissioner Landis gave diamond-studded watches to each Yankee player to commemorate the 1928 Yankee world championship.

For the first time, the Yankees sported numbers on the backs of their uniform jerseys. They were assigned mainly for where a player batted in the lineup:

EARLE COMBS, 1

MARK KOENIG, 2

BABE RUTH, 3

LOU GEHRIG, 4

BOB MEUSEL, 5

TONY LAZZERI, 6

LEO DUROCHER, 7

JOE GRABOWSKI, 8

George Pipgras, number 14, was the starter, and Fred Heimach, number 17, got the win. In his first time at bat, the newly married Babe Ruth slammed a home run. Rounding second base, he doffed his cap to his bride, Claire, who smiled at him from the stands.

That last season of the 1920s had a tragic moment on May 19th. In the fifth inning of a game against Boston, a severe cloudburst dropped heavy rain. Fans scattered to exits. Many panicked. Two died, and 62 were injured. Yankee owner Jake Ruppert subsequently ended forever the practice of selling more tickets than there were seats.

Despite the tragedy of the stampede, the Roaring Twenties was a boom time for the Yankees, now settled comfortably into their big ballpark in the Bronx.

*"It was so large and the fans there were so rabid.
It was amazing for me to go out there and stand on the mound and look around
and realize that was the place that Ruth built."* —**BOB FELLER**

CHAPTER

THIRTIES

On July 5, 1930, Negro League teams played at Yankee Stadium for the first time. Jacob Ruppert had allowed his stadium to be used for a game to benefit the Brotherhood of Sleeping Car Porters. The New York Lincoln Giants and the Baltimore Black Sox split a doubleheader before 20,000.

	YEAR	POSITION	WON	LOST	PCT.	MANAGER	ATTENDANCE
	1930	THIRD	86	68	.558	BOB SHAWKEY	1,169,230
	1931	SECOND	94	59	.614	JOE McCARTHY	912,437
	1932*	FIRST	107	47	.695	JOE McCARTHY	962,320
	1933	SECOND	91	59	.607	JOE McCARTHY	728,014
	1934	SECOND	94	60	.610	JOE McCARTHY	854,682
	1935	SECOND	89	60	.597	JOE McCARTHY	657,508
	1936*	FIRST	102	51	.667	JOE McCARTHY	976,913
	1937*	FIRST	102	52	.662	JOE McCARTHY	998,148
	1938*	FIRST	99	53	.651	JOE McCARTHY	970,916
	1939*	FIRST	106	45	.702	JOE McCARTHY	859,785

YANKEES YEAR BY YEAR 1930–1939

*WORLD CHAMPIONS

ROGER KAHN: Raised in the Grand Army section of Brooklyn, Ebbets Field was the ballpark I went to most. Later, when I began to go to the Stadium, I was impressed by the vastness of it all. I went with some friends. We really couldn't see the game very well because of the smoke. Everybody smoked in those days. It would come out of the lower deck and would result in kind of a hazy view of activity around home plate.

BILL WERBER: I returned to the Yankees in 1930 with my degree from Duke completed. Now spent a month with the team in 1927. Before, I had roomed downtown, but now I was living at the Concourse Plaza Hotel, about two or three blocks up from Yankee Stadium. It was a very nice hotel, where quite a few of the Yankees lived. I just walked to work.

I recognized there was camaraderie among the players. They played all kinds of jokes on each other. Lazzeri and Ruth were fond of each other. Ruth would refer to Lazzeri as "the wop" or "the dago," even through he knew his name. But it was in fun. No animosity was ever evident. He called me "kid," which sounded like "keed." Bill "Bojangles" Robinson, the noted tap dancer, was friendly with the Babe, and he would come into the clubhouse, always dressed in a nice coat, and put on dancing exhibitions.

MONTE IRVIN: In the 1930s and 1940s, Yankee Stadium was rented by the Black Yankees of the Negro National League when the Yankees were on the road. Playing there as a member of the visiting Newark Eagles, it was like being on hallowed ground. But we didn't get into the Yankee dressing rooms. We all had to dress together with the Black Yankees in the visitors' dressing room.

ARTHUR RICHMAN: I started going to Yankee Stadium in the early 1930s, when I was around six years old. My daddy would take me. I don't know if he paid or if I went under the turnstile. It was the Depression, so nobody really had much money. I saw Babe Ruth, and Lou Gehrig, who gave me a penny postcard and wrote on it in pencil, "Good wishes, Arthur."

The bleacher seats were about 55 cents, grandstand was a dollar ten. Games started about 3:15. Many a day I would stand outside the press gate waiting for someone, perhaps a fan who had an extra ticket or reporters who could help me get in.

PAGE 48: Joe DiMaggio readies his bat before a game
ABOVE: Lou Gehrig scores in the 1932 World Series
OPPOSITE: Fans wait to enter the Stadium for game one of the 1932 Series

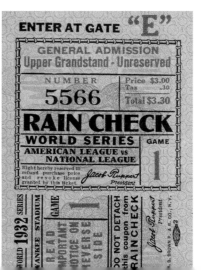

BETTING IS PROHIBITED
TEAMS 1 2 3 4 5 6 7 8 9 10 11 12 R. H. E.
ST.LOU
CHICO
CLEVE
DETRT
PHILA
WASH
BOST
TEAMS 1 2 3 4 5 6 7 8 9 10 11 12 R. H. E.
PITTS
CINTI
CHICO
ST.LOU
PHILA
BOST
AT BAT
STRIKES
BALLS
OUTS
UMPIRES - PLATE
BASES
429 ft
GEM

WHITEY FORD: When I was nine years old, I went to my first Yankee game and sat in the center-field bleachers. I never imagined I would be pitching one day on that mound.

Joe McCarthy took over as Yankee manager in 1931. Jake Ruppert told him, "I don't like finishing second."

"Neither do I," said McCarthy.

A strict disciplinarian, the man they called "Marse Joe," McCarthy allowed no shaving in the Yankee clubhouse. He had the card table in the clubhouse chopped into kindling wood. "This is a clubhouse and not a clubroom," he snapped.

His "Ten Commandments of Baseball" were made clear to every Yankee:

1. Nobody ever became a ballplayer by walking after a ball.
2. You will never become a .300 hitter unless you take the bat off your shoulder.
3. An outfielder who throws back of the runner is locking the barn after the horse is stolen.
4. Keep your head up and you may not have to keep it down.
5. When you start to slide, S-L-I-D-E. He who changes his mind may have to change a good leg for a bad one.
6. Do not alibi on bad hops. Anybody can field the good ones.
7. vAlways run them out. You can never tell.
8. Do not quit.
9. Do not find too much fault with the umpires. You cannot expect them to be as perfect as you are.
10. A pitcher who hasn't control, hasn't anything.

One of his favorite lines was "Guys who rush in and out of the clubhouse rush in and out of the big leagues."

He had Yankee uniform caps cut squarer and larger to emphasize the power mystique of the team. Uniforms were made larger, making his players look bigger and stronger.

The 1931 Yankees averaged six runs plus per game, led the majors in runs scored, hits, homers, RBIs, total bases, bases on balls, batting average, on-base percentage, and slugging percentage.

But even with all that they had going for them offensively, the Bronx Bombers finished 13 1/2 games behind Philadelphia, even though they scored 209 more runs than the A's.

As the 1932 season began, it had been four years since the Yankees recorded their last world championship. Among the prime-time players left from the 1927 Yankees were Babe Ruth, Lou Gehrig, Tony Lazzeri, Earle Combs, George Pipgras, and Herb Pennock.

On Opening Day the Yankees hit five home runs at the Stadium, winning the game, 8–3. Babe Ruth, 12 pounds lighter from a battle with the flu, hammered one of the dingers.

Power personified was what the '32 Yanks were all about. They would bat .286 as a team. Winning 107 games, playing before 962,320 at home, the Yankees would score more than a thousand runs—league leaders in that area for the third straight season.

The Bronx Bombers finished 13 games ahead of second-place Philadelphia, copping their seventh pennant. In the World Series, manager Joe McCarthy led his team against the Cubs, who had fired him in 1930. The Yankees, outscoring Chicago in the total Series 37–19, swept the Cubbies in four and happily took the winner's share of $5,232.

The tradition of honoring their legends at the Stadium started on Memorial Day of 1932, when a monument for Miller Huggins, the little manager who had passed away at age 50 on September 25, 1929, was placed in deep center field. Its inscription reads "A splendid character who made priceless contributions to baseball." Monuments would later be erected for Lou Gehrig and Babe Ruth. Others would follow.

Located in straightaway center field, they were part of the playing field, standing near the flagpole about ten feet before the wall. There were times when long drives rolled behind the monuments, and retrieving the ball became an odd and "ghoulish" task for an outfielder jockeying around the "gravestones."

On June 23, 1932, Lou Gehrig had played in his 1,103rd straight game. Less than a year later the streak was at 1,249 straight when he and manager Joe McCarthy were tossed out of a game for arguing with the umpire. The Yankee manager was given a three-game suspension. Gehrig played on. On August 17, 1933, Gehrig broke the record of playing in 1,308 straight games set by Everett Scott.

OPPOSITE: In an attempt to draw fans during the Great Depression, Babe Ruth pitches in a 1933 game
ABOVE: Joe McCarthy and Ed Barrow shake hands in 1938

The final game of the season was played on October 1, 1933. Attempting to draw fans for a meaningless contest in the depths of the Great Depression, the Yankees gave Ruth a pitching start. Babe's appearance attracted 20,000 fans, more than doubling the attendance of the day before. The thirty-eight-year-old pitched a complete game, nipping his old Boston team, 6–5. He also batted cleanup and went one-for-three, with a home run. It was the last game he pitched, his fifth since he joined the Yankees 13 years earlier.

During the 1934 season, Lou Gehrig's failing health became evident. The problem was diagnosed as lumbago. On July 13, 1934, his pain became so severe in the first inning of a game against Detroit that he had to be assisted off the field. The next day, listed first in the Yankee batting order and penciled in to play shortstop, The Iron Horse singled in his first at bat but was then replaced by a pinch runner.

September 24, 1934, was the date of Babe's last game as a player in "The House That Ruth Built," a sad and poignant day for him and his many fans. Twenty-four thousand were there, including many youngsters in "Ruthville." In three at-bats, he went hitless. Disappointed and dejected that his fabulous career in pinstripes was over, he could never imagine how his name and legend would gain more and more luster as the years passed. Today a Google search for "Babe Ruth" results in almost 8 million hits. A Sotheby's auction of his 1919 contract netted $996,000.

In 1935, without the Sultan of Swat on the scene for the first time since 1920, the Yankees now were 32-year-old Lou Gehrig's team, and he would show he was up to the challenge.

The Yankees lost their season home opener, 1–0, to Boston on April 16, 1935. A throwing error by pitcher Lefty Gomez made it possible for the game's lone run to be scored by former Yankee Bill Werber, whose contract had been purchased by the Red Sox in 1933.

Gehrig's consecutive-game streak almost ended in 1935. He was in a collision on June 8 with Carl Reynolds of the Red Sox at first base and was forced to leave the game with an injured arm and shoulder. But there was a rainout the next game, and then an extra day off due to an open date. That downtime enabled The Iron Horse to be up and running again.

The Yanks finished out of the money, in second place—three games behind Detroit. If Lefty Gomez had had a typical year, New York probably would have won another pennant. But this season, he was only 12–15.

As the story goes, during off-season contract negotiations, Colonel Ruppert proposed cutting Gomez's salary from $20,000 to $7,500. The pitcher replied: "You keep the salary. I'll take the cut."

As the 1936 season got under way, The Iron Horse had already played in 1,600 straight games. His supporting cast included Red Rolfe, George Selkirk, Bill Dickey, Frank Crosetti, Tony Lazzeri, Red Ruffing, Lefty Gomez, and a rookie born as Giuseppe Paolo DiMaggio, whom everyone called Joe.

Four years had passed since the Yankees were in the World Series. Now, with the Yankee Clipper on the scene, they would not only make it to the fall classic but also cop four straight world championships.

The 1936 Yankees were loaded. In April they won 10 of 15 games. Eddie Brannick, the secretary of the New York Giants, was at one of the games at Yankee Stadium.

"What do you think of the Yankees?" a reporter asked.

"Window-breakers," was his response.

May 1936 was a wonderful month for two Italian American Yankee ballplayers, Joseph DiMaggio and Anthony Lazzeri.

An estimated 25,000, including many Italian Americans, showed up to witness 21-year-old Joe DiMaggio's major league debut on May 3. He'd

missed the first 15 games of the season, having burned his foot in a heat-therapy machine. Now, wearing number 9, the highly heralded rookie batted ahead of Lou Gehrig in the lineup. Joe tripled, singled twice, and scored three runs in the 14–5 rout of the St. Louis Browns. Three days later he hit the first of what would be 361 career home runs, a 400-foot shot off Philadelphia pitcher George Turbeville at the Stadium. The Yankees that day took over first place, and that's where they stayed to the season's end.

_____

MARIO CUOMO: Growing up in Queens in the 1930s, you had to be a Yankee fan. If you were Mario Cuomo, and they had a guy by the name of Joe DiMaggio, not to mention Frankie Crosetti and Phil Rizzuto, but mostly Joe DiMaggio, then you were for all time fated to be a Yankee fan. The first baseball game I ever saw was with Joe DiMaggio.

_____

DiMaggio had said: "A ballplayer has to be kept hungry to become a big leaguer. That's why no boy from a rich family has ever made the big leagues."

Joe DiMaggio was no longer a "poor boy." His 1936 salary was $8,500 ($127,000 in 2007 dollars), third highest on the club behind Red Ruffing at $12,000 and Lou Gehrig at $31,000.

Tony Lazzeri also came from a modest background. He lit up American League pitching. Yankee Stadium rang with the cheers of his faithful: "Poosh 'em up, Tony. Poosh 'em up, Tony."

Though the Sultan of Swat was no longer on the scene, there always seemed to be something in the air at the Stadium that led to "Ruthian feats." And the feats were accomplished not just by Yankees.

One June 3, the great black star Josh Gibson hammered a shot just two feet below the rim of Yankee Stadium, 580 feet from home plate, according to reports. Had the drive cleared the roof, it is estimated that the ball would have traveled nearly 700 feet.

On September 19, Hank Greenberg slammed the first home run ever into the center-field stands at the Stadium, highlighting an 8–1 Detroit win.

But the fans came out to the Stadium and on the road to see the Yankees do their thing, and more often than not in that Great Depression year, the fans got their money's worth.

On May 24, the Yanks romped, 25–2, over Philly. It was the most runs in a game ever for the Yankees. On fire, Tony Lazzeri racked two grand-slam dingers, and Ben Chapman got on base seven consecutive times.

Lou Gehrig appeared in his 1,700th consecutive game on June 5. On August 3, still slugging away, Lou Gehrig appeared in his 1,900th straight game before a Monday crowd of 66,767.

Yankee slugging power was on display on August 28, 1936. The Bombers won the opener of a double-header, 14–5. Lou Gehrig hit his 41st and 42nd homers of the year. The Yanks had a cakewalk, 19–4, in the second game, called after seven innings. New York pitcher Johnny Murphy ripped five singles in five at-bats.

In an MVP season that included 49 home runs, 152 RBIs, and a .354 average, Henry Louis Gehrig was the motor making the Yankees run. Winning 102 games, and losing just 51, the Bronx Bombers won their eighth pennant, finishing 19½ games ahead of Detroit.

Not only were the Yankees of '36 one of the top Yankees teams, they also were one of the best big league clubs ever: five players had more than 100 RBIs, their team fielding percentage was .973, and their 1,065 runs scored were the most to that time by a pennant winner. They defeated the New York Giants in six games in a World Series where Joe D. batted .346, Gehrig homered twice, and Lefty Gomez won two games. It was the Yanks' first world championship without Babe Ruth, but with

21-year-old Joseph Paul DiMaggio, they had their new young star in place.

During the winter of 1936–1937, concrete bleachers replaced the Stadium's wooden ones. Straightaway center field was reduced from 490 to 461 feet. The seating capacity shrunk from the 80,000s to the 70,000s. During the season, second and third decks were added in right center. The right-field stands were enlarged, and the right-field grandstand was extended, allowing for "upper deck" home runs in both directions. Triple decks were extended past the foul pole in right field. A ball hitting the foul pole in the 1930s was now considered in play, not an automatic home run.

In 1937, Stadium attendance was just 998,148 in 79 games, an average of 12,635 per contest. People just did not have the money to come out, as Babe Ruth had once said, "in droves." Yet the 1937 team was outstanding. It included not only DiMaggio and Gehrig but also Bill Dickey, Tony Lazzeri, Tommy Henrich, Red Ruffing, and Lefty Gomez, to name a few.

In spite of the hard times, Joe DiMaggio's salary rose to $17,000; only Gehrig earned more on the team. And the Yankee Clipper was worth every penny. He would bat .346 that season, drive in 167 runs, and hit 46 home runs. Gehrig did not do too badly either hitting .351, smacking 37 home runs, and driving in 157 runs.

Salaries for the pair of Yankee superstars went up again in 1938: The Iron Horse was salaried at $39,000, while the Yankee Clipper made $25,000. Frugal to a fault when it came to paying his players and insisting they put a $30 deposit on their uniforms every year, Jake Ruppert knew where to put his money when it came to those two icons. Sadly, he hardly got the chance to see them play that year. Suffering from phlebitis and then a liver infection, he attended only Opening Day and eight innings of another game.

An estimated 4,903 women attended the Stadium's first Ladies' Day, on April 29, 1938, when

the Yanks got by the Red Sox, 6–4, and Lou Gehrig singled twice and moved his consecutive-games-played streak to 1,977.

A franchise record crowd of 83,533 watched the Yankees sweep the Red Sox in a doubleheader on May 30, 1938. More than 6,000 fans were turned away; 511 were issued refunds. Behind Red Ruffing, the Yanks took two from Boston, 10–0 and 5–4. The second game was highlighted by a fight between Yankee outfielder Jake Powell and Boston player-manager Joe Cronin.

The first no-hitter at Yankee Stadium was recorded on August 27, 1938, a day the Yankees played their sixth straight doubleheader. Joe DiMaggio tripled three times in the first game of the twin bill, an 8–7 New York win over Cleveland before 40,959. The second game saw Montgomery Marcellus Pearson, out of Oakland, California, on the mound for the Bombers. Possessed of much talent but also of control problems and illnesses, real and imagined, Pearson was generally not one to toe the mound unless he felt tip-top. This day he did, coming into the contest with a nine-game winning streak. He ran the streak to ten, no-hitting Cleveland, 13–0.

As the season of 1938 neared its end, the Yankees were as powerful as ever, finishing with 99 wins and their 10th pennant. It was clear, however, that something was terribly wrong with two pillars of the franchise. Jake Ruppert was too ill to attend the World Series. And it was becoming increasingly clear that something was not right with Lou Gehrig. The great strength had ebbed. His hand trembled when he held a cup of coffee. But he played on and through the World Series, a Yankee four-game sweep of the Cubs, the final two games at the Stadium. With that victory, the Bronx Bombers became the first baseball club to win three straight world championships.

DICK GROAT: Growing up in Pittsburgh, I was a Pirate fan, but one of my early baseball memories was going with my father to a game at the 1938 World Series at Yankee Stadium. I was eight years old. Little did I realize I would be there again playing shortstop in two World Series in the 1960s.

BILL GALLO: In the late 30s, the end of the Depression, we kids, 12-year-olds from Astoria, would travel to the Stadium, and it was like going to the Taj Mahal. You'd get an usher, a kindhearted man, who would turn around, and we'd be in, trying to get what seats we could get. We would be chased around until we finally settled down.

We did that a lot of times, and I saw all the greats. Lou Gehrig, he was the man. DiMaggio and Frank Crosetti. Lefty Gomez—"Goofy," who was a great pitcher and a great character.

Vernon "Lefty" Gomez was one of the most animated and colorful of any Yankee—ever. In the 1930s he compiled a won-lost record of 165–89 and was in the top ten in MVP voting three times. At first a hard thrower, he sustained arm injuries in 1933, 1936, and 1939, and became a finesse-type hurler. He was a self-deprecating type, famous for one-liners such as, "I want to thank all my teammates who scored so many runs, and Joe DiMaggio, who ran down so many of my mistakes."

BILL GALLO: Getting autographs in those days was no big deal. If you waited outside after the game was over, you'd see a sprinkling of guys coming out. You'd ask for autographs. They were worth nothing then. It was just a thing that we did. We didn't know what memorabilia was then; we couldn't even spell it. We'd get the autograph on a book, on a piece of paper. Never on a ball.

Hot dogs were a nickel, later a dime. It was a nickel on the subway, but we saved that by sneaking under the turnstile and getting a free ride to and from. We were good kids; we just were poor.

WHITEY FORD: Growing up in Astoria, Queens, I'd be taken to Yankee Stadium by my father or my uncles. We'd sit in the bleachers. That was when I was about 10. So that was 68 years ago. I never dreamed of pitching there. I wasn't even playing baseball. There were no baseball fields in Astoria.

On January 4, 1939, Jacob Ruppert suffered a heart attack. Friends and family started gathering at the Yankee owner's home at 1120 Fifth Avenue. Nine days later the 71-year-old owner slipped into a coma and died. With the end of his 24-year ownership of the team came the end of an era. At the time of his death, the New York Yankees were valued at $7 million to $10 million, a tribute to the will, dedication, and intelligence of Jake Ruppert.

As the season began, it looked like a challenging year was shaping up for the Yankees, particularly when Joe DiMaggio's leg injury kept him sidelined for the first two weeks. But those who followed the team knew that it would be a challenging season for the American League rivals of the Bronx Bombers, the seven teams characterized by sportswriters as the "Seven Dwarfs."

In the fifth inning of the Yankees' Opening Day on April 20, 1939, Boston's star pitcher Lefty Grove—who had once called Lou Gehrig "the toughest man I've ever faced"—intentionally walked Joe DiMaggio to face Gehrig, batting fifth in the order. Appearing in his 2,124th consecutive game, the "Pride of the Yankees" weakly grounded into a double play. The Iron Horse went zero-for-four against Grove. A week into the season, Gehrig had driven in just one run; his batting average was well below .200. He would play in just six more games and then call it a career.

Boston rookie Ted Williams smacked the ball off the 407-foot sign in right-center field at Yankee Stadium in that game. It was his first major league hit, a double. It also would be the only game in which Williams would play against Gehrig.

"On a chilly Sunday in 1939," author and baseball fan James T Farrell wrote, "I went to see my first game of the year. The sports pages had been full of stories about Lou Gehrig. He was not himself, they said. Something was wrong. The Yanks won with ease. But Gehrig was sluggish, he swung without power. He was no veteran slowing up. His reflexes were so far off, you could not but observe the fact. I didn't know it was to be one of Gehrig's last games."

One of the most poignant moments in Yankee Stadium history occurred on the Fourth of July 1939, a beautiful Bronx day, when Lou Gehrig Appreciation Day was staged before 61,808. Gehrig's uniform number 4 was the first in baseball history to be retired.

The Yankees had a doubleheader to play against the Senators. In the large crowd were Gehrig's mother and father; his wife, Eleanor; Postmaster General James Farley; Mayor Fiorello LaGuardia; and other dignitaries.

In the 40-minute ceremony between games, a parade led by the Seventh Regiment Band escorted former Yankees Babe Ruth, Waite Hoyt, Bob Meusel,

RIGHT: Yankee Stadium before a World Series game

Herb Pennock, Bob Shawkey, Joe Dugan, Tony Lazzeri, Mark Koenig, Benny Bengough, Wally Schang, Everett Scott, Wally Pipp, and George Pipgras, who now was an American League umpire, to the center-field flagpole. A banner was raised in salute to the 1927 Yankees. Players, officials, writers, and employees of Yankee Stadium all had gifts for the Yankee great.

Gehrig's teammates presented him with a silver trophy inscribed with their signatures, along with a poem by John Kieran:

We've been to the wars together;
We took our foes as they came;
And always you were the leader,
And ever you played the game.
Idol of cheering millions;
Records are yours by the sheaves;
Iron of frame they hailed you,
Decked you with laurel leaves.
But higher than that we hold you,
We who have known you best;
Knowing the way you came through
Every human test.
Let this be a silent token
Of lasting friendship's gleam
And all that we've left unspoken.
                    —*Your pals of the Yankee team*

Assembled near the pitchers' mound, the group of former Yankees and the Senators formed a semicircle that extended around a microphone at home plate.

"We want Lou! We want Lou!" screamed the crowd. Directed out of the dugout by Yankee president Ed Barrow, Gehrig removed his cap. He fought to hold back tears.

"Ladies and gentlemen, Lou Gehrig has asked me to thank you all for him. He is too moved to speak."

LEFT: Lou Gehrig Appreciation Day, before a crowd of almost 62,000

The chanting picked up again. "We want Lou! We want Lou!"

With encouragement from Joe McCarthy, Gehrig wiped his eyes, blew his nose, and slowly moved toward the microphone. Then he delivered the speech that has gone down in baseball history:

Fans, for the past two weeks you have been reading about a bad break I got. Yet today, I consider myself the luckiest man on the face of the earth. I have been in ballparks for seventeen years and I have never received anything but kindness and encouragement from you fans.

Look at these grand men. Which of you wouldn't consider it the highlight of his career just to associate with them for even one day?

Sure, I'm lucky. Who wouldn't have considered it an honor to have known Jacob Ruppert? Also, the builder of baseball's greatest empire, Ed Barrow? To have spent six years with that wonderful little fellow, Miller Huggins? Then to have spent the next nine years with that outstanding leader, that smart student of psychology, the best manager in baseball today, Joe McCarthy? Sure, I'm lucky.

When the New York Giants, a team you would give your right arm to beat and vice versa, sends you a gift, that's something. When everybody down to the grounds-keeper and those boys in white coats remember you with trophies, that's something. When you have a father and mother work all their lives so that you can have an education and build your body, it's a blessing. When you have a wife who has been a tower of strength and shown more courage than you dreamed existed, that's the finest I know. So I close in saying that I might have had a bad break, but I have an awful lot to live for.

Until the end of that 1939 season, The Iron Horse was there, on the dugout bench at the Stadium, on every road trip, sitting through all the games of the 1939 World Series.

He was on hand as an honorary member of the American League team the week after Lou Gehrig Day when the seventh All-Star Game was played

at the Stadium before 62,892, coinciding with the New York World's Fair.

When the American League lineup was announced, a fan yelled, "Make Joe McCarthy play an All-Star American League team. We can beat them, but we can't beat the Yankees."

Six starters were Yankees: Red Rolfe, Bill Dickey, George Selkirk, Joe Gordon, Red Ruffing, and Joe DiMaggio, who homered in the 3–1 American League triumph. With manager Joe McCarthy and nonstarters Frank Crosetti, Lefty Gomez, and Johnny Murphy, there were 10 Yankees on the All-Star team.

The SRO crowd was especially charged up seeing Yankee favorite hurler Red Ruffing start the game and Joe DiMaggio hit a home run.

After the All-Star break, the Yanks went on a tear, winning 35 of 49 games. The Yankee Clipper finished first in batting average, second in RBIs, and third in home runs Bill Dickey, George Selkirk,

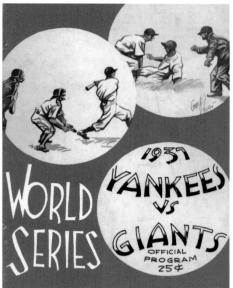

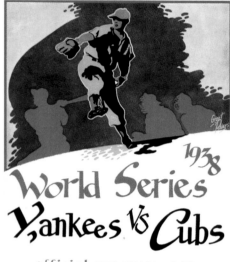

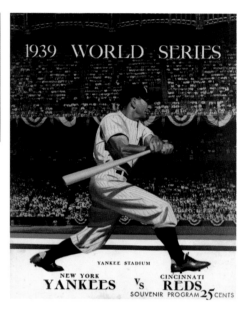

Joe Gordon, and Joe DiMaggio drove in more than 100 runs each. The Yankees led the league in home runs, RBIs, slugging percentage, walks, runs, and fielding percentage. Allowing nearly 150 runs fewer than any other team in the league, the Yankees outscored their opponents by 411, a greater run differential than any other team in history. They took the pennant, finishing 17 games ahead of second-place Boston.

And although the Yanks outdrew all American League teams in their home park, the 859,785 who came through the Stadium gates that last year of the 1930s was a disappointing number for the only baseball club that played at a .700 clip that season.

The Yankees swept the Reds in four for their fourth consecutive world championship, giving them a 28–3 record over their last 31 Series games. Then the Bronx Bombers boarded the train in Cincinnati and returned to Manhattan for a big celebration at the Commodore Hotel.

The Great Depression was grim and taxing. The Yankees coped with tears and tragedy within their own family. But they also took pride in their triumphs and towering achievements on the baseball field, their domination of the national pastime. In the decade ahead there would be many changes at Yankee Stadium, bringing it into an entirely new era.

LEFT: World's Fair patch conspicuous on 1939 Yankee uniforms
RIGHT: Fans enjoying the game on a sweltering summer day

CHAPTER

FORTIES

As the new decade dawned, America was still at peace in a world at war, and baseball retained its hold on the nation's consciousness. The Yanks had won 106 games in 1939; they'd notched their fourth straight world championship and were favored to do it again. More than ever, Yankee Stadium was a terrific place for watching baseball.

	YEAR	POSITION	WON	LOST	PCT.	MANAGER	ATTENDANCE
	1940	THIRD	88	66	.571	JOE McCARTHY	988,975
	1941*	FIRST	101	53	.656	JOE McCARTHY	964,722
	1942	FIRST	103	51	.669	JOE McCARTHY	922,011
	1943*	FIRST	98	56	.636	JOE McCARTHY	618,330
	1944	THIRD	83	71	.539	JOE McCARTHY	789,995
	1945	FOURTH	81	71	.531	JOE McCARTHY	881,845
	1946	THIRD	87	67	.565	McCARTHY/BILL DICKEY/JOHNNY NEUN	2,265,512
	1947*	FIRST	97	57	.630	BUCKY HARRIS	2,178,937
	1948	THIRD	94	60	.610	BUCKY HARRIS	2,373,901
	1949*	FIRST	97	57	.630	McCARTHY/HUGGINS/ART FLETCHER	2,283,676

YANKEES YEAR BY YEAR 1940–1949

*WORLD CHAMPIONS

RED FOLEY: Prior to the Second World War, box seats at the Stadium were regular wooden chairs that went back two or three rows from third to first base. They cost about $2.50. You had the low fences in left and right field only about three feet high. Players could lean in and make a catch. On the other hand, there were a lot of pillars and people sat behind them and couldn't see very well. It was called "an obstructed view."

PAGE 62: 1941 World Series game one
LEFT: Mickey Owen slides in for a triple in game one of the 1941 World Series
ABOVE: The last World Series game before the U.S. joins World War II

The 1940 season would be one of the tightest American League races ever. As it got under way, reverence for the past was displayed at the Stadium on April 16 when a plaque in Jake Ruppert's memory was placed on the center-field wall close to the flagpole. It read:

TO THE MEMORY OF
JACOB RUPPERT
1867–1939
GENTLEMAN, AMERICAN — SPORTSMAN
THROUGH WHOSE VISION AND
COURAGE THIS IMPOSING EDIFICE,
DESTINED TO BECOME THE HOME
OF CHAMPIONS, WAS ERECTED AND
DEDICATED TO THE AMERICAN GAME OF BASEBALL

Jake Ruppert had passed. Lou Gehrig was no longer on the scene. Joe DiMaggio, victim of a sprained knee in an exhibition game just before the season started, was ailing. The Bombers lost five of their first eight games and all season long played catch-up in the American League pennant race, chasing Boston, then Cleveland, and finally Detroit. The Yankees would wind up in third place, with an 88–66 record, two games behind Detroit. Had the Yanks been as good on the road as they were at home, they would have run away with the pennant. Their Yankee Stadium record was 52–24; their road log was 36–43.

JOE DIMAGGIO'S
56-Game Hitting Streak, 1941

GAME	DATE	PITCHER(S)	TEAM	AB	R	H	2B	3B	HR	RBI
1	MAY 15	EDDIE SMITH	CHICAGO	4	0	1	0	0	0	1
2	MAY 16	THORNTON LEE	CHICAGO	4	2	2	0	1	1	1
3	MAY 17	JOHNNY RIGNEY	CHICAGO	3	1	1	0	0	0	0
4	MAY 18	BOB HARRIS	ST. LOUIS	3	3	2	1	0	0	1
		JOHNNY NIGGELING				1				
5	MAY 19	DENNY GALEHOUSE	ST. LOUIS	3	0	1	1	0	0	0
6	MAY 20	ELDEN AUKER	ST. LOUIS	5	1	1	0	0	0	1
7	MAY 21	SCHOOLBOY ROWE	DETROIT	5	0	1	0	0	0	1
		AL BENTON				1				
8	MAY 22	ARCHIE MCKAIN	DETROIT	4	0	1	0	0	0	1
9	MAY 23	DICK NEWSOME	BOSTON	5	0	1	0	0	0	2
10	MAY 24	EARL JOHNSON	BOSTON	4	2	1	0	0	0	2
11	MAY 25	LEFTY GROVE (HOF)	BOSTON	4	0	1	0	0	0	0
12	MAY 27	KEN CHASE	WASHINGTON	5	3	1	0	0	1	3
		RED ANDERSON				2				
		ALEX CARRASQUEL				1				
13	MAY 28	SID HUDSON	WASHINGTON	4	1	1	0	1	0	0
14	MAY 29	STEVE SUNDRA	WASHINGTON	3	1	1	0	0	0	0
15	MAY 30	EARL JOHNSON	BOSTON	2	1	1	0	0	0	0
16	MAY 30	MICKEY HARRIS	BOSTON	3	0	1	1	0	0	0
17	JUNE 1	AL MILNAR	CLEVELAND	4	1	1	0	0	0	0
18	JUNE 1	MEL HARDER	CLEVELAND	4	0	1	0	0	0	0
19	JUNE 2	BOB FELLER (HOF)	CLEVELAND	4	2	2	1	0	0	0
20	JUNE 3	DIZZY TROUT	DETROIT .	4	1	1	0	0	1	1
21	JUNE 5	HAL NEWHOUSER (HOF)	DETROIT	5	1	1	0	1	0	1
22	JUNE 7	BOB MUNCRIEF	ST. LOUIS	5	2	1	0	0	0	1
		JOHNNY ALLEN				1			0	
		GEORGE CASTER				1				
23	JUNE 8	ELDEN AUKER	ST. LOUIS	4	3	2	0	0	2	4
24	JUNE 8	GEORGE CASTER	ST. LOUIS	4	1	1	1	0	1	3
		JACK KRAMER				1				
25	JUNE 10	JOHNNY RIGNEY	CHICAGO	5	1	1	0	0	0	0
26	JUNE 12	THORNTON LEE	CHICAGO	4	1	2	0	0	1	1
27	JUNE 14	BOB FELLER (HOF)	CLEVELAND	2	0	1	1	0	0	1
28	JUNE 15	JIM BAGBY	CLEVELAND	3	1	1	0	0	1	1
29	JUNE 16	AL MILNAR	CLEVELAND	5	0	1	1	0	0	0
30	JUNE 17	JOHNNY RIGNEY	CHICAGO	4	1	1	0	0	0	0
31	JUNE 18	THORNTON LEE	CHICAGO	3	0	1	0	0	0	0
32	JUNE 19	EDDIE SMITH	CHICAGO	3	2	1	0	0	1	2
		BUCK ROSS				2				
33	JUNE 20	BOBO NEWSOM	DETROIT	5	3	2	1	0	0	1
		ARCHIE MCKAIN				2				
34	JUNE 21	DIZZY TROUT	DETROIT	4	0	1	0	0	0	1
35	JUNE 22	HAL NEWHOUSER (HOF)	DETROIT	5	1	1	1	0	1	2
		BOBO NEWSOM				1				
36	JUNE 24	BOB MUNCRIEF	ST. LOUIS	4	1	1	0	0	0	0
37	JUNE 25	DENNY GALEHOUSE	ST. LOUIS	4	1	1	0	0	1	3
38	JUNE 26	ELDEN AUKER	ST. LOUIS	4	0	1	0	0	0	1
39	JUNE 27	CHUBBY DEAN	PHILADELPHIA	3	1	2	0	0	1	2
40	JUNE 28	JOHNNY BABICH	PHILADELPHIA	5	1	1	1	0	0	0
		LUM HARRIS	WASHINGTON			1				
41	JUNE 29	DUTCH LEONARD		4	1	1	1	0	0	0
42	JUNE 29	RED ANDERSON	WASHINGTON	5	1	1	0	0	0	1
43	JULY 1	MICKEY HARRIS	BOSTON	4	0	1	0	0	0	0
		MIKE RYBA				1				
44	JULY 1	JACK WILSON	BOSTON	3	1	1	0	0	0	1
45	JULY 2	DICK NEWSOME	BOSTON	5	1	1	0	0	1	3
46	JULY 5	PHIL MARCHILDON	PHILADELPHIA	4	2	1	0	0	1	2
47	JULY 6	JOHNNY BABICH	PHILADELPHIA	5	2	2	1	0	0	2
		BUMP HADLEY				2				
48	JULY 6	JACK KNOTT	PHILADELPHIA	4	0	2	0	1	0	2
49	JULY 10	JOHNNY NIGGELING	ST. LOUIS	2	0	1	0	0	0	0
50	JULY 11	BOB HARRIS	ST. LOUIS	5	1	3	0	0	1	2
		JACK KRAMER				1				
51	JULY 12	ELDEN AUKER	ST. LOUIS	5	1	1	1	0	0	1
		BOB MUNCRIEF				1				
52	JULY 13	TED LYONS (HOF)	CHICAGO	4	2	2	0	0	0	0
		JACK HALLETT				1				
53	JULY 13	THORNTON LEE	CHICAGO	4	0	1	0	0	0	0
54	JULY 14	JOHNNY RIGNEY	CHICAGO	3	0	1	0	0	0	0
55	JULY 15	EDDIE SMITH	CHICAGO	4	1	2	1	0	0	2
56	JULY 16	AL MILNAR	CLEVELAND	4	3	2	1	0	0	0
		JOE KRAKAUSKAS				1				
				223	56	91	16	4	15	55

DAVE "BOO" FERRISS: In 1941, I played summer baseball in a college league, the Northern League in Brattleboro, Vermont. After the season ended, the Red Sox gave me a uniform and had me pitch some batting practice at Fenway Park. Then Boston player-manager Joe Cronin invited me to come along to a weekend series with the Yankees at the Stadium. I stayed with the team at the Hotel Commodore. Ted Williams took me for a walk down to Times Square.

I rode out on the subway with Mr. Cronin. It was the first time I had ever been on a subway. We came right up on the track right above Yankee Stadium looking down on the field and I will never forget that sight I saw.

I pitched batting practice at the Stadium. I got to see Lefty Gomez pitch that first game for the Yankees and battle with Ted Williams, who was to hit over .400 that season. Ted got three hits off Lefty. I never dreamed that in a few years I would be pitching for Boston against the Yankees at the Stadium in a real game.

The 1941 season was the 39th for the New York Yankees, their 18th at Yankee Stadium. It would be the last season before the United States entered that world at war. Anticipating the conflict that was to come, Yankee president Ed Barrow offered Civil Defense the use of Yankee Stadium as a bomb shelter, indicating that the area under the stands could provide protection in case of attack.

It was the season when 23-year-old Phil Rizzuto broke in as Yankee shortstop. As the story goes, Lefty Gomez called him over and asked: "Kid, is your mother in the stands?"

"Yes," said Rizzuto.

"Well," the fun-loving hurler told him, "stay here and talk to me a little, and she'll think you're giving advice to the great Lefty Gomez."

Joe DiMaggio did not get off to a quick start in 1941; there were those who claimed he was in a bit

BELOW: Joe DiMaggio ties the record for hitting in the most consecutive games

of a slump. On May 15, before a small crowd at the Stadium in a game against Chicago, he batted four times and managed a single off stubby southpaw Edgar Smith. The hit was little noticed. More was made of the fact that the home team now had lost eight of its last 10 games with this 13–1 drubbing by the White Sox.

Over the next two months, however, the Yankee center fielder notched at least a hit a game. Joe DiMaggio was in a hot groove. And his fire added fuel to the Yankee engine. The team began winning.

"I became conscious of the streak when the writers started talking about the records I could break," the Yankee Clipper said.

Newspaper stories and radio commentary dramatized what Joe DiMaggio was doing. Since virtually all games in that era were played in the afternoon, radio announcers would routinely interrupt programs with news of the Yankee Clipper's progress. Day and night, radio disc jockeys played the Les Brown band recording:

Who started baseball's famous streak
That's got us all aglow?
He's just a man and not a freak,
Jolting Joe DiMaggio.
Joe...Joe...DiMaggio
we want you on our side.
From coast to coast, that's all you hear
Of Joe the one-man show.
He's glorified the horsehide sphere,
Jolting Joe DiMaggio.
Joe...Joe...DiMaggio
we want you on our side.
He'll live in baseball's Hall of Fame,
He got there blow by blow
Our kids will tell their kids his name,
Jolting Joe DiMaggio.

(COPYRIGHT 1941 BY ALAN COURTNEY)

At Yankee Stadium on June 17, official scorer Dan Daniel of the *New York World-Telegram* credited DiMaggio with a hit on a ground ball to short that bounced up, hitting Chicago's Luke Appling on the shoulder. It was a call that would be questioned— one of several during the streak where scorers strove to be as diligent as possible. The questioning did not matter; DiMag later slapped a single.

With 30 straight games of hitting safely, the George Sisler American League consecutive-game-hit record of 41 was not that far away. And neither was "Wee Willie" Keeler's mark of 44 straight.

Then, before 52,832 at Yankee Stadium on July 1, the Yankee Clipper torqued a doubleheader sweep of Boston with two hits in the first game off Mike Ryba. The first hit was controversial—a ground ball to Jim Tabor in the fourth inning. Rushing, the third baseman made an errant throw to first. DiMag wound up on second base. Hit or error? It was Dan Daniel time again. The official scorer raised his right arm in the press box, signaling "hit!"

The nightcap was called after five innings because of rain, but Joe D. managed a first-inning single that tied the 43-year-old major league mark of 44 set by Keeler.

On Wednesday, July 2, 1941, despite the 95-degree heat, Joe DiMaggio was into it. The chance was there for him to break Keeler's record. Star veteran hurler Lefty Grove rested because of the heat, and the Red Sox started rookie Heber (Dick) Newsome, who would win 19 games in 1941.

The chief of American League umpires, Tom Connolly, came up to DiMaggio near the Yankee clubhouse. The vigorous Irishman had known Keeler. "Boy, I hope you do it," he told the Yankee Clipper. "If you do, you'll be breaking the record of the finest little fellow who ever walked and who never said a mean thing about anyone in his life. Good luck to you."

In his first at-bat against Newsome, DiMag hit a long drive. It was run down by outfielder Stan Spence, who made a leaping catch. The second time up, DiMaggio grounded out.

With two teammates on the bases and a 2–1 count in his third at-bat, Joe D. blasted the ball into the seats in lower left field. It was his 18th home run of the season. Taking big strides, rounding the bases, tipping his hat,

the elegant superstar bounded into the dugout, where his joyous teammates congratulated him.

The record for most consecutive games with a hit was now his: 45! Yankee Stadium rocked.

Relaxed after the game ended, sitting in front of his locker, talking slowly and smoking a cigarette, DiMaggio had some thoughts about the streak:

"I don't know how far I can go, but I'm not going to worry about it now," he said. "I'm glad it's over. It

got to be quite a strain over the last ten days. Now I can go back to swinging at good balls. I was swinging at some bad pitches so I wouldn't be walked. The pressure has been tough off the field as on it. It was a great tribute to me, and I appreciated it, but it had its drawbacks, too. I got so much fan mail—there was

some kind of good luck charm in every letter—that I had to turn it over to the front office."

A center-field monument to Lou Gehrig was unveiled on July 6, and the Yankee Clipper rapped out six hits in a doubleheader. The streak was extended to 48 games.

On July 16, when the Yankees came to Cleveland, DiMaggio had hit in 55 straight games. Facing Al Milnar in the first inning, "Joltin' Joe" singled: 56!

The next day 67,468 were there (40,000 of them had bought tickets ahead of time) to witness baseball history play out.

They were in the right place. The noise level was unbearable. DiMag showed no emotion. In the eighth inning, he came up with the bases loaded and grounded into a double play. The streak ended.

"I can't say I'm glad it's over," DiMag said after the game. "Of course, I wanted it to go on as long as it could." After the streak ended, the Yankee Clipper went off on another one, hitting in 17 straight games. Joltin Joe had a fabled 1941 season, and so did the Yankees. Going on a tear back in July, winning 25 of 29 games (an .862 percentage, the best in American League history for one month), the Yanks clinched the pennant on September 4—the earliest date to that time in big league history.

Red Ruffing pitched the Yankees to a 3–2 win over the Dodgers in the opening game of the World Series, and the Bombers went on to win their ninth world championship taking four of the five games played. It was the first time the Dodgers and the Yankees had met in the World Series, the Subway Series. In that and the following 15 seasons they would meet seven times.

In retrospect there was poignancy to the '41 Series, which concluded on October 6 at Ebbets Field. No one knew it then, but December 7 was just two months and a day away, a date that not only would live in infamy but would also affect the lives of millions of people around the globe.

At the major league meetings after Pearl Harbor it was decided to allow only seven night games per team due to wartime exigencies. Ed Barrow, always a tough guy, made the point that Yankee Stadium did not have night baseball lights, which he deemed a fad, and that he had no plans to have them installed.

"If night baseball is stopped," Barrow exclaimed, "I will not be the one to cry. It is a wart on the nose of the game."

On January 15, 1942, President Franklin Roosevelt sent a "green-light letter" to baseball commissioner Kenesaw Mountain Landis, urging that for the good of the nation organized baseball continue despite the war. Games became opportunities for patriotic events, bond rallies, exhibitions, homes away from home for service personnel. And Yankee Stadium, with its prominent "Buy War Stamps and Bonds" advertising sign, was in the forefront of such actions.

Before the season got under way, Johnny Sturm enlisted in the army air corps. Near the end of the season Tommy Henrich would join the coast guard. By 1943 Phil Rizzuto, Joe DiMaggio, Buddy Hassett, Red Ruffing, and other Yankees would be in the military.

JIM REISLER: My father was in the marines. He told how they would let servicemen in for free. If he couldn't find a seat, he would just sit on the steps.

MARIO CUOMO: I saw Babe Ruth, believe it or not, face Walter Johnson at a World War II bond rally game. He was quite sick. He fouled off a couple. Then, damned if he didn't hit one into the right-field stands. They started cheering and demanding that he run. He didn't want to run. And they kept hollering. And so he pulled his cap down the way he would, and did that little short jog he did with his belly hanging out in front of him.

That game at the Stadium, on August 23, 1942, drew 69,000. It pitted New York against Washington and raised $80,000 for army–navy relief.

For the first time since 1926, the Yankees received the losing player's share, of $3,352, for the 1942 World Series. They lost in five games to the Cardinals, as they were defeated in games three, four, and five at Yankee Stadium. It was a good Series for Phil Rizzuto, who batted .381 to pace all regulars.

To reduce the strain on essential services, in 1943, teams set up their spring training sites close to home. The Yankees were headquartered in Asbury Park, New Jersey.

On July 25, 1943, the second game of a doubleheader against the White Sox was interrupted with the announcement that Italian dictator Benito Mussolini had resigned. The Stadium erupted with cheers and applause.

Three days later, a Red Cross benefit exhibition game matched Babe Ruth's team of ex-Yankees against Ted Williams's team of University of North Carolina Cloudbusters. The Bambino's crew lost, 8–5.

But despite patriotic assemblages, attendance was at an all-time low at "The House That Ruth Built": just 618,330 in 1943. Still it remained tops in the American League.

And the New York Yankees remained the top team in the big leagues. Winning their 14th pennant, they faced off against the Cardinals in the World Series of 1943. It took just five games for the Yanks to notch another world championship. The Cards were only able to eke out a 4–3 win, in the second game, played at the Stadium before 68,578.

Spring training in 1944 was in Atlantic City, New Jersey. Many more Yanks were in the armed forces, including Bill Dickey, George Selkirk, Charlie Keller, Red Ruffing, and Joe Gordon.

Although more than half of the players in the 400-man Yankee organization were in the service, on January 25, 1945, Larry MacPhail, Dan Topping, and Del Webb purchased the Yankees from the estate of Jake Ruppert for $2.8 million. The players were part of the deal that included the Stadium, parks in Newark and Kansas City, and leases on minor league ballparks.

It was business as usual in the Bronx for 1945's opening day, sort of. Soaking and steady rain held attendance down to just 13,923. But Mayor Fiorello LaGuardia braved the elements and threw out the first ball. A seven-run seventh inning sealed the Yankees' 8–4 win over the Red Sox.

PATRICK MACKIN: Snuffy Stirnweiss had been my favorite player. Now playing in the majors in his third season, he was having a great year. I was eighteen years old in 1945 and had already been called up for the draft. Knowing I would be going away, I wanted to see the Yankees play their last game that season. I sat in the bleachers. That was all I could afford.

I had grown up in Kearney, New Jersey, and had gone to several Newark Bears games. They were the number one farm team of the Yankees, and they played at Ruppert Stadium, a short bus ride and walk from where I lived. A dollar from my mother would get me on the bus, admission, and a bag of peanuts.

Now at Yankee Stadium at last, I knew Snuffy had a shot at winning the batting title, even though the leader for that prize was Tony Cuccinello of the White Sox. As it turned out, Cuccinello's last two games were rained out, so he was stuck at .308. He couldn't improve.

Stirnweiss, on the other hand, got three hits in that game. His last hit — I learned all about this after the game — was too hot to handle. It was first ruled an error by the official scorekeeper, who then changed the ruling to a hit. That gave him the batting title. He batted .309, the lowest average to win a batting championship.

The 1945 Yanks finished fourth, their lowest finish since 1925. Part of the problem was the large amount of Bomber talent in the military. Part of the problem was the cumulative effect of neglect on the franchise in the wake of Ruppert's death.

But the new ownership had the means, the money, and the desire to turn things around. By 1946, in the spirit of the postwar boom, a $600,000 renovation began. Irish turf was put down to create greener and healthier grass. A new paint job made the Stadium greener and bluer. Dugout locations were changed: the visiting team was moved to the third-base side of the infield. The Yankee dugout was shifted to the first-base side.

New promotions were added to the scene: foot races, free nylon stockings for women attending games, archery contests. And the Stadium Club made its debut. It consisted of two rooms on the mezzanine level, one done in the Art Deco chrome-and-leather motif of the time, and the other in an old English tavern style.

PAUL DOHERTY: Nat Cohen, who ran the Stadium Club, wouldn't let you pass through the club to get to the elevator that brought you to the media area unless you were wearing a jacket. There was a "jackets only" policy at the Stadium club, whether you were a guest or a Yankee employee.

The Stadium Club was a place to see and be seen, to eat and to drink at what was the largest bar in New York State. It spurred the creation of luxury boxes: $600 for a four-seat box, which gave one access to a private lounge, bar, and restaurant. Priority for tickets to postseason games and other sporting events at the Stadium also was part of the package.

Among the appetizers at the Stadium Club were shrimp cocktail for $1.85 and herring in sour cream for $1.00. There was crème vichyssoise for $0.60, entrées such as French poached salmon with butter sauce for $4.95, and roast prime rib of beef au jus for $5.95. Sides of baked, whipped, or French fried potatoes, sliced tomatoes, or the vegetable du jour cost $0.60. To accompany the meal, a "delicate and fruity" half bottle of Beaujolais for $2.85 or a "light and vigorous" half bottle of Chablis for $3.65 could be ordered from a modest wine list.

PAUL DOHERTY: The precursor to the Yankees' "bat in the hat" emblem debuted. MacPhail commissioned the noted graphic artist Lon Keller. But the Yankee co-owner wasn't entirely satisfied with Keller's initial image. His suggested refinement was to place a baseball around the word "Yankees" and make the "K" into a baseball bat. With those changes, the logo remains in use.

On April 30, 1946, there were 54,826 on hand — a new Yankee Stadium record for Opening Day.

BILL GALLO: In 1946, I came out of the marines, and the first thing I wanted to do was see a ball game. Now I was on the _Daily News_. I wrote

RIGHT: (l to r) Joe DiMaggio, Ted Williams, and Dom DiMaggio on Opening Day, 1941

captions and was a cub reporter. I did not have press access, but I got my ticket from the paper. I sat way up on top and watched Bob Feller pitch a no-hitter against the Yankees, striking out 11. He went the nine in the Bronx and the fans cheered him.

"I would rather beat the Yankees regularly than pitch a no-hit game," Feller said after his lights-out performance.

Before a Friday 64,183 Ladies' Day crowd on May 10, the first-place Red Sox rolled to their 15th straight victory, 5–4 over the Yankees. Earl Johnson's four scoreless relief innings helped the Beantown club, while a Joe DiMaggio grand slam accounted for all the Yankee runs.

Thirty-five games into the season, Joseph Vincent McCarthy quit—some said he was fired—as Yankee manager. "He was drinking too much," Joe DiMaggio told reporters. "He wasn't eating right, and he was worried about the team because it was playing so lousy." His relationship with the new Yankee owners was also "lousy," so Marse Joe moved on and was replaced by Bill Dickey, who was replaced later that season by Johnny Neuse.

Ed Barrow, whose relationship with the new owners was also "lousy," was not too happy when Larry MacPhail had most of the flagpoles removed from the Stadium's roof and replaced with structures that held hundreds of electric lights.

A press release hyped that there was now illumination equal to that of 5,000 full moons. On May 28, 1946, the first night game at Yankee Stadium was played. The curious crowd numbered 49,917, and the Senators nipped the Yankees, 2–1.

Barrow must have had a fit on August 9 when for the first time all big league games were staged at night—four in the National League and four in the American for a total of almost 200,000 fans, 63,040 at Yankee Stadium.

BOBBY BROWN: Late that 1946 season I along with Yogi Berra and Vic Raschi were brought up to play for the Yankees. We drove over from Newark to the Stadium for a Sunday doubleheader against Philadelphia. Yogi and I played every one of the remaining seven games. Vic Raschi pitched in the regular turn.

WHITEY FORD: Out of high school, I pitched for the 34th Avenue Boys in Queens and we ended up winning the New York City Sandlot championship in 1946 at the Polo Grounds, right across the river from Yankee Stadium.

Teams were bidding for my services. I signed at the Stadium in the fall of '46 for $7,000. The Yankees were playing Philadelphia. Paul Krichell, the famous head of scouting, had me sitting in the front row there next to the dugout.

"I want you to meet somebody," Krichell said. "He just came up from our Newark Bears farm team."

He says: "Larry Berra, this is Eddie Ford."

That was how Yogi and I were first introduced to each other. I never thought I would be pitching to him through all those great times.

Throughout 1946, innovations and improvements plus a very appealing Yankee team created new highs in Yankee attendance. On June 9, 66,000 had crowded into the yard for a doubleheader against Cleveland. That pushed Yankee attendance for the season to more than 1 million, the quickest

any team had ever reached that mark. The team went on to set records for average-single game attendance, 29,442, and total season attendance at the Stadium, the first two-million gate, 2,265,512—up significantly from 1945's 881,845. In fact, 1946 kicked off the first of five straight seasons when the Yankees would draw 2 million or more into the big ballpark in Bronx.

April 27, 1947, was one of those memorable, marker times: "Babe Ruth Day" at Yankee Stadium and at all organized leagues in the United States and Japan. The Stadium program was broadcast nationally and piped into all big league parks. The American League presented Babe Ruth with a bronze plaque with his picture on it. The National League gave him a leather book with signatures of all the players in the league.

A feeble-looking Babe, holding back tears, delivered his speech in a raspy voice to the crowd of almost 58,500:

Thank you very much, ladies and gentlemen. You know, this baseball game of ours comes up from the youth. That means the boys. And after you're a boy and grow up to play ball, then you come to the boys you see representing clubs today in your national pastime. The only real game in the world, I think, is baseball. As a rule, people think that if you give boys a football or a baseball or something like that, they naturally become athletes right away. But you can't do that in baseball. You got to start from way down, at the bottom, when the boys are six or seven years of age. You can't wait until they're 14 or 15. You got to let it grow up with you, if you're the boy. And if you try hard enough, you're bound to come out on top, just as these boys here have come to the top now. There have been so many lovely things said about me today that I'm glad to have had the opportunity to thank everybody.

SAM MELE: When I first got to Yankee Stadium, I was a player with the Red Sox. It was in 1947.

I stood on the dugout steps and looked out, and I felt like I didn't belong there with all those legends. I am a New York guy originally, grew up in Astoria, Queens. Strange — I played baseball all the time but had never gone to Yankee Stadium as a kid.

I hit my first home run at Yankee Stadium with my mother and father watching from the stands. Our traveling secretary went out to the stands and got the guy who caught the ball to trade it for a new ball. I signed the ball I hit for my mother.

The attraction of night baseball and the attractiveness of the New York Yankees combined to pull 74,747 for a night game on May 26.

With Bucky Harris at the helm the entire 1947 season, the Yankees won 94 games and the American League pennant and squared off against their age-old rivals the Dodgers in the World Series opener at Yankee Stadium on September 30. This was the first World Series to be shown on television, although coverage was limited to New York City and its surroundings. The Bombers scored five times in the fifth inning and won 5–3 before a record crowd of 73,365, who paid a total gate of $325,828.

October 5, 1947, was a beautiful day for baseball. The Yankees had a 3–2 lead in games in the Series. Most of the 74,065 there had come out to see the home team notch another world championship.

Allie Reynolds was pitted against small southpaw Vic Lombardi for the Dodgers. The Yanks had squandered a 5–4 lead and trailed 8–5 as the bottom of the sixth inning got under way. Dodger manager Burt Shotten inserted five-foot, six-inch Al Gionfriddo for defensive purposes. Just two days before, the little outfielder had scored Brooklyn's winning run as "Dem Bums" beat Yankee pitcher Bill Bevens, who not only lost the game but also his no-hitter attempt.

Now Gionfriddo was in left field. Joe Hatten was on the mound for the Dodgers. A walk to George Stirnweiss. A single by Yogi Berra. Two on. Two out. Joe DiMaggio up.

RED BARBER (GAME CALL, OCTOBER 5, 1947):

Swung on, belted… it's a long one… back for it Gionfriddo… back-back-back… he-e-e… makes a one-handed catch against the bullpen! Oh, Doctor!

With the crack of the bat, Gionfriddo had sped toward the bullpen railing. Losing his cap, turning, leaping, he put out his glove and caught the ball to the left of the 415-foot marker in front of a low metal gate.

Joe DiMaggio, who was not one to show emotion, saw the Gionfriddo catch as he neared second base. Shaking his head, he kicked at the dirt.

Thirty-eight players were used in that sixth game, which took three hours and 19 minutes. Brooklyn won, 8–6, forcing a seventh game. The Yankees won it on October 7, 5–2. World champions again.

In the clubhouse celebration, with his team savoring yet another world championship, Larry MacPhail, cigarette in one hand, beer bottle in the other, announced his resignation as Yankee general manager and owner.

"My heart can't stand it anymore. I'm through," he said. The flamboyant MacPhail had threatened to resign before, but this time he meant it. Dan Topping and Del Webb bought out his one-third interest in the club for $2 million. Exit the man who pushed the Yankees and the park they played in to new dimensions.

The Dodger–Yankee rivalry was still red hot on April 18 as the 1948 season got under way. At Yankee Stadium, 62,369 fans, the largest crowd ever for an exhibition game, watched as the Bums edged the Yankees, 5–3.

The Red Sox–Yankee rivalry took a backseat on June 13 to Babe Ruth, who returned for a final appearance at the house that he had built.

MEL PARNELL: Guys on my Boston team all wanted to go over and shake Ruth's hand. But at the time he looked awfully bad and had a sort of gray pallor to his face. You could tell that he still followed the game and knew our names when we mentioned them to him. Ted Williams was one of those who spoke to him. I didn't think to ask the Babe for an autograph. It certainly was a sad moment for me, for all of us. It was obvious what was coming.

The plan was to retire Babe Ruth's uniform number 3 and to celebrate Yankee Stadium's 25th anniversary and that of the 1923 Yankees. A shadow of his former self, Ruth socialized in the Yankee clubhouse with his teammates from the 1923 team, who played a brief exhibition game against veterans from other years.

It was a rainy and raw New York day. A camel's hair coat was placed over his shoulders. One by one, his old teammates were introduced. Finally, announcer Mel Allen called him. The coat was removed from his shoulders. Using a bat he had gotten from Bob Feller as a temporary cane, Babe Ruth shuffled to home plate to a booming ovation. And the crowd of 49,647 sang "Auld Lang Syne."

The Babe spoke of how filled with pride he was to have hit the first homer in Yankee Stadium history. The he added: "Lord knows who'll hit the last."

In the Yankee locker room afterward, ceremonies completed, his old buddy Joe Dugan poured a beer for him.

"So, how are you?"

"Joe, I'm gone," the Babe said. And he started to cry.

On August 16, 1948, after a two-year battle with cancer, the Babe passed away. He was 53 years old. For the next two days, his body lay in state at the entrance to Yankee Stadium. More than 200,000 came to say farewell.

GENE CONLEY: The Hearst Annual All-Star Game was at first supported by Babe Ruth. After he died, it became a memorial to him.

The summer the Babe died I played in the All-Star Game. I had been picked to play in a doubleheader with kids from all over the State of Washington, where I pitched and struck out a whole bunch of batters and also was the only guy who hit a home run. As a result of that, Monte Stratton and the comedian Joe E. Brown selected me to represent the State of Washington in the All-Star Game. I traveled from Seattle to New York by train accompanied by a writer from the *Seattle Post-Intelligence*.

DICK GROAT: As a junior and senior in high school, 1947 and 1948, I won trips to New York representing the City of Pittsburgh playing shortstop in the Hearst Annual All-Star baseball competition.

You practiced at Yankee Stadium. You always went out to look at the statues, to touch them. But you played the All-Star Game at the Polo Grounds.

GENE CONLEY: While I enjoyed the whole experience, my biggest thrill was working out at Yankee Stadium. I was a westerner; I'd never seen the Stadium before. It was like being in the bottom of a cellar, in a dream. We were all goggle-eyed, walking around, looking around. That evening when we went over to the Polo Grounds, I just couldn't believe how close the two stadiums were.

RALPH HOUK: Yankee Stadium for me was a home away from home without a doubt. Those were really the best years of my life. The first time I saw it I could hardly believe it was a place to play baseball in. It was so big and awesome. I was born in Kansas and raised on a farm and I had played in the Kansas City ballpark a little bit. In 1947, I played in the Texas League ballparks. But I never expected anything like the Stadium.

It was especially amazing to me when I walked out on the field and saw the people sitting in the high stands looking down and the trains going by outside right field. The women were all dressed up and the men wore hats and jackets. It just didn't seem where you ought to be playing baseball.

When I began, I was one of three catchers along with [Aaron] Robinson and Yogi. I was catching against lefthanders, Aaron was catching against righthanders, and Yogi was playing right field.

RIGHT: Fans pay their respects as Babe Ruth's body lies in state at Yankee Stadium
FAR RIGHT: Laying a wreath at Ruth's monument
OVERLEAF: Fans rush the field after 1947 World Series win over the Brooklyn Dodgers

My locker from the start was right next to the manager's office. I can always remember DiMaggio coming in on the other side and going down to the end, and equipment manager Pete Sheehy bringing him a cup of coffee. He didn't ask for one—Pete always knew when he wanted one.

DiMaggio became one of my better friends on the club, believe it or not. He knew I had been in the war. I was pretty quiet then, and he was more of a loner. He invited me to dinner a few times. In those days, my best friend was anyone who wanted to see me.

"In the late forties, I hit a ball about four hundred feet to left center," Joe DiMaggio recalled. "We were playing the Red Sox, and my brother Dom had no trouble making the catch." Joe Gordon followed and hit one about 420 feet to the same area. Dom caught it. "Yogi Berra cracked a line drive into the right-field seats near the foul line. If you remember there was a low railing out there about three feet high. The ball barely cleared it. Yogi couldn't have hit the ball more than 300 feet. Joe Gordon and I watched him trot around the bases with a big grin on his face. We looked at each other and shrugged our shoulders. If we were born left-handed, our shots would've landed in the bleachers. They didn't name left-center field Death Valley for nothing."

SAM MELE: I remember Dom going toward left field, making one hell of a catch off his brother. I was running from the outfield into the dugout along with Dominic and when Joe passed him going out to center field, he just looked at his brother admiringly, yet a look that said "Damn you— you just robbed me of a double or triple." Dom and Joe hardly ever spoke to each other on the field.

RALPH HOUK: I spent lots of years in the bullpen. There were mostly all Yankee fans around. They treated us real good. But we would never autograph during a game.

There was a wire gate in front of the bullpen. I can tell the story now: We would sit on the benches with our feet on that fence. When a ball was hit that way, if a right fielder on the other team came to the fence to get the ball, we'd push the fence so he would have trouble getting at it. If one of our guys hit it there, we would try and pull the fence back. I don't know if we ever accomplished much, but that was what we did.

BARRY DEUTSCH: One sunny Saturday in 1948, my father took me, then eight years old, to my first baseball game at the home of the team I worshiped. We parked our car in a grimy parking lot that my father said charged too much and walked a few blocks. My mother had packed us a lunch because she said the food would cost too much.

We walked up a slight ramp, through a gateway, and there it was—the greenest grass I ever saw, the whitest baselines and bases, whiter than the sheets my mother hung up on the clothesline my father had strung among the television antennas on the roof of our apartment house. The horseshoe shape of the field was a panorama that was impossible to capture on our black-and-white Majestic television set. There were mobs of people, more than I had ever seen in one place.

During pregame ceremonies at the season's opener against the Senators on April 19, 1949, a granite monument to Babe Ruth was unveiled. Plaques were also presented honoring Lou Gehrig and Miller Huggins. Mrs. Babe Ruth, Mayor William O'Dwyer, Governor Thomas E. Dewey, and the baseball team from the Babe's old school, St. Mary's Industrial School in Baltimore, were all at Yankee Stadium that day.

JOE CARRIERI: My brother was the Yankee batboy in 1949. When the visiting batboy joined the marines, I got his job. I am 13 years old. First day. April. Exhibition game. The Brooklyn Dodgers come in for a night game. I am a Catholic boy. I cannot eat meat on Friday, so my mother makes me a pepper and egg sandwich on a roll. The game starts at 8:05. I am sitting on the trunk. I pull out my brown bag, pull off the cellophane, and start munching. Who comes over but Jackie Robinson.

"Son," he says to me, "your sandwich looks dry. Take a soda. And mark it on my bill."

In those days your name was up on the wall, and if you took cigarettes, candy, or soda, you just put what you took next to your name. And after your time at the Stadium was done, you had to pay the clubhouse man for what you had, plus a tip. I was seven years there at Yankee Stadium and no one else ever bought me a soda. Jackie Robinson saw me for ten seconds and bought me a soda.

During games I would make sure the bats were in order and that I gave the right bats to the right player. If a bat was broken, it was my responsibility to make sure a second bat was ready so the game was not delayed.

There was always smoking during the game. Players would leave the dugout and go down the steps into the passageway or the dressing room. Hank Bauer would smoke during a game. DiMaggio was winded by the time I was there, but he would not smoke during the game. Jerry Coleman would have a smoke, Yogi Berra, Whitey Ford. Tommy Henrich would smoke a cigar and let it lie there during the innings and go back and have a couple of puffs. On the other hand, Phil Rizzuto, who advertised for Chesterfield, didn't smoke.

LEIGH MONTVILLE: I grew up in New Haven, Connecticut. My father was a Red Sox fan, and that's how I became a Red Sox fan. He gave me the Democratic Party, the Catholic Church, and the Red Sox.

Yankee Stadium was where we went to watch big games. My father would take me and another kid from the neighborhood. We'd go down in the Studebaker.

The players all parked their cars right along the side of the street next to the Stadium. Kids would come down with penny postcards, slide one of them through the window of the car, and it would fall into the seat. You had your home address on it, and you hoped the player would send you the card back with an autograph. I did get some back autographed—Phil Rizzuto for one.

PHIL RIZZUTO: I knew every nook and cranny in the Stadium. The fans were behind us. Being from New York, it meant a lot for me to play in my hometown.

ELI S. BELI: I was born and raised on the Lower East Side of New York City. I am a diehard Yankee fan. One day I went to a game courtesy of the New York City Police Athletic League (PAL). The Seventh Precinct Station regularly gave out free tickets to underprivileged kids in the area, with seats in the upper deck not far from the WINS [radio] booth. That afternoon, I got to the Stadium early and was waiting outside the Yankee player entrance hoping to get Joe

D.'s autograph, when I heard running footsteps in back of me.

I turned, and there was this little guy. He stopped, said, "Hi, young fella," patted me on the head, reached into his bag, and handed me a baseball.

I thanked him. He gave me a great smile and headed into the Stadium. It was only when I looked at the ball and saw the Phil Rizzuto signature that I realized who he was.

I put the ball away in an old suitcase with Yankee scorecards. In 1950, I enlisted in the U.S. Air Force. When I came back from the Korean War, my suitcase was nowhere to be found. My mom had given it to a neighbor's kid going to summer camp.

I lost the ball, but I will never lose the memory of that day and the wonderful person who was kind enough to make me feel like the richest kid in the world.

BERT PADELL: I came to Yankee Stadium in August of 1948 to be a substitute batboy and became the regular Yankee batboy in 1949 and 1950.

When there was a night game, I would sleep on the dressing table so I would not have to go home if the next day was no school. But I never missed school. I went to the High School of Commerce because Lou Gehrig went there and because I wanted to become another Gehrig.

The assistant dean gave me a schedule where I started at eight o'clock and left at 12 o'clock. In those days the games did not start until 2:30. So I took the train—Commerce was downtown—got there in time for batting practice, picked up the bats, and everything was ready. I never, ever, missed a game.

To be there, to walk down the runway and climb up the steps to the field—it was sensational, like God hit me. I just loved what I

did even though my pay was a dollar a day. A dollar a day. My check was left usually on the table in the front of the dressing room. Joe DiMaggio says to me:

"Don't worry Bert, nobody will ever steal it—if anything, they'll put money into it."

I did everything. I used to get five, six dozen balls signed every day from the whole team. I helped carry players off the field on stretchers if they got hurt. I helped clean off their spikes. I bought pickles for my favorite Yankee players. I protected all the equipment—one time a fan got into the dugout and stole a bat and I ran the whole length of the field, tackled him, and got the bat back.

I used to hold the players' bats in the home on-deck circle. They didn't have to look around for it. I knew everyone's bat as they were coming up. I would rub it up myself, give the bat to the player, and say, "It's gonna happen, it's gonna happen."

I did not have a locker. I dressed in the drying room, where they dried all the jock straps and stuff like that. I was very active, catching batting practice, and other things. I had two or three uniforms, and sometimes it was so hot I had to change because I sweated.

I answered fan mail for some of the guys. Joe Page used to tell me, "Take the mail, smell all the envelopes. If any of the envelopes smell from perfume, don't even open 'em up. Put 'em aside for me. All the rest you answer."

Frank Sinatra used to come in. He was friends with Rizzuto. Phil used to hang up on the rafter and make noises like "Oink, oink, oink!" and Yogi used to chase him.

I loved them all—Gene Woodling, Ralph Houk, Joe DiMaggio, Tommy Byrne, Phil Rizzuto. They were so nice to me.

Autumn in New York City—baseball on center stage again. Casey Stengel was in as Yankee manager, and Bucky Harris, who had led the team to a third-place finish in 1948, was out. The Yankees were one game behind the Red Sox in the standings as former Yankee manager Joe McCarthy's team had won 59 of its last 78 games. Boston needed just one win in the two-game series the weekend of October 1 and 2 at Yankee Stadium to clinch the title.

MEL PARNELL: The Red Sox–Yankee rivalry was one of the most unique things in baseball history. We were criticized as being a country club ball club pampered by Mr. Yawkey. The differences were that we were probably a step slower than the Yankees. They also had more depth.

I really liked Yankee Stadium. A lot of times I would sit down in the bullpen in the sunshine. I wasn't actually there to pitch. They used to store the peanuts down there and pitchers who would not expect to come in until late in the game would stretch out on the peanut sacks and get a little sleep time. The box seats were on the left side and on the bleachers were on the right side. We would get friendly with the fans. They knew their baseball.

In 1949, I won 25 games and Ellis Kinder won 23. As the season came to its end, we were either in the game or in the bullpen for 19 consecutive days. We were pretty well worn out. Every time we Red Sox came into Yankee Stadium it seemed that Ellis and I opposed Allie Reynolds and Vic Raschi, two outstanding pitchers. So we knew we had our hands full.

It was Joe DiMaggio Day at Yankee Stadium on October 1, 1949. And despite having viral pneumonia, the great star was ready to play all out. More than 140,000 would be on hand for the two games. Many, without tickets, moved about outside the park, listening to the games on big portable radios.

The "Joe DiMaggio Special" came down from New Haven, nine cars transporting 700 fans. Dom DiMaggio was in center field for Boston. Mom Rosalie DiMaggio had flown in from California as well as a brother, Tom, and Joe Jr., Joe's son. The great Ethel Merman sang.

A reporter asked Mrs. DiMaggio, "Which team and which center fielder do you favor?"

Dom DiMaggio cut him off. "Mom is impartial."

Among the scores of gifts showered on the great DiMag that day included a Dodge for him and a Cadillac for his mother.

And there was a Chris-Craft boat, Longine Baro Thermo calendar watch, Waltham watch chain knife, a wallet with religious gifts, golf cuff links, a gold belt buckle, 14-karat gold cuff links and tie pin, a 51-inch loving cup trophy, Admiral television set, Dumont television set, deer rifle, bronze plaque, $100 fedora hat, golf bag, General Electric blanket and radio, Thermos water jug set, a 14-karat gold key chain autographed in links. Also a silver loving cup, 25 volumes of Joe DiMaggio Capitol records for Yankee Juniors, a set of Lionel trains for Joe Jr., driving glasses and sunglasses for Yankee Juniors, Christmas candy and baseball and bat, 500 Joe DiMaggio shirts in Joe's name to Yankee Juniors, a ship's clock, an oil painting of Joe DiMaggio, carpeting for his living room in Amsterdam, New York, a Westinghouse toaster, a 14-karat gold money clip, open house privileges at the Concourse Plaza and Martinique hotels in the Bronx (these hotels also provided a four-year college scholarship for a boy of Joe's selection).

And there was more. The Il Progresso newspaper medal of honor, 300 quarts of Cardini ice cream for any institution designated by Joe, a statuette neckerchief and clip from the Boy Scouts of America, an air-foam mattress and box spring, Fond du Lac Wisconsin cheese, a 14-karat gold watch with diamond numerals from the Italian Welfare Association of Elizabeth, New Jersey, a case of shoestring potatoes, a case of Ventura County oranges, a sack of walnuts, a case of lemonade and frozen lima beans, a handpainted tie, a polished wood paperweight, a leather wallet, a metal good luck elephant. Also, sterling silver rosary beads for Joe Jr., a portrait from Frank Paladino of Brooklyn, New York, a Sporting News plaque, a dozen gold balls, an ashtray, a Thermo tote bag, a Columbia bicycle for Joe Jr., fishing tackle, luggage, a cocker spaniel from the American Spaniel Club, a plaque from the Columbia Civic Club of Newark, New Jersey, a traveling bag, a certificate of recognition from the Italian Historical Society of America, a Lux Clock Company traveling alarm clock, a sterling silver money clip, handpainted ties for Joe and Joe Jr., and taxi service for 300 fans from Newark ("This ride is on Joe D.") from the Brown and White Cab Company of Newark.

After the presentations, the Yankee Clipper, in his typically laconic way, said, "I want to thank the Good Lord for making me a Yankee."

The game began. Mel Parnell faced Allie Reynolds. Grantland Rice observed: "For blocks around Yankee Stadium...before the game started there was a sort of carnival hum in the air."

PHIL RIZZUTO: We were behind, 4–0. We were behind but not beaten. Casey had told Joe Page who came in for Allie, "Just hold them, Joe, just hold them."

I went up to hit and Boston catcher Birdie Tebbetts, who always talked to me, this time got me angry. "'Oh, Phil,' he said, 'we're gonna be drinking a lot of champagne tonight and we're gonna have a party because we're gonna clinch the pennant today and a kid from the minors will be pitching for us tomorrow.'"

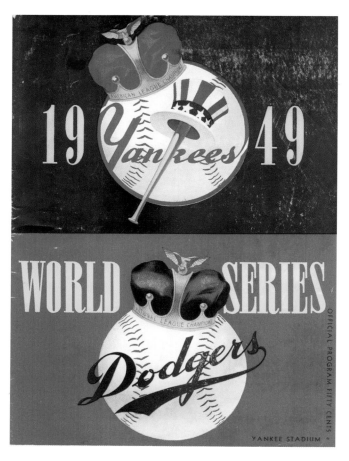

Holy cow, I was annoyed. I told Casey and some of the other guys when I got back to the bench, and they weren't happy with what he had said either. I don't think that was the only factor in getting us back in the game, but it sure helped.

MEL PARNELL: I don't make excuses. I was tired, but I was a professional, and professionals are paid to pitch. The Yanks scored four times, and then Joe Dobson came in to relieve me and Johnny Lindell hit the eighth-inning home run that beat us, 5–4.

Eighteen hours before the Sunday, October 2, game time, the line for bleacher seats coiled out more than a block long. Nearly 70,000 excited fans were jammed into Yankee Stadium. Ellis Kinder started for Boston. Vic Raschi took the mound for the New Yorkers. That game was the first time all season that Joe DiMaggio, Tommy Henrich, and Yogi Berra were in the lineup together.

Going into the eighth inning, Raschi held a 1–0 lead. Autumn's shadows started to fill Yankee Stadium. Kinder had been touched for just two hits, yet trailed, 1–0. Joe McCarthy, the man they called the "push-button manager," pushed a button and pinch-hit for Kinder. No dice. He then summoned Mel Parnell from the bullpen to hurl the bottom of the eighth inning. Parnell, weary from pitching the day before, and an unlucky Tex Hughson, who followed him, were tagged for four runs. A Sox rally fell a bit short. And the Yankees won the game, 5–3 and the pennant, their 16th.

In the locker room, Casey Stengel savored the moment. "Fellas, I want to thank you all for going to all the trouble to do this for me. I want to thank you all for giving me the greatest thrill of my life. And to think they pay me for managing so great a bunch of guys."

The 1949 World Series was a magical matchup: the Dodgers of Brooklyn against Casey Stengel's New York Yankees. It was a special event in New York City as thousands came into Manhattan creating the biggest hotel room shortage since World War II. Hundreds of police were assigned to Yankee Stadium and Ebbets Field in Brooklyn around the clock to minimize any chance of incidents. Subways had hundreds of extra police riding the rails to help keep unruly fans in check.

Game one, staged before 66,224 at Yankee Stadium, saw Don Newcombe make history as the first black pitcher to start a World Series game. Allie Reynolds was the Yankee starter.

RED BARBER (GAME CALL, OCTOBER 5, 1949):

Two balls, no strikes. Two and oh. Newcombe looking into the dirt....Two nothing pitch is...swung on...drilled out toward right field, going way back...that's...the ball game! A home run for Tommy Henrich!

There's Henrich now between first and second. Bill Dickey, the first-base coach, almost jumps on his back, then realizes that's a tender back and he'd better not. Henrich's coming into third. He is trotting his home run home. Look at him grin, big as a slice of watermelon! Wow! Old Reliable hit one...that's all!

Well, they call him Old Reliable, and they're not jokin'. He hit a two-nothing pitch. Way up there in the straightaway right-field stands.

Henrich's home run was the first game-ending one in World Series history. Reynolds, yielding just two hits, and fanning nine, got the win. Rookie Newcombe pitched brilliantly, giving up just five hits and striking out 11.

The Yankees split the first two games at the Stadium and then swept the Dodgers in three games at Ebbets Field, winning their 12th World Series, the first of a record five consecutive world championships. The winners' share was $5,627 per player. The Dodger shares were $4,273 each.

It was a magical exclamation point to the 1940s for the team that played in the big ballpark in the Bronx.

CHAPTER

FIFTIES

It was business as usual as the New York Yankees began play at the start of the second half of the 20th century. They were the elite of baseball on the playing field and at the box office, where they would draw more than 2 million fans to Yankee Stadium for the fifth straight season.

YANKEES YEAR BY YEAR 1950 – 1959		YEAR	POSITION	WON	LOST	PCT.	MANAGER	ATTENDANCE
		1950*	FIRST	98	56	.636	CASEY STENGEL	2,081,380
		1951*	FIRST	98	56	.636	CASEY STENGEL	1,950,017
		1952*	FIRST	95	59	.617	CASEY STENGEL	1,629,665
		1953*	FIRST	99	52	.656	CASEY STENGEL	1,537,811
		1954	SECOND	103	51	.669	CASEY STENGEL	1,475,171
		1955	FIRST	96	58	.623	CASEY STENGEL	1,490,138
		1956*	FIRST	97	57	.680	CASEY STENGEL	1,491,784
		1957	FIRST	98	56	.636	CASEY STENGEL	1,497,134
		1958*	FIRST	92	62	.597	CASEY STENGEL	1,428,428
		1959	THIRD	79	75	.513	CASEY STENGEL	1,552,030

*WORLD CHAMPIONS

PAGE 84: Mickey Mantle at batting practice
ABOVE: Clubhouse keeper Pete Sheehey
OPPOSITE: Yankee Stadium in the foreground and the Polo Grounds, once the Yankees' home, across the way in Manhattan

RUDY GIULIANI: My first baseball game was in 1950 or 1951. It was between the Yankees and the Red Sox, with Joe DiMaggio playing for the Yankees and Dominic DiMaggio playing for the Red Sox. As a five- or six-year-old at Yankee Stadium, I found that fascinating—that brothers would be on two different teams. It was really weird to me. I remember asking my father, "How come they're playing for different teams? Are they angry at each other?"

JOE CARRIERI: In 1950, I became the regular Yankee batboy. Typical day—I'd go to Cardinal Hayes High School, three blocks from Yankee Stadium. I would get out at 12 o'clock with permission from the monsignor. I walked to the Stadium through McCombs Dam Park and got there a little after noon.

I dressed in the dryer room next to the jock straps. It was my own room. It was private. I had a Yankee uniform but it did not have a number or anything on the back of it. I would bring all the bats out through the clubhouse to the dugout. I made sure the bats were in the proper order because Casey Stengel had five lineups. That day's lineup would be hung over the bats. If Rizzuto was batting first, for example, the first hole would house his bat, etc., etc. Once I had the bats the way I wanted them, I would go out on the field and shag flies.

I'd sit on the stool outside the dugout, and when the ball was hit off the screen, I would fetch it and give it to coach Frank Crosetti. He would take all the old balls, count them, number them one to 20, whatever, and have them ready for the next day for batting practice. Back then a baseball could last a whole inning. Now it's something if it lasts one swing.

When the umpires were out of balls, Crosetti would send me to their room to get another dozen, two dozen balls. I would rub them up. Frank Crosetti told me, "If the Yankees are winning, rub 'em up dark. If the Yankees are losing, rub 'em up shiny." That was so the Yankees could see the balls better.

That was the time when my parents got their first television set and I could come home from Yankee Stadium and my mother would say, "I saw you today with Joe DiMaggio."

WHITEY FORD: My major league debut was July 1, 1950. I was 21 years old. I won my first nine decisions as a starter before losing a game in relief. A lot of the guys I'd played with in sandlot would come to the games at the Stadium. My mother and father came, my uncles. It was like the greatest dream to be with the great Yankees in the great Stadium. I had first been there, as I said, when I was 10, maybe 11 years old. To get there, playing, it was great.

The Yanks won their second straight pennant in 1950 and came up against the "Whiz Kids," the Philadelphia Phillies, in the World Series.

WHITEY FORD: Casey picked me, a rookie, to start the fourth game of the 1950 World Series against the Phillies at the Stadium on October 7. I had to buy World Series tickets for a lot of people. I got 30 or 40 tickets for the game I pitched in. They were four dollars and six dollars.

I was up 5–0 on the Phillies going into the ninth inning. There were two on and then I got Andy Seminick to hit a fly ball to the outfield. Gene Woodling lost it in the sun. He dropped it. Had he caught it, the game would have ended. Two runs came in. So Casey took me out and brought in Allie Reynolds. He didn't say too much when he was taking you out of the game. He might say "Nice job," something like that, and grab the ball from you.

I remember as I was walking off the mound going back to the dugout, people started booing. I thought they were booing me. But they were booing Casey, who was walking about 20 feet behind me, for taking me out of the game. We won anyway, 5–2.

The Yankees claimed their 13th world championship in 1950, backed by superb pitching that yielded just three earned runs and recorded a combined ERA of 0.73 in the Series. Vic Raschi hurled a 1–0 shutout in the first game. Allie Reynolds won the second game, 2–1. Eddie Lopat, who liked to talk about "The bell in the clubhouse . . . when it rang we were ready," started the third game. It was, however, Tom Ferrick who got the decision in relief in the 3–2 Yankee squeaker at the Stadium.

JOE CARRIERI: Mickey Mantle came up in 1951. He was shy, a nondrinker. The first few days he would take off his shirt near his locker and Casey Stengel would say, "Oh, my God, I've never see a physique like that in my life. Look at the muscles on that kid." Back in those days, baseball players did not have huge chests, forearms, or big shoulders. They were built in the main like ordinary people.

Mickey Mantle made his major league debut on April 17, going one-for-four in a 4–0 Yankee win over the Red Sox at Yankee Stadium. Whitey Ford, wearing his army uniform, tossed out the first ball. It was also debut day for a rookie public address announcer who was born when the Yankees were still called the Highlanders. He replaced Red Patterson, the public relations director, who had done PA since the mid-1940s.

BOB SHEPPARD: The Yankee team was made up of Johnny Mize, at first base, Jerry Coleman at second, Phil Rizzuto was the shortstop. Billy

LEFT: The way they used to do it—fans exiting onto the field when the game is over
ABOVE: Allie Reynolds drinking in the moment after a no-hit performance

Johnson played third base. Jackie Jensen was in left field. Joe DiMaggio was in center, and a rookie was in right field, Mickey Mantle. The catcher was Yogi Berra. The pitcher was Vic Raschi. That was some team. Five of them are in the Hall of Fame, and if Whitey Ford had been pitching that day there would have been six out of nine.

I thought Yankee Stadium had a cathedral-like quality. I had been in St. Patrick's Cathedral many, many times. But getting into Yankee Stadium I felt it was almost like St. Patrick's Cathedral. It had a kind of dignity, a quietude that many ballparks did not seem to have. I liked it. And I think it fit my style more than the Polo Grounds or Ebbets Field, where I had worked as a PA announcer.

Just about a month after his big-league debut, on May 16, 1951, Mickey Mantle hammered the first of his 206 homers at the Stadium.

At Old-Timers' Day, September 8, 1951, when former Yankee manager Joe McCarthy was honored, even the legends who had gathered took notice when Mantle slugged a home run into the last row of the right-field bleachers and Eddie Lopat shut out the Senators, 4–0.

A day later, the second game of a doubleheader was called after the sixth inning because of darkness, giving the Yankees a 2–0 win. Unlike in the National League, American League games could not use ballpark lights on Sundays.

On September 28, Allie Reynolds, who had pitched a no-hitter earlier in the season, was on the mound in the first game of a doubleheader against the Red Sox and Mel Parnell before 40,000. The Yanks needed just two wins to clinch their third straight pennant, one win for a tie.

MARVIN POLANSKY: It was Friday afternoon. My uncle, who was a big Yankee fan, called and said, "I have tickets."

I was 16 years old, a big Yankee fan, a student at Stuyvesant High School, which was on a double session. I got out at 12:30 and ran like a demon. The brass plate on the box at Yankee Stadium said: "ORO." My uncle told me that was for Ogus, Rabinowitz, and Ogus. Some business firm.

The day was cloudy and raw. It was a pretty full house. The Yankees were up 5–0 by the fourth inning. It was one of Joe DiMaggio's last games. He was my idol.

The game moved to the top of the ninth inning. With the Yankees way out ahead, 8–0, the main focus of the day was the no-hitter in progress.

Ted Williams was the final batter for Boston, all that was standing between Allie Reynolds and a no-hitter.

"Most times I tried to walk the damn guy," Reynolds said later. "In my opinion it was just stupid to let an outstanding hitter like him beat you."

Fastball, strike one. The next pitch—fastball again. Ball popped up behind home plate. The ball bounced off Berra's glove, and Yogi bounced off Reynolds backing up the play.

The fatigued Reynolds said, "Don't worry, Yogi, we'll get him next time."

A giant groan was unleashed all over the Stadium.

MARVIN POLANSKY: I remember saying to my uncle: "The worst thing you can do is give a hitter like Williams another chance."

It got very, very quiet.

Berra returned and took up his catcher's position.

An angry and annoyed Williams snapped: "You sons of bitches put me in a hell of a spot. You blew it, and now I've got to bear down even harder even though the game is decided and your man has a no-hitter going."

"I called for the same pitch, the same fastball," recalled Berra.

On the next Reynolds offering, Williams again popped the ball up. Foul ball, near the Yankee dugout. Berra raced back. "Lotsa room, Yogi, lotsa room!" screamed Tommy Henrich. "You can get it!" This time Berra squeezed it. Reynolds had his second no-hitter of the season, clinching at least a Yankee tie for the pennant.

MARVIN POLANSKY: When Berra caught the ball, he was directly in front of me. I was in the first row of seats on the left-hand side of the Yankee

LEFT: Joe DiMaggio posed and primed for retirement

dugout. We went wild, my uncle and I and all the fans there.

That night I told my friends what had happened. Most of them were Dodgers fans, and it was a bit unusual for me, who lived in Brooklyn to be a Yankee fan. Still, they were interested in my story. I had seen this marvelous, wonderful game that everyone was talking about.

We got the *Herald Tribune* for free at Stuyvesant. The next day, I looked through it, and there was a picture of me, in my gray jacket, with both my arms up. I was right behind Berra, who was catching the foul pop-up.

In the second game of the doubleheader, the Yankees locked up their third straight flag under Casey Stengel. Vic Raschi coasted to an 11–3 win, his 21st victory. And Joe DiMaggio recorded the final regular-season homer of his fabled career, a three-run shot.

The World Series competition for the Yankees in 1951 was the Giants of New York. They had a storybook season, chasing, catching, and then conquering their hated rival Brooklyn Dodgers in the deciding contest of a three-game play-off on Bobby Thomson's "Shot Heard 'Round the World."

EDDIE LOPAT: All the reporters told us to watch out. "The Giants are hot," they said. "They beat the Dodgers coming out of nowhere." We didn't believe what anybody told us or what they printed in the newspapers. The other teams had to beat us on the field. That was where it counted.

MONTE IRVIN: We were still on a high after beating the Dodgers in 1951 in that play-off game when we went up against the Yankees in the World Series. Without a chance to rest, we reported to

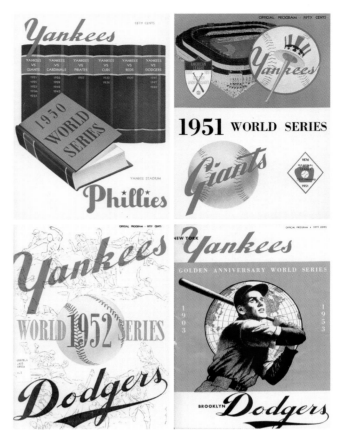

the Stadium the next day. I got four straight hits and also stole home in the first inning.

My last time up, Yogi Berra said, "Monte, I don't know what to throw you. You have been hitting high balls and low balls and curveballs. I'm gonna have you get a fastball right down the middle."

I really didn't believe Yogi. But sure enough, Reynolds threw me a fastball right down the middle. I hit a line drive. The ball was caught. I really wanted that hit. No one had ever gone five for five in the World Series.

Fielding the first black outfield in World Series history—Hank Thompson, Monte Irvin, and Willie Mays—the Giants defeated Allie Reynolds and the Yankees, 5–1, with Dave Koslo going the distance for the win in the first game.

from the outfield grass. He lay there, motionless. His right knee had snapped, and he was lost to the Yankees for the rest of the Series.

No matter—the Yankees were loaded with talent, and though the Giants had momentum, it was another world championship for Stengel's guys on October 10, 1951, as Vic Raschi bested Koslo, 4–3 before 61,711. That was the last World Series game Joe DiMaggio ever played in.

BOB WOLFF: When you approached Joe DiMaggio at the Stadium to do an interview, you had to almost check out what he was like that day. He was a very, very shy man, somber in his mood and difficult to speak to. It was like getting an appointment with royalty. As far as I could ascertain, he was the same way with teammates. A world apart from others in stature and communication.

WHITEY FORD: I didn't have much of a relationship with Joe DiMaggio, who was finishing up when I was on the scene and mostly stayed to himself. But I got to have a lot of good friends on those teams—Roger Maris, Mickey Mantle, Billy Martin, Yogi, Elston Howard. . . .

STEVE SWIRSKY: I was 10 years old and a Yankee fan. My dad didn't have a lot of money, but he came home one day with two tickets for the second '51 World Series game.

I remember everything about that day—the smells, the walking around to the little shops, my dad digging deep to buy a cap and a hot dog for me. It almost glowed in my heart 'cause I used to listen to the Yankee games on the radio from all over the country even though there were times I could barely hear it.

We sat down the left-field line underneath the overhang—20 rows back. In those days poles held up the overhang. My seat had an obstructed view. But you know how some women are about little boys. A woman switched seats with me so I could see. It was Willie Mays who hit the fly ball that Mantle, playing right field, chased. Mantle was not the superstar that he was going to be, but there was a big hush when he went down. It seemed like the world stopped.

The 19-year-old Mantle, attempting to avoid a collision with Joe DiMaggio, twisted his ankle in the fifth inning on a sprinkler-head cover protruding

PAUL SHEPPARD: I was a kind of mini-ballboy in '52 and '53, a couple of my high school years. I sat next to the Yankee dugout and would phone up to Dad [Bob Sheppard] any changes in the lineup.

In between games of a doubleheader, I'd get the new lineup from Casey Stengel. Charlie Silvera, the backup catcher, was usually outside

ABOVE: With the famous facade as a backdrop, Phil Rizzuto demonstrates his bunting skills

the door waiting to see the lineup because the only time he had a chance to play in place of Yogi Berra was in the second game of a double-header. Most times I would say, "Sorry, Charlie, not today." But in 1952 or 1953, the Yankees had clinched the pennant and were about 10 games up. And Casey Stengel said to me, "What kind of a lineup do you think we should have for the second game? You pick it, Paul."

So I picked it. All my favorites. Hank Bauer, at third base, someone who was not a third baseman. Johnny Mize, number 36. I loved him and put him in the lineup. And, of course, I had Charlie Silvera catching.

I called the lineup to my dad.

"Paul," he goes, "are you sure?"

I said, "Casey said I could do it."

And he said, "Sure, yeah."

Dad used to sit in the open air and do his announcing and he'd catch foul balls. He was a terrific athlete; he'd been a seven-letter man at St. John's. In those days, the early years, there was little or no recognition of him. The voice, while impressive, was not something that people talked about.

The original "Subway Series" games were actually bus rides for most New York City baseball players. For the 1952 World Series, the Yankee team bus had a police escort from Yankee Stadium to Ebbets Field and back. On one trip, a red sports car attached itself to the cavalcade headed back to

the Stadium. A motorcycle cop pulled up along the flashy auto to shoo it away. Then he saw the driver was Phil Rizzuto, who had come along for the ride from his home in New Jersey.

It took the Yankees seven games to defeat the Dodgers (for the third time in half a dozen years in the World Series). A game-saving catch by New York in the seventh game was described by Mel Allen this way: "It's a high pop-up . . . Who's going to get it? Here comes Billy Martin digging hard . . . and he makes the catch at the last second! How about that!"

JOE CARRIERI: When I was 15 years old, I had the chance to go on a road trip with the Yankees to St. Louis and Kansas City, etc. My mom said, "You're too young. You can't go."

The next day at the Stadium I told Phil what my mother had said.

"What's your mother's phone number?"

"Motthaven 5-5959."

He picked up the phone. "Mrs. Carrieri, this is Phil Rizzuto. I've got your son Joey here. Let your son go on the road trip and I will watch him. I'll be his mentor."

On the road I'd have my own room. But Phil had me come to his room to watch a little TV. He'd order up a sandwich and a Coke from room service.

At one point I became Phil's secretary. He would get hundreds of letters every day, and I had to answer them. I would take them home and send each fan a postcard with Phil's signature engraved on it, just to keep the goodwill going.

In 1953, the Yankees just kept rolling along, winning their fifth straight pennant. At home, they posted a 50–27 won-lost record. Before 62,370 at the Stadium on October 5, 1953, the Yankees captured

their record fifth consecutive world championship, eliminating the Brooklyn Dodgers in six games. The World Series winners' shares were a record $8,240 per player.

On April 15, 1954, a plaque that read "molder of a tradition of victory" was dedicated to Ed Barrow by the Yankees. It was hung on the center-field wall near the flagpole and close by the monuments to Babe Ruth, Lou Gehrig, and Miller Huggins.

In the meantime, Mickey Mantle just kept chugging along. His determination was on display at the Stadium on May 21 when Frank Sullivan, a hurler with little big-league experience pitched for the Red Sox. The Mick, having a hard time against a pitcher he had never seen, struck out three times. Then he figured it out, torching Sullivan for a home run that went over the auxiliary scoreboard and landed in the right center-field bleachers.

Although the Yankees led the league in attendance with 1,475,171 in 1954, only 1,912—a Yankee Stadium game low in attendance to that point in time—showed up on September 21, 1954, as rookie Bob Grim posted his 20th victory, four-hitting Washington, 3–1. It was the 101st Yankee win. They wound up finishing the 1954 season with 103 victories and just 51 losses, 54–23 with one tie at home. But that record was only good enough for second place, eight games behind the Indians, who won 111 games. Yankee fans had the consolation of knowing that their '53 team's .669 winning percentage was the highest ever for a second-place team. Cleveland was just better.

In the 1955 season opener, on April 13, the Yanks torched the Senators, 19–1. Winning pitcher Whitey Ford stroked three hits and allowed but two. Mickey Mantle, Yogi Berra, and Bill Skowron smashed home runs, while Bob Cerv and Andy Carey tripled.

On April 14, 1955, Elston Howard, the first black player on the Yankees, singled in his first at-bat in a game against the Red Sox.

FRANK PRUDENTI: Ellie Howard was one of the nicest gentlemen you would ever want to meet. Mickey Mantle gave him the nickname "Freddy the Freeloader," but it was good-naturedly.

We used to get a lot of things delivered to the clubhouse. One day cases of the hair tonic Brylcreem came in. There's Ellie going home with a case of it. Another time we got Gold Bond powder, cases of it; the Yankees used it all the time. Pete Sheehy had it out in the shower room where the players shaved. Ellie got a lot of that, too. All the guys took stuff. It just seemed Ellie took more than his share.

It was Friday the 13th in May 1955. But that didn't bother Mickey Mantle who homered from both sides of the plate for the first time. Mantle actually notched three home runs that day—the first two batting left-handed against Detroit starter Steve Gromek, the third batting right-handed off Bob Miller. It was The Mick in classic mid-1950s form—all the home runs reached the deep parts of the right center-field bleachers. He virtually single-handedly helped the Yanks defeat the Tigers, 5–2. With three home runs, Mantle, along with Tony Lazzeri, Ben Chapman, and Bill Dickey became one of four Yankees to hit three homers in one game at the Stadium.

The mighty Mantle was at it again on June 21. In the first inning at Yankee Stadium, he slammed a 461-foot shot, the first home run to ever reach the center-field bleachers. It came off Philadelphia's Alex Kellner.

BILL CHUCK: As a kid, whenever I couldn't fall asleep at night, I would think of Tony Kubek taking a ground ball in the hole and using that sidearm throwing motion, making the throw right on a line to Moose Skowron. And the next thing I'd know, I'd be fast asleep.

BOBBY RICHARDSON: After I signed with the New York Yankees in August 1955, I took the train from Sumter, South Carolina, to New York. I checked into the Hotel New Yorker and took a cab up to Yankee Stadium. Then I walked into the clubhouse and got a locker. Two good people, Kubek and Crosetti, had lockers on either side of me. I got a uniform from Pete Sheehy, the equipment manager. A very quiet man, Pete was one of those I admired most in all of baseball.

JOE CARRIERI: Pete never came past the top step of the dugout, never came out on the field. He had his own little room in the back of the clubhouse with a locker and a folding bed with a nice, soft mattress. When the Yankees were home, he would never leave. He got his food from the Stadium Club and would eat right in the clubhouse. He'd call up and tell them what he wanted, usually steak, mashed potatoes, and salad. When the team was on the road, he would go home to his apartment in the 80s by York Avenue.

After the games I would help Pete Sheehy with the chores, picking up the socks, getting the uniforms collected, and putting them in the washing machine and dryer. He kept the clubhouse, which was his home, immaculate.

There was a secret door about 20 feet across from the clubhouse. One day, he took me over there and opened the door. On the other side were trunks of baseball gloves, hats, and uniforms, all kinds of coveted Yankee memorabilia.

"Joe," he said, "take anything you want."

I took a Joe DiMaggio bat.

Where the door was, that area has been cemented over. I always wonder whether all those valuables are still in there or whether they were taken out. Only Pete Sheehy would know.

BOBBY RICHARDSON: My first day at the Stadium, I put on a uniform and was told to take batting practice with the regulars before the game. I come from a town that had about 12,000 people. I started to see people coming into the ballpark, making for a crowd that was several, several times more than the population of my whole town.

I stood by the batting cage but was not about to walk in. I did not want to get in front of Yogi Berra, Hank Bauer, or any of those.

Then Mickey Mantle came over, put his arm around me, and said, "C'mon kid, come in here and take some swings." That started a friendship that lasted a lifetime—a dozen years as teammates.

I worked out for four days with the Yankees and got to know the ballpark, the team a little bit. They had a pregame television show with Joe E. Brown and I was on that show. He asked me, "How long do you think it will be before you come back and play here?" I don't remember my answer. And then I was sent out to work my way back up through the farm system.

It was claimed that the groundskeepers at Yankee Stadium wet an area close by the catcher's box when Ford was slated to pitch. Catcher Elston Howard was allegedly adept at coating one side of the ball with mud. Scuffing the ball, according to reports, was a way Ford enhanced his pitching ability.

WHITEY FORD: If a guy blew a game because he came to work late after a long night of drinking or bouncing around, that's when somebody like Hank Bauer settled it in a hurry. He'd grab you in the dugout and look you right in the eyes and growl, "Don't fuck around with my money." And that's maybe the main thing that kept the guys straight, the idea that you're not only screwing yourself but you're also taking money out of everybody else's pocket if you screw up.

DON CRONSON: The 1950s were my time. My dad was a big Yankee fan. He got me into it. We'd go to the games and then after you could literally walk out onto the field, not the infield, which was ringed by ushers, but the outfield, where Mickey Mantle had been standing ten minutes before, where the Babe had been some years before.

GARY LEFKOWITZ: You could exit the Stadium via the warning track through the Yankee bullpen. I actually got to touch the auxiliary scoreboard. I got dust on my fingers. At first I was annoyed and then I said, "Wait a minute, this is holy dust."

DON CRONSON: To this day I remember the outfield distances going from right to left: 296, 344, 407, 461 in center out by the monuments on the playing field. Three of them—for Miller Huggins, Babe Ruth, and Lou Gehrig—were placed in front of the flagpole.

When I was able to go to games myself, I always sat in the upper deck behind home plate in the grandstand seats. They were super, unobstructed if you got there early enough. My big thing was going to Sunday doubleheaders. I'd have a bag full of food. My mother always packed string beans and carrots and other good things, and I'd have my pick of hot dogs. I'd watch batting practice. Just to watch Ted Williams when the Red Sox came in, hitting rifle shots all over the field was special. But I loved Mickey Mantle best. He was my hero.

May 30, 1956. Mort Schneider, my best friend, Bruce's, father, let us use his two season tickets, section seven, row one, upper deck. Front row, literally on the rail overlooking the field. Great seats. It's the Washington Senators, a doubleheader.

Hitting lefty, Mantle, in the second game, tags a pitch from Camilo Pascual. I had been in the Stadium so many times that as soon as a fly ball was hit I knew where it was going. Fifth inning, he hits a shot, and I jump up and start screaming, "It's going up! It's going out!" I knew it was going out. It was not a rocket shot. It was towering, and it was literally on its way down when it hit about 18 inches below the roof itself. That was Mantle's 20th home run of the season—the first time someone had hit 20 before June.

LEIGH MONTVILLE: In my senior year of high school sometime in the 1950s, we went down to New York. I was friends with a guy whose aunt lived on the Grand Concourse, and she let us stay over her house and sleep on the floor. The Yankees played the Tigers, and we saw all 18 innings. Afterwards, the kid and I got on a subway train and went all the way down to the Brooklyn Fox, where we saw Murray the K's Rock 'n Roll Show with Jerry Lee Lewis and Jackie Wilson. All this, plus an Audie Murphy movie. I always thought that maybe was one of the great days of my life.

FRANK PRUDENTI: I started as a Yankee batboy in 1956, succeeding my cousin Frank Carrieri. I was 14. You began on the visitors' side and you worked your way over to the Yankee side, where I was from 1959 to 1961. Those were the great years, the glory years.

Before I began working at Yankee Stadium, I used to go there every Saturday and Sunday with my one-dollar allowance. I would take the

ABOVE: Billy Martin in the Yankee dugout with his favorite piece of lumber

subway for 10 cents and sit in the bleachers for 50 cents. There was a lot of the same crowd there all the time, and you got to become friends.

It was so much different in that era. Players came in through an entrance back of first base, walked down a flight of steps, and they were immediately in the clubhouse. There were beautiful offices, too. You came into the lobby and went downstairs through a stairway and to the left was a hallway with five offices. The last one was for the ticket manager, with windows that faced outside into the lower lobby behind home plate. Across the street from the Stadium there was a one-level parking lot that probably held a maximum of 300 cars.

There are tunnels underneath Yankee Stadium that led out to the bullpens. You would leave the clubhouse and walk to the right up a little ramp into the Stadium and had to actually cross in front of the fans for about eight feet. It was such a joke—there were players in uniforms running that eight feet. Most times players ran through without anyone noticing them, but there were always a couple of fans hanging around knowing about that secret way to the bullpen. It really was like a secret passageway, very dark, very few lightbulbs. There were old chairs under there, lockers, gloves.

The players would wind up in the corner of right field, where they had a little room about eight feet by eight feet with a water cooler, a small bathroom, and a telephone. They would just wait for the call from the dugout. So many Yankee pitchers walked that tunnel through the years.

A lot of fans hung out maybe 30 feet down the right-field line, where the tarp cover was. When the game would end, they would be the first ones out on the field, as Mickey Mantle would run for that dugout as quick as he could because the fans were charging toward him.

One time a fan ran and reached out and grabbed the top of Mantle's shirt. Mickey turned a little and twisted his left shoulder. For a few days it bothered him when he was batting left-handed — that was the power shoulder.

The Yankees decided they needed to prevent that kind of stuff from happening, so they took the ushers and had them hover around the right-field corner, and when the last out was made, all of them would run for Mickey. He would tuck in behind them, and they'd run together to the dugout. Those ushers were called "the Suicide Squad." They only used the younger ushers — the older guys couldn't keep up with The Mick.

One August afternoon Whitey Ford was pitching, and it was almost a hundred degrees and humid. We wore wool uniforms back then, and Whitey was sweating. At the end of his pitching in an inning, he would come in and take off his shirt. I would dry him down. He would put on a nice dry T-shirt and his shirt over it, and I would place a light jacket on him.

Now he was sitting in the corner of the dugout, and I hear him calling, "Frankie, Frankie."

"What's the matter?" I ask.

"Go and tell Gus [Gus Mauch, the trainer] I want to take a shower at the end of this inning."

Whitey got the last out of the inning. He ran into the dugout and down the little runway into the clubhouse. He was the "Chairman of the Board"; his locker was in the corner when you entered the clubhouse, and it was the biggest.

Ripping off his clothing, he ran into the shower. Pete Sheehy and Gus Mauch waited for him to get out. We told each batter coming up to slow down just a little bit because Whitey was taking a shower.

He takes a nice, cool shower, not rushing. And he made it in just enough time to get out there and pitch and win the game. That was Whitey — a cool character.

Those teams I worked for had great camaraderie. Everybody was a brother, respected one another. If you were Bob Hale, the 25th man, or Mickey Mantle or Yogi Berra, it didn't matter. You were respected the same way by everybody.

That was all part of the atmosphere Casey Stengel projected and protected.

JOHNNY BLANCHARD: In 1955, I was 22 and had led the Eastern League in home runs and RBIs. After our last game of the season was over, I was in a pizza parlor with the ball club when the phone rang. It was for me.

"John, this is George Weiss," the voice on the other end says. "I want you in New York tomorrow morning."

I hung up. I thought it was a prank call. The phone rings again. I pick it up and I hear, "Don't you ever hang up on me again!"

I drove to the Bronx. The Yankees were playing the Red Sox. It was a doubleheader. A packed house. I was scared to death. I had never seen that many people in my life. I thought all these people were taking the oxygen right out of the ballpark.

I was sitting in the bullpen. About the eighth inning, Charlie Silvera, the coach, yelled, "Hey John, they want you to come up and pinch-hit."

I said, "There's no way I can make it. I can't get over that little iron railing." It was very short, about three feet high, but for me to run from there to the dugout and then to home plate with all those people watching . . . "Tell 'em my leg's broke, anything, I don't care."

Then he broke up laughing. "Just kidding, John. They want a relief pitcher." And then everybody started laughing. They got me good. Talk about butterflies.

Pete Sheehy gave me my number: 38. They gave all the lower numbers to the stars or guys they thought were going to be stars. I called it my "football number," meaning I thought I had no

prayer of staying with the ball club, especially since they sent me back to the minors. I wouldn't come back until 1959.

But while I was in New York, the *New York Times* wrote a story on me. They came up to the Concourse Plaza Hotel and took a picture of me looking out the window at Yankee Stadium. I spoke a lot about the life in the minor leagues and some of the difficulties there. I thought it was a pretty nice article.

Then there was a pink slip in my locker: "See Mr. Weiss immediately."

Oh, boy, I didn't know what to think. Maybe I would be catching the next train to Memphis or something.

I went up there. He was dressed slick, sitting behind his desk. He was a grouchy old bag. I never saw the man smile.

"Sit down."

I sat down.

"I'd really appreciate it if you'd keep your mouth shut," he said.

Then he showed me the newspaper article. And he went on about the good money he paid to his scouting staff trying to get the best players to sign with the Yankees, and their parents are reading the newspapers, and things I said about how tough the minor league conditions are makes their job more difficult.

The bottom line was, "Rookie, keep your mouth shut."

FRANK PRUDENTI: George Weiss, in his business suit, was on the scene and in control, ruling with an iron first. He was a tough man. He'd sit ten seats over from the screen, third or fourth row back, the best seats in Yankee Stadium. He did not sit right next to the dugout. There was a crown in the infield, which was a lot higher than it is now. So sitting in the dugout or in the first two rows of seats, you actually had to lift your head up and strain to be able to see ground balls hit to third base. You couldn't see Yogi Berra standing in left field.

In 1955, the Dodgers of Brooklyn were probably the best team in all of baseball. Their team batting average and slugging percentage were tops in the National League, their pitchers had the best ERA, most saves, and most strikeouts. The Dodgers stole more bases, hit more home runs, and scored more runs than any other National League club.

JACK LANG: It was an awesome collection of talent. They knew they were good, but they had this sense that they could not beat the Yankees in the World Series.

The Brooklyn Dodgers had never won a World Series. Their last five losses were to the Yankees. Now it was the 1955 World Series. They were knotted at three wins apiece with the Yankees in the seventh and deciding game on October 4th, before 62,465 at Yankee Stadium.

Johnny Podres, 23, was the Brooklyn pitcher. He was matched up against veteran Tommy Byrne. Hits by Gil Hodges in the fourth and sixth innings gave the Dodgers a 2–0 lead. Junior Gilliam came in from left field to play second base in the bottom of the sixth inning. Speedy Sandy Amoros took his place in the outfield.

Mantle drew a walk to start the Yankee sixth. Gil McDougald managed a bunt single. Berra was next.

MEL ALLEN (GAME CALL):
The outfield swung away toward right. Sandy Amoros is playing way into left center. Berra is basically a pull hitter. Here's the pitch. Berra swings and he does hit one to the opposite field, down the left-field line. Sandy Amoros races over toward the foul line . . . and he makes a sensational, running, one-handed catch! He turns, whirls, fires to Pee Wee Reese. Reese fires to Gil Hodges at first base in time to double up McDougald. And the Yankees' rally is stymied!

JERRY COLEMAN: It wasn't so much that Amoros made a great catch. It was the way he went after it in the sun. A better fielder would have made it easier. The circumstances were such that we may have had a tied ball game. But as it turned out, that was our last chance.

The Yankees were down to their last out in the bottom of the ninth inning. Mel Allen, in the moment, turned the microphone over to Dodger announcer **VIN SCULLY:** *"Howard hits a ground ball to Reese. He throws to Hodges . . . the Brooklyn Dodgers are world champions!"*

Afterward, Arthur Daley wrote in the *New York Times*, "Conscience-stricken by the many shabby tricks she had played on the Brooks through the years . . . Lady Luck put wings on the feet of Amoros and glue in his glove."

The talk all over baseball but particularly in New York and especially in Brooklyn was all about the "Dem Bums" finally beating the Yankees in the World Series. Most experts expected the two powerhouse ball clubs to meet again in 1956, in another "Subway Series."

As the season got under way, Mickey Mantle, despite physical ailments that included strained muscles in his thigh, was in midseason form. On April 21 he smacked a home run for the second straight day against the Red Sox and went three for five.

Four days later The Mick ripped a shot that slammed dead center into the bleachers and caromed back onto the field. Boston center fielder

Jimmy Piersall held Mantle to a triple, getting a strong throw into third. An animated Casey Stengel trudged out to argue that the shot was a home run. He protested a bit too much and was thrown out of the game.

Billy Crystal, who was born in 1948, recalled, "My first Yankee Stadium game was in 1956. I sat in Louis Armstrong's seats (my family was in the music business), and Mickey [Mantle] signed my scorecard and hit a home run. From then on when I went to the Stadium I thought that Mickey Mantle knew I was there and was telling himself, 'Billy's here. I'd better have a good day. I'd better try to hit one for him.'"

It may or may not have been the day young Billy Crystal showed at the Stadium. But on May 5, the young

and powerful Mickey Mantle was all over the ball, as he was all that season. His tape-measure shot that day struck the right-field facade at Yankee Stadium, high-lighting the Yankee win over Kansas City, 5–2.

———

LEIGH MONTVILLE: I went to the Stadium with my Boy Scout troop. Our seats were way up in the third deck. We all had our gloves with us, and we all said we were going to catch a ball. Our scoutmaster disillusioned us. "Balls never come up, you know," he said.

Then, the very next day, Mantle hit that one off the facade. They had a picture in the *Daily News* **with the dotted line showing how the ball went. I wanted to show that to the scoutmaster.**

ABOVE: The great Jackie Robinson steals home in a 1955 game at Yankee Stadium

In the first game of a doubleheader, Mantle faced Pedro Ramos and slugged a high drive toward right field. Those there looked at the ball in flight climbing above the Stadium roof. A stiff breeze brought it down against the right-field facade, about 18 inches from clearing the roof.

———

BOB WOLFF: Unlike Babe Ruth, who hit balls high in the air, which then descended, usually into the lower deck, Mantle hit home runs which soared upward. That shot off Ramos was on its ascendancy when it hit about a foot from the

top. It was still going upwards. I thought that one would have gone as much as 700 feet.

Despite the slightly varying accounts of what happened that May 30, the facts are impressive, some would say mind-boggling. Mantle homered twice: once off Pedro Ramos and in the nightcap off Camilio Pascual. Both shots were "Ruthian." Both paved the way for Bomber victories. Both further enhanced the image of the Yankee center fielder as a premier power hitter.

ROGER KAHN: I suppose a highlight of the time I covered the Yankees was being in the bar in the press room where Casey Stengel used to hang out. He had writers divided into two categories: "my writers" and "the other guys." I was one of his writers, and he would go on and on to me about all subjects.

BOB WOLFF: Casey Stengel was a charming man, always great copy. I would get to the Stadium early to get comments from him in the Yankee dugout. He was always there. He would talk to you in a voice that made it seem as if you were 100 yards away: "Well, Bob, let me tell you about today's lineup." People would hear his voice booming across the Stadium, and a crowd would start to arrive. Then after I got what I wanted, I had to fight my way out through the hunk of people who were there around him. He was like the pied piper of Yankee Stadium. He would talk to anybody who would listen—fans, opposing players, groundskeepers, anyone.

ROGER KAHN: When *Sports Illustrated* was a new magazine, they offered me a job, but they wanted me to write a sample story. They liked my idea of Allie Reynolds, a portrait of an aging ballplayer. I went to Reynolds, whom I knew well, and he agreed. He was in the locker room. We walked around. Reynolds had a towel on his head; otherwise he was nude. He talked about being a scared Indian kid, he didn't say Native American. He spoke about how he developed and learned how to pitch. It was a wonderful exposition. His back was bothering him, and after about 25 minutes he hopped in the whirlpool tub and soaked for a while. When he got out he dried himself with the towel. That was why it was on his head.

I went to Stengel the next day and told him about the Reynolds piece. He was in his usual pose at the bar in civilian clothes with a drink. He didn't become silly or incoherent. He said he didn't like magazines because they held things for a few weeks and when it comes out you can't believe you said it. "But you are one of my guys so I gotta help you."

And he said something like this: "Reynolds is the greatest two ways—starting and relieving. And I've seen the great Mathewson and Cy Young and I wondered who that fat old guy was which shows you what a dumb young punk I was and you could look that up."

As the story goes, one day some of the older writers were comparing notes and they didn't know who was pitching the next day and they sent a junior member of the Stadium baseball writing corps to go down and ask Stengel. The young writer disappears for about a half an hour and then comes back.

The older writers ask, "All right, all right, who's pitching tomorrow?"

And the response was, "I'm not sure, but I think it's Christy Mathewson."

Down the home stretch of the 1956 season, the Yankees picked up outfielder Enos Slaughter. Phil Rizzuto was asked to go over the postseason roster with management at the Stadium to suggest the player to cut to make room for the ex-Cardinal. For each player the little shortstop suggested be cut, management gave reasons why that player should stay.

On August 25, 1956, Rizzuto was given his unconditional release. The Yankees came to the conclusion that their only expendable player was the Scooter.

Slaughter helped the Yankees, but Mickey Mantle and Whitey Ford were the siege guns for the team in its 54th season, both on top of their game, torquing New York to a nine-game runaway over the Cleveland Indians and another pennant. The Mick won the Triple Crown and the MVP award. The Chairman of the Board was 19–6 and led the AL in winning percentage and ERA.

The Yankees were ready for revenge against the "Bums" from Brooklyn, who had finally beaten them in a World Series the year before.

For a while it looked like Dem Bums were going to have their way again with the Yankees as they won the first two games, at Ebbets Field, 6–3 and 13–8. But the Yankees took the third and the fourth games played at the Stadium, 5–3 and 6–2.

The fifth game, played before 64,519 at Yankee Stadium, is one that has gone down as a classic in baseball history.

BOB WOLFF: Mel Allen was with Vin Scully on TV that World Series game five, October 8, 1956. I was sitting on the first mezzanine looking down on the ball field. The radio booth was separate from the press box. The only other person near me was the other radio announcer, Bob Neal, from Cleveland. My Mutual Broadcasting System account went around the country and throughout the world on the Armed Forces Radio Network.

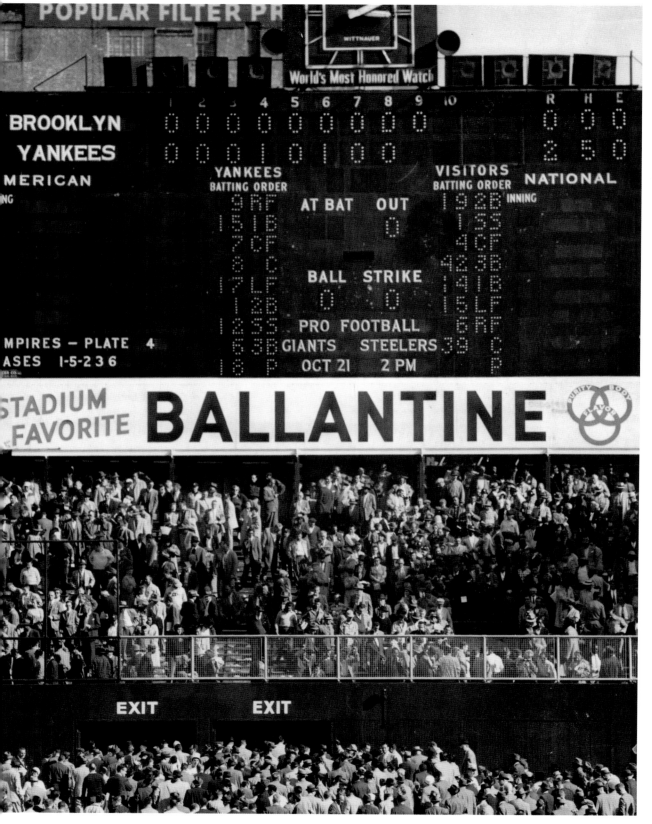

Don Larsen had started game two of the Series against Brooklyn, walked four, and was tagged for four runs in 1 2/3 innings. Nevertheless, Casey Stengel, always a hunch player, tabbed him to start game five.

Autumnal shadows, smoke and haze, and a great deal of noise were part of the environment that day along with the big crowd and World Series buntings on railings along the first- and third-base lines. Zeroes on the scoreboard kept going up for the Dodgers of Brooklyn, inning after inning.

A second-inning Jackie Robinson line drive off the glove of Andy Carey at third was picked up by Gil McDougald. Out at first. Mantle's great jump on a fifth-inning line drive by Gil Hodges put him in position for a backhand grab of the ball. A screamer by Hodges in the eighth inning down the third-base line was turned into an out by Andy Carey. Brooklyn's Sandy Amoros and Duke Snider sent shots into the right field seats—foul.

BOB WOLFF: Don Larsen did not wind up. I had to say, "He's ready, here's the pitch." You had the swelling of noise after an out or a strike. And then complete silence. And also a hum and roars. After a while I was not conscious of anybody [or] focused on anything but the no-hitter in progress, whether they were Brooklyn or Yankee fans.

The Yankees had scratched out a couple of runs off Sal "the Barber" Maglie. The game moved to the bottom of the ninth inning.

PREVIOUS SPREAD: The play that saved Don Larsen's perfect game; An overjoyed Yogi Berra and Don Larsen after the last out
LEFT: The scoreboard tells the story—a World Series game for the books

ROGER KAHN: It was over before you realized the tremendous impact of what was happening. It was not like some of the special Dodger-Yankee games that took forever.

"If it was 9–0, Larsen would've been paying little attention," Berra said. "It was close and he had to be extremely disciplined. He was. I went to the mound and reminded him that if he walked one guy and the next guy hit one out, the game was tied."

DON LARSEN: The last three outs were the toughest. I was so weak in the knees that I thought I was going to faint. I was so nervous I almost fell down. My legs were rubbery. My fingers didn't feel like they belonged to me. I said to myself, "Please help me, somebody."

Carl Furillo flied out to Hank Bauer in right field.

Roy Campanella grounded out weakly to Billy Martin at second base.

Left-handed hitting Dale Mitchell pinch-hit for Sal Maglie.

BOB WOLFF (GAME CALL):

Count is one and one. And this crowd just straining forward on every pitch. Here it comes—a swing and a miss! Two strikes, ball one to Dale Mitchell. Listen to this crowd! I'll guarantee that nobody—but nobody—has left this ballpark. And if somebody did manage to leave early, man, he's missing the greatest! Two strikes and a ball. Mitchell waiting, stands deep, feet close together. Larsen is ready, gets the sign. Two strikes, ball one, here comes the pitch. Strike three! A no-hitter! A perfect game for Don Larsen!

Yogi Berra runs out. He leaps on Larsen, who is swarmed by his teammates. Listen to this crowd roar.

Pandemonium broke out all over Yankee Stadium as thousands of fans managed to get onto the playing field.

PAUL DOHERTY: There really wasn't any "security" as we know it today. People ran past the ushers—several of the ushers headed for Larsen, too.

The 27-year-old Larsen, overcome by the moment, busted loose and into the relative sanctuary of the Yankee dugout and then the clubhouse.

The game lasted but two hours and six minutes. The final pitch, Larsen's 97th of the game, was the only one that stirred some controversy.

"The third strike on Mitchell," Berra was adamant, "was absolutely, positively a strike on the outside corner. No question about it. People say it was a ball and that I rushed the mound to hug Larsen to make the umpire think it was a strike. Nonsense. It was a perfect strike."

Afterward sportswriter Louis Effrat asked Casey Stengel, "Was that the best game you have ever seen Larsen pitch?"

"So far," was the Yankee manager's response.

DON LARSEN: I pitched for 14 years with eight different clubs and won only 81 games. I wish my record had been better, but I was very pleased to get into the World Series and pitch the perfect game. And I guess that is what I will always be remembered for. They can never break my record. Everybody is entitled to a good day, and mine came at the right time. I still find it hard to believe I really pitched the perfect game It's almost like a dream, like something that happened to somebody else.

ARTHUR RICHMAN: Don Larsen and I were friends. We still are. That night we went to the Copa to celebrate. I had called up for a table and they said there was no room but when I told them I was bringing Don Larsen, they brought a table down front and set us up. We ate and drank and Joe E. Lewis, the great comic, introduced Don to the audience. When the check came, we had ordered so much we didn't have the money to pay. But Joe E. Lewis picked up the tab. It was a perfect day and night for Don.

BOB WOLFF: Don Larsen signed my scorecard, which I still have. My arm was stiff for a week afterwards because doing the broadcast, I kept pitching that last half inning with Larsen pitch by pitch.

BOB SHEPPARD: If Nolan Ryan had done it, if Sandy Koufax had done it, if Don Drysdale had done it, I would have nodded and said, "Well, it could happen." But Don Larsen?

A LETTER TO DON LARSEN:

Dear Mr. Larsen: It is a noteworthy event when anybody achieves perfection in anything. It has been so long since anyone pitched a perfect big league game that I have to go back to my generation of ballplayers to recall such a thing and that is truly a long time ago.

This note brings you my very sincere congratulations on a memorable feat, one that will inspire pitchers for a long time to come.

With best wishes,

Sincerely,

Dwight D. Eisenhower

President of the United States

The Dodgers won game six, setting up the seventh and final game of the back-and-forth World Series. That was no contest. Behind the three-hit pitching of Johnny Kucks and home runs slammed by Yogi Berra (two), Elston Howard, and Bill Skowron, the Yankees cakewalked their way, 9–0, to another world championship. No one knew then, but it would be the last World Series game ever played between the Brooklyn Dodgers and the New York Yankees.

BOBBY RICHARDSON: I played in 11 games in 1955 and five in 1956 and was voted a third share in '55 and a fifth share in '56. I came back in 1957, this time as a full member of the Yankee roster. That was an even bigger thrill.

It was my first full year with the Yankees and I was in and out of the lineup. We had a lot of good infielders: Jerry Coleman, Billy Martin, Gil McDougald. I went to George Weiss and told him that I would like to be traded where I could play every day.

He said, "Just be patient. You'll get your chance. We are not going to trade you."

Tony Kubek and I had roomed together in the minor leagues and now in the major leagues. He was my closest friend. We were dubbed by Casey "the Milkshake Twins." Stengel said of me, "Look at him. He don't drink, he don't smoke, he don't chew tobacco, he don't stay out too late, and he still don't hit .250!" Later he changed it to "He's the best .260 hitter I've ever seen."

Casey Stengel was a lot smarter than most people gave him credit for. He also was smart enough to have the best coaches. I was friendly with him, but I am not sure he ever knew my name.

FRANK PRUDENTI: Casey didn't talk to me much, since I was only a Yankee batboy. But when he talked you would understand him clear as could be. On the other hand, when he was talking to the press, it was that Stengelese that got everyone confused. A reporter asked him about Roger Maris and he didn't want to answer the question so he started to talk first about our pitching staff, and then about times he played in close games, and then he began to talk about a guy in this drugstore from long ago who was making him an ice cream soda.

They said Casey slept on the bench. Sometimes he did. He would doze off, and Coach Crosetti had the job of keeping Casey awake by whistling to the shortstop to come back a step, move up a step. Only he never really was moving the shortstop—he was trying to wake up Casey.

BROOKS ROBINSON: I saw Yankee Stadium for the first time in 1957. I always felt the Yankees had an advantage. You left the hotel and drove through all the traffic to get there and got off the bus and then came into contact with those kids who said "Youse'r gonna get it."

And we usually got it. In that era when I began with the Baltimore Orioles, I was always coming up against the cream of the crop at Yankee Stadium. They were loaded.

Playing there was something else. I was always in awe knowing the history and tradition. I'd go out to the monuments. I took the subway up there many times all by myself just to experience the whole thing.

As time went on, Clete Boyer of the Yankees became one of my best friends. He was a third baseman like me, a great defensive third baseman. I always told him: "If there's ever a fight at the Stadium, I'm gonna look for you, and we are going to just dance around."

On June 23, 1957, Prime Minister Kishi of Japan, sporting a Yankee cap, was just one of the 63,787 fans at the Stadium. The Yanks split a doubleheader with Chicago. Mickey Mantle was six-for-nine.

The Yankees wound up in the World Series for the eighth time in nine years as they finished eight games ahead of the White Sox.

ROGER KAHN: We flew back from Milwaukee after the Braves had taken games four and five of the 1957 World Series. I was with Stengel at the Stadium and a TV guy put a microphone in his face and said, "Did your guys choke up out there?"

And Stengel said, "Do you choke up on that fucking microphone?" And then he turned around and scratched his buttocks and kept talking.

Stengel later said to me, "We've gotta put a stop to them terrible questions. When I said "fuck," I ruined his audio. When I scratched my ass, I ruined his video."

The Braves of Milwaukee ruined the Yankees' time, taking down the New Yorkers in seven games. The pivotal game was the last one, on October 10, 1957, at Yankee Stadium before 61,207. Lew Burdette was on his game, and in total control, hurling a 5–0 shutout over the Yanks.

The team that played its home games in the big ballpark in the Bronx may have lost the World Series, but as it prepared for the 1958 season there were all kinds of optimism. The Yankees still had all those stars in their prime of primes, especially Mickey Mantle.

ROGER KAHN: In the early years, Mantle was not that nice. He became nicer as he went along. I was sports editor at *Newsweek*. They decided that they wanted a cover [story] on him. The Yankees ordered him to cooperate, but he

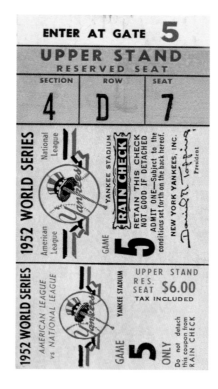

was militantly uncooperative. I spent two weeks knocking around a lot at the Stadium with Mickey, and to all my questions he gave grudging answers.

During that time he went on "The Ed Sullivan Show." Later, I asked him what he got for that appearance.

"$500."

"Only $500?"

"Yeah, but Kim Novak was on the show and I got to spend the night with her."

The 1958 Yankees showed that winning was everything at the July 5th game in Boston. The Red Sox had a 5–3 lead in the top of the eleventh inning. The Yanks stalled so that the 11:59 game curfew was triggered, and the game wound up reverting to the 3–3 score that existed at the end of the tenth inning. It was a move that delighted the hometown fans.

But the hometown fans were not delighted on September 21, when Baltimore's Hoyt Wilhelm hurled a 1–0 no-hitter against their team. The knuckleballer came into the Stadium on that drizzly night with a 2–10 won-lost record. The Yanks had clinched the pennant. Ironically, the Yankee pitcher in that game opposing Wilhelm was Don Larsen, two years away from his World Series perfect game.

Revenge was the theme for the Yankees as they matched up against Milwaukee in the 1958 World Series. Games four and five, at the Stadium, drew 71,563 and 65,279, respectively. They had to go seven games, but the Yankees won another world championship.

In April 1959 the first electronic message scoreboard was in place at Yankee Stadium.

PAUL DOHERTY: Installed in time for Opening Day, the message scoreboard was designed by Lon Keller, who had created the famous Yankee "hat" brand still used today. The previous Yankee board, installed in 1946, was taken apart and delivered to the Phillies' Connie Mack Stadium.

One of the low moments of the '59 season took place on May 20. The Yankees were mired in the American League basement, last place, for the first time since May 8, 1940. They went 7–8 in April and 12–15 in May and played catch-up the rest of the year.

On July 17, Ralph Terry had a no-hitter going into the ninth. Jim McAnany singled to left for the White Sox. Mel Allen, aware of the taping of the game for Red Barber's postgame show, asked WPIX director Jack Murphy for a replay. One batter later, the rewound tape revealed that McAnany's single did drop in front of Norm Siebern. And thus was instant replay born at Yankee Stadium.

In 1959, the Yankees finished in third place, the lowest in Casey's Yankee time. Nearing age 70, increasingly impatient, peevish, a gulf widening between him and the younger players, Stengel seemed to have lost a few steps. And he was making some game moves with pinch hitters, pitching changes, lineups, that were odd even for him.

Except for 1954 and 1959, the Yankees under Casey Stengel as manager won pennants in each year he was there. When he assumed command of the Yankees in 1949, there were 37 different players on the roster at one time or another that season.

As the 1960 season beckoned, the only player who remained from Casey's start with the Yankees was Lawrence Peter Berra, "Yogi." A new addition to the team was Roger Maris who had been traded to the Yankees from Kansas City.

OPPOSITE: Casey Stengel bids farewell toward the end of his dozen years as Yankee manager
OVERLEAF: Yankee Stadium gets a face lift in the fifties

OFFICIAL TIME
LONGINES
GATE 2
GATE 4
GATE 4
GATE 4
GATE 6
157 ST.
NO PARKING

CHAPTER

SIXTIES

When Roger Maris came to the Yankees in 1960, he was just another player added to the roster. He had not come up through the Yankee farm system. The Mick, who had blasted 52 homers in 1956, was the fan favorite. The talk had always been that if anyone would break Babe Ruth's single-season home-run record, it would be the "Commerce Comet."

YANKEES YEAR BY YEAR 1960–1969	YEAR	POSITION	WON	LOST	PCT.	MANAGER	ATTENDANCE
	1960	FIRST	97	57	.630	CASEY STENGEL	1,627,349
	1961*	FIRST	109	53	.673	RALPH HOUK	1,747,725
	1962*	FIRST	96	66	.593	RALPH HOUK	1,493,574
	1963	FIRST	104	57	.646	RALPH HOUK	1,308,920
	1964	FIRST	99	63	.611	YOGI BERRA	1,305,638
	1965	SIXTH	77	85	.475	JOHNNY KEANE	1,213,552
	1966	TENTH	70	89	.440	KEANE/HOUK	1,124,648
	1967	NINTH	72	90	.444	RALPH HOUK	1,259,514
	1968	FIFTH	83	79	.512	RALPH HOUK	1,185,666
	1969	FIFTH	80	81	.497	RALPH HOUK	1,067,996

*WORLD CHAMPIONS

BOB WOLFF: Mantle was getting more and more mature. He had a sly way of speaking, an impish grin, and a self-deprecating type of humor. I had seen all the famous home run hitters — Babe Ruth and all the rest. No one hit them as far and hard as Mantle. No one could hit home runs to left or right field with equal power the way Mantle did as a switch hitter. Nobody.

At the Yankee Stadium home opener on April 22, 1960, Mickey Mantle blasted a fourth-inning homer off Hoyt Wilhelm. New York trimmed Baltimore, 5–0. Another season and The Mick and the Yanks were at it again.

From 1959 to 1962, Major League Baseball staged two All-Star games. Yankee Stadium was the site for a second 1960 All-Star Game, on July 13. Seven Yankees were on that American League squad: The starters were Whitey Ford (starting pitcher), Yogi Berra (catcher), Mickey Mantle (outfield), Roger Maris (outfield), and Bill Skowron (first base). Jim Coates (pitcher) and Elston Howard (catcher) were reserves. Only 38,362 showed up — maybe fans were "all-starred" out. The National League used six hurlers and won, 6–0.

At the Old-Timers' Day on August 13, three days after his 86th birthday, Herbert Hoover threw out the first ball.

On September 6, in his final game at Yankee Stadium, Ted Williams hit his 518th career homer.

The Yankees drew 1,627,349 in 1960, their best home attendance since 1952. They notched their 25th pennant and faced off against Pittsburgh in the World Series.

BILL VIRDON: In newspaper comparisons of center fielders I might have gotten the worst of it, but that didn't bother me. To be compared with Mantle, I was flattered.

Like many others, I was impressed with the Stadium when I came in there for the World Series. It was the only center field that I got into for the first time, looked around, and did not think I could cover. I was a speedy outfielder, but it was that huge, especially in left center.

The monuments were right behind me in center field. I didn't think they had any business being there on the playing field. As a center fielder you had to be very cautious — you didn't want to run into one of them.

DICK GROAT: It was special for me to return to Yankee Stadium for the World Series, the place my father had taken me to as a kid and where I had practiced as a high school all-star. Our Pirates were the underdogs to the Yankees, and we were impressed with them. But we were not in awe.

Despite Richardson and Mantle and Berra and Ford and Maris and the others, the Yankees went down to defeat. The word was that Stengel had not utilized Whitey Ford properly, giving him just two starts in the Series, both of which were shutouts.

The climactic moment was the bottom of the ninth in game seven, in Pittsburgh. Bill Mazeroski led off against Yankee pitcher Ralph Terry and slugged his World Series–winning homer over the left-field wall. Terry, the critics said, had warmed up four times but left his best stuff in the bullpen.

Stengel took the heat. Two days after the World Series ended, the New York Yankees announced that the highest-paid manager in baseball ($90,000) was retiring. For several years, Yankee owners Dan Topping and Del Webb wanted to dump their superstar manager and replace him with Yankee coach Ralph Houk. Now it was rumored that the decorated World War II major, who commanded men during the Battle of the Bulge, was being wooed by other teams. And the Yankees wanted to lock him up.

RALPH HOUK: When Casey got fired, that hurt me. He was a great guy. I was at Yankee Stadium from 1947 to 1955 as a player and came back in 1958, replacing Bill Dickey as a coach at first base. It was Casey Stengel who made me a coach. I learned a lot from him.

I moved into the manager's office in 1961, and the great clubhouse guy Pete Sheehy had everything ready for me. It had all I wanted: a room, a desk, a place to keep my records. Most of my memories of that office was bringing guys in and telling them things they didn't want to hear.

I was usually down at one end of the Yankee dugout, managing from a standing position with one leg up. I stood rather than sat on the bench. I was always moving.

PAGE 112: Sal Durante catches Roger Maris' 61st home run ball
PREVIOUS SPREAD: Whitey Ford in action during the 1960 World Series
ABOVE: Whitey Ford shows off his 1961 Cy Young Award
OPPOSITE: The Stadium and surroundings in 1960

Managing in Yankee Stadium you tried to take advantage of our right-field little wall and have guys on your team who could hit the ball there. You tried to have pitchers make the other team hit the ball to the big part of the field.

In freezing rain on Opening Day, April 17, 1961, only 1,947 hardy souls showed up. Whitey Ford got the Yankees off to a good start, blanking Kansas City, 3–0. Still, the Yankees moved out slowly that season.

Just 9–19 in spring training, 18–15 as the season got into full swing, the Yankees in their first 33 games managed only 34 homers. But that would change.

Through 10 games in 1961, Roger Maris was homerless. On May 17 he hit his first Stadium homer of the season, off southpaw Pete Burnside of Washington. That gave the quiet outfielder four for the season. But there would be many more—24 in his next 38 games. By the end of May, Maris had a dozen homers. By the end of June, he had 27.

On July 1, 1961, the Senators led the Yankees 3–0, when a Mickey Mantle shot, a few feet left of the 456-foot sign in left field, put the Yanks on the scoreboard. Washington moved ahead, 5–1. The Yankees closed the gap to 5–4 on a Mantle three-run homer. Then in the ninth inning, Maris pounded a two-run homer, his 28th. New York won, 7–6.

JOHNNY BLANCHARD: Roger Maris had the locker next to mine. When he was popping those long ones out of the park, I had to get out of my own locker because 20, 30 writers would flock around him, and they would sift into my locker space. Roger was an introvert and did not like all the bright lights. That was what gave him the reputation of being nasty. But he was not.

LEFT: The feared Yankee sluggers, "The M&M Boys"

By the end of July, Maris had 40 home runs. That placed his record six ahead of Babe Ruth's pace. The Sultan of Swat had set his record of 60 homers in a 154-game season. But this year Major League Baseball had added two expansion teams to the roster and eight games to the schedule. Accordingly, Baseball Commissioner Ford Frick ruled that if Maris broke Ruth's record, an asterisk would be placed next to the solidly built Yankee's name in the record books.

While all the focus seemed to be on the home-run race that '61 season, other Yankees had big moments, too, but none as big as Maris would have. On July 26 Johnny Blanchard, the man they called "Super Sub," hammered his third and fourth straight home runs at Yankee Stadium, powering a 5–2 New York win over the Chicago White Sox. Blanchard's four home runs in a row over three games tied a major league record.

On August 4 Maris clubbed home run number 41 at the Stadium off Camilo Pasqual of Minnesota. Home runs 52 and 53 were slammed at "The House That Ruth Built" on September 2 off Frank Lary and Hank Aguirre of Detroit.

ROGER KAHN: I had a freelance assignment for *Sports Illustrated* **for a story on Maris. He was**

fine, just a few little outbursts of temper. There were times when he got 50 reporters around him asking the same question. He'd answer them but he was annoyed.

One day after he finished an interview he turned to Elston Howard and said, "I'm just sick of all these questions, all this attention."

And Howard told Maris, "If I had 55 home runs, questions would not make me sick."

In the clubhouse, Maris would tell Mickey, "I can't take it anymore, I just can't."

And Mantle would say, "I'm telling you, Roger, you've got to take it."

When it got to the point where he could not "take it" anymore, Maris would retreat to the training room or sit at a huge oak table in the center of the clubhouse smoking Camels and sipping coffee while playing for hours with a contraption trying to manipulate a steel ball through a 40-hole maze.

He was the talk of the town, the big news in the Bronx. But another Yankee who was having a spectacular season was the "Chairman of the Board," Whitey Ford. And on September 9, many were on hand to see one of their all-time favorites honored.

PAUL DOHERTY: According to most reports, Whitey was very pleased with all the accolades and gifts, but anything but happy over the "Life Savers" gimmick, which he thought a bit tacky.

Meanwhile, fame's relentless spotlight continued to bear down on Roger Maris, especially since Mickey Mantle, hobbled by injuries, managed to hit but one home run from September 10 on. Without Mantle as a contender for the home-run title and with the Yankees having clinched their 26th pennant, it was truly showtime for Maris.

On September 18, the Yankees arrived in Baltimore for a four-game series. Maris had 58 home runs. He did not homer in a twinight doubleheader, games 152 and 153. But on September 20, a night game where there were about 21,000 in the stands, Maris batted against Milt Pappas in the third inning and slammed a shot that went almost 400 feet into the bleachers in right field. Number 59.

On September 26, the announced attendance was just 19,401 at Yankee Stadium. In the third inning Jack Fisher of Baltimore threw an elevated curveball.

"The minute I threw the ball, I said to myself, that does it. That's number 60," Fisher remembered.

Number 60, the one that tied the record set by Babe Ruth in 1927, was a shot into the third deck. It pounded onto the concrete steps of the sixth row. Bouncing back onto the field, the ball was snatched by Baltimore right fielder Earl Robinson, who tossed it to umpire Ed Hurley, who gave it to Yankee first-base coach Wally Moses, who rolled it into the Yankee dugout. Maris, running out the 60th home run, arrived in the dugout at about the same time as the ball did.

BILL CHUCK: My dad and I came up by subway from Stuyvesant Town especially for Whitey Ford Day. I was very excited. It cost us three, maybe four dollars total for the two general admission tickets. We sat between first and third, upstairs looking down, watching the ceremony. Whitey's wife was out there and his three kids.

The "day" was not enormously sponsored, as it is now. And unlike today, where a "day" for a player is given after his career is over, Ford got his in the midst of one of his great years, when he ended with 25 wins.

The gifts, considering the money the ballplayers were making then, were pretty big deals to them. But there were no big gifts. There were things such as patio furniture, movie cameras, color TVs, a trip to somewhere.

After all the other gifts had been given out, Mel Allen said, "Whitey, we've got one last surprise for you."

Out of one of the bullpens comes a car pulling an eight-foot-tall Life Savers package, peppermint—blue and white, of course. It drives up. It stops. Out pops Luis Arroyo who had saved Whitey so many times. He gives Whitey a big hug. Even from the upper deck, you could see the look of surprise and happiness on Whitey's face. We all went crazy.

ABOVE: Roger Maris connects for a record-breaking 61st home run in 1961
RIGHT: Maris in the Yankee dugout before a 1961 World Series game

The Yankee slugger picked up the ball, barely looking at it. Then he emerged from the dugout and stood on the top step and waved his cap to the cheering fans.

The quest to set a new record came down to the final three games of the 1961 season.

It was fittingly Yankees versus Red Sox.

It was Maris versus Ruth.

The man from Fargo, North Dakota, failed to homer in the first two games against Boston pitching at the Stadium.

Tired, tense, bedraggled, Maris faced the 24-year-old Red Sox righthander Tracy Stallard on October 1 before just 23,154.

Out in right field, in the Yankee bullpen, pitchers and catchers watched. A $5,000 reward had been pledged to the one who caught the ball. Maris said: "I told them that if they got the ball not to give it to me. Take the $5,000 reward."

Stallard retired Maris in his first at-bat. In the fourth inning, Maris came up again.

———

SAL DURANTE: I was with my girlfriend Rosemarie, who's my wife now, and my cousin John and his girl. We were hanging out in Coney Island doing nothing. So I made a suggestion that we go to the last game at Yankee Stadium. I knew that Maris was going after the 61st home run. I knew about the promised $5,000 reward for the guy who caught the ball. I had read all about it in the [Daily] News.

I was a Yankee fan as far back as I can remember, although not really a Roger Maris fan. I was a Mickey Mantle fan and watched every Yankee game as I was growing up because of him.

We asked the ticket guy for four seats in right field. I never expected there would be any. The guy thumbed through tickets like a deck of playing cards, "Yeah, I've got four seats."

I had no money. Rosemarie paid for the tickets. We were in Section 33, Box 163D, the sixth row of the right-field lower deck. In those days you had six seats to a box. I was sitting in the row below Rosemarie, with John and his girl. Rosemarie was sitting by herself in seat four. I switched seats with her so she could talk to them. It was the smartest thing I did.

———

**PHIL RIZZUTO
(GAME CALL, WCBS RADIO):**
They're standing, waiting to see if Maris is gonna hit number 61. We've only got a handful of people sitting out in left field, but in right field, man, it's hogged out there. And they're standing up. Here's the windup, the pitch to Roger. Way outside, ball one. And the fans are starting to boo. Low, ball two. That one was in the dirt. And the boos get louder. Two balls, no strikes on Roger Maris. Here's the windup. Fastball, hit deep to right! This could be it!

———

SAL DURANTE: As soon as Maris hit the ball, I knew it was going to be a home run that would go over my head. I jumped up on my seat and reached as high as I could (see photo, page 112). The ball hit the palm of my hand. It didn't hurt. It was a thing from heaven that knocked me over into the next row.

———

**PHIL RIZZUTO
(GAME CALL, WCBS RADIO):**
Way back there! Holy cow, he did it! Sixty-one for Maris! And look at the fight for that ball out there! Holy cow, what a shot! Another standing ovation for Maris, and they're still fighting for that ball out there, climbing over each other's backs.

SAL DURANTE: There was a bit of a scramble. I got hit in the face. Two security guards picked me up off the ground. I was swinging so that nobody could get the ball out of my hand. They calmed me down.

———

Roger Maris rounded first base rapidly and sped around the bases. Rounding third, he headed home, shaking hands with third-base coach Frank Crosetti. Maris stepped on home plate, shook hands with Yogi Berra first, then the batboy, and then a young man in a plaid jacket who had jumped out of the stands via the gate next to the home-plate side of the Yankee dugout.

Down the steps of the dugout past Houk, Maris turned left and took off his helmet, all the while shaking teammates' hands, receiving pats on the back. Then putting on his cap, Maris went up a couple of steps. He tipped his hat and several times mouthed a smiling "Thank you."

As he started back down the steps to the dugout, the cheers grew louder. Several players pushed him back up for a second curtain call. Looking almost incredulously at the players, motioning his arms to indicate "Hey, come on!," Maris went back up a step or two, turned his head up to the crowd, tipped his cap once more, and acknowledged the fans.

Mel Allen, seated with Red Barber in the WPIX booth, commented on-air, "This is most unusual. Most unusual."

———

SAL DURANTE: That $5,000 was a year and a half's pay for me. I was taking home $60 a week, driving a truck, delivering auto parts. I was 19 years old. I gave my mom and dad half of the reward. That money also helped me to marry Rosemarie. I caught the baseball October 1 and we were married October 29.

ROGER MARIS
61 HOME RUNS IN 1961

#	GAME	DATE	OPPONENT	H/A
1	11	APRIL 26	DETROIT	A
2	17	MAY 3	MINNESOTA	A
3	20	MAY 6	LOS ANGELES	A
4	29	MAY 17	WASHINGTON	H
5	30	MAY 19	CLEVELAND	A
6	31	MAY 20	CLEVELAND	A
7	32	MAY 21	BALTIMORE	H
8	35	MAY 24	BOSTON	H
9	38	MAY 28	CHICAGO	H
10	40	MAY 30	BOSTON	A
11	40	MAY 30	BOSTON	A
12	41	MAY 31	BOSTON	A
13	43	JUNE 2	CHICAGO	A
14	44	JUNE 3	CHICAGO	A
15	45	JUNE 4	CHICAGO	A
16	48	JUNE 6	MINNESOTA	H
17	49	JUNE 7	MINNESOTA	H
18	52	JUNE 9	KANSAS CITY	H
19	55	JUNE 11	LOS ANGELES	H
20	55	JUNE 11	LOS ANGELES	H
21	57	JUNE 13	CLEVELAND	A
22	58	JUNE 14	CLEVELAND	A
23	61	JUNE 17	DETROIT	A
24	62	JUNE 18	DETROIT	A
25	63	JUNE 19	KANSAS CITY	A
26	64	JUNE 20	KANSAS CITY	A
27	66	JUNE 22	KANSAS CITY	A
28	74	JULY 1	WASHINGTON	H
29	75	JULY 2	WASHINGTON	H
30	75	JULY 2	WASHINGTON	H
31	77	JULY 4	DETROIT	H
32	78	JULY 5	CLEVELAND	H
33	82	JULY 9	BOSTON	H
34	84	JULY 13	CHICAGO	A
35	86	JULY 15	CHICAGO	A
36	92	JULY 21	BOSTON	A
37	95	JULY 25	CHICAGO	H
38	95	JULY 25	CHICAGO	H
39	96	JULY 25	CHICAGO	H
40	96	JULY 25	CHICAGO	H
41	106	AUGUST 4	MINNESOTA	H
42	114	AUGUST 11	WASHINGTON	A
43	115	AUGUST 12	WASHINGTON	A
44	116	AUGUST 13	WASHINGTON	A
45	117	AUGUST 13	WASHINGTON	A
46	118	AUGUST 15	CHICAGO	H
47	119	AUGUST 16	CHICAGO	H
48	119	AUGUST 16	CHICAGO	H
49	124	AUGUST 20	CLEVELAND	A
50	125	AUGUST 22	LOS ANGELES	A
51	129	AUGUST 26	KANSAS CITY	A
52	135	SEPTEMBER 2	DETROIT	H
53	135	SEPTEMBER 2	DETROIT	H
54	140	SEPTEMBER 6	WASHINGTON	H
55	141	SEPTEMBER 7	CLEVELAND	H
56	143	SEPTEMBER 9	CLEVELAND	A
57	151	SEPTEMBER 16	DETROIT	A
58	152	SEPTEMBER 17	DETROIT	A
59	155	SEPTEMBER 20	BALTIMORE	A
60	159	SEPTEMBER 26	BALTIMORE	H
61	163	OCTOBER 1	BOSTON	H

The 1961 Yankees pounded 240 home runs, tops to that point in time. Winners of 109 games that season, they were almost unbeatable at home in the Bronx, losing just 16 times, winning 65 times for a percentage of .802. With all their weapons, they were heavily favored to defeat the Reds of Cincinnati in the World Series.

In the opener, on October 4, 1961, at Yankee Stadium, Whitey Ford spun a 2–0 beauty, moving his scoreless streak to 27 innings, three straight shutouts in the October classic.

He extended the streak to 33 1/3 innings in game four but was forced to leave in the sixth inning with an injured ankle. The Yankee took four of five from the Reds, outscoring Cincy 27–13 to win their 19th title in 39 seasons.

Mickey Mantle, Roger Maris, and Bill Skowron had blasted a total of 143 home runs in 1961. On Opening Day 1962, the sluggers picked up where they left off. Each homered, propelling the Yankees to a 7–6 triumph over Baltimore.

JIM BOUTON: As a kid, I was a Giants fan. I never had a feeling about Yankee Stadium. The Polo Grounds was the magical place of my childhood. The Yankees only came into play when the World Series came around, and we'd root for the Yankees to beat the Dodgers; if you were a Giants fan, you hated the Dodgers. So I got to know something about the Yankees, how Tommy Henrich was the reliable guy and how you could always count on Yogi for the clutch hit.

My first time in Yankee Stadium as a rookie pitcher was in 1962, when the team arrived a day or two before Opening Day for a workout at the ballpark. I got down there very early that day, about eight in the morning—we didn't have to be there until one. The only other person around was the clubhouse man, Pete Sheehy.

The clubhouse was carpeted wall-to-wall in a nice grayish-green; the pipes and ceiling were painted in beautiful gray-green and mauve tones. The furniture was like something out of an expensive showroom. And the uniforms were hung in the lockers with military precision.

I saw my uniform, and of course I had to try it on, to see if it fit. I went over to the mirror and put my hat on. It looked pretty good.

Then I wondered what it would be like to sit in the dugout. So I walked out of the locker room down the runway into the dugout and sat on the bench and looked out on the field. You couldn't see left field because of the hump, the elevated infield for draining purposes. Then I wondered what it would be like to stand on the mound. So I walked out to the mound and stood on it. I looked to home plate and up above, the three tiers of stands: the main level, the mezzanine, and the upper deck. I'd never pitched in a ballpark with three tiers. I thought it was like the [Los Angeles] Coliseum.

It was very quiet. The only sounds were the pigeons and the rumble of the elevated train going by. It was pretty magical being out there, just me and the pigeons and the elevated trains.

My first game at Yankee Stadium, I started against the Washington Senators. It was part of a doubleheader. I was very nervous, very jacked up, very sky-high. I walked the first three batters. The bases were loaded, nobody out. The next batter I got three and one on, and then I threw what I thought was ball four. But the umpire called it a strike. So now it was three and two. Ralph Houk had taken a step out of the dugout. He was going to come and get me if I walked a run in. But then when the umpire called it a strike, he took a step back into the dugout. I got the batter out on the next pitch. And then I got out of the inning with no runs scored.

I struggled the whole game. But it was a shut-out. They never scored on me; it was a complete game. It was also the worst shutout in the history of baseball. Seven walks, seven hits. After the game, Houk said to me, "Any more shutouts like that, we're gonna need a new bullpen." They were warming up every inning.

It was only recently that I learned I held the record for the longest number of shutout innings by a rookie. My first 15 innings were scoreless. I didn't know they kept such a record until Joba Chamberlain had 14 1/3 scoreless innings [in 2007], and they said he's 2/3 of an inning away from breaking Jim Bouton's record. He went on to pitch 15 1/3 and then gave up a run. So he broke my record by 1/3 of an inning. If he hadn't done that, I'd have never known I had that record.

My nickname came from that game. After the game, the reporters were crowding around Elston Howard's locker asking what he thought of this new kid. And Elston said, "He's a real bulldog."

When the rest of the team went on into the clubhouse, I was held back in the dugout to do an interview with Jerry Coleman and Red Barber on their television show. After it was over, I stepped into the clubhouse, and there was a path of white towels. Arranged in a semicircle, they went from the front door to my locker, where Mickey Mantle was laying down the last towel. He was giving me the "white-carpet treatment" for my first start at Yankee Stadium.

Ralph Houk was a great manager. He didn't have much to say. It was all wisecracking stuff, all very positive. Players loved him, particularly the older guys, who thought he was much better than Casey Stengel, the strong silent type. To him everyone was "partner." "What do you say, partner?"

The 1962 Yankees had Bouton and Rookie of the Year Tom Tresh and all kinds of talent. The son of former major leaguer Mike Tresh, Tom was turned on by his first year: "Out of everybody in the country, how come I was the one playing in Yankee Stadium, standing there with my locker next to Mickey Mantle's, going out to dinner with Bobby Richardson after a game? It was just a great feeling."

It was a great feeling for the Yanks and their fans: a third straight pennant. Posting a mark of 96–66, outscoring the opposition 817–680, the pennant-winning Bombers squared off against the Giants in the World Series.

Rain was the prevailing climate condition in a series that stretched out over 13 days, tying it with the 1911 fall classic for the longest ever. The teams split the first two games, at Candlestick Park. The Yanks took two out of three at the Stadium. Back in San Francisco for game seven, Ralph Terry spun a four-hit shutout and the Yanks won, 1–0.

Whitey Ford had his season of seasons in 1963. He was first in wins, innings pitched, games started, and winning percentage. Winding up with a 24–7 record, he was the big constant on a team of solid performers.

So was Mickey Mantle until he broke his foot and ended up playing in only 65 games that season. But when he was on the field, he was a wonder. On May 17, 1963, in the bottom of the ninth inning, Mantle blasted the game winner against the A's. It knocked against the upper-deck facade in right field. No fair ball had ever come closer to exiting Yankee Stadium.

Tremendous tape-measure shots by The Mick were becoming almost routine, but they continued to astonish the baseball world. On May 22, 1963, at the Stadium he led off the eleventh inning against Bill Fischer of Kansas City and smashed a 2–2 pitch that almost cleared the right-field roof. Mantle had borrowed the bat from Dale Long and said later that "it was the hardest ball I ever hit, the only

homer I ever hit that the bat actually bent in my hands." There are estimates that if the ball had not struck the facade, it would have gone 620 feet. Talk about tape measure.

———

GARY LEFKOWITZ: The first Mayor's Trophy Game was played at the Stadium the night of June 3, 1963. For Casey Stengel, now managing the Mets, it was a very important game. He was back in the place where he'd had all that glory. The Mets took it seriously. But to the Yankees, it was just another game.

Jimmy Piersall was playing center field for the Mets, and he was clowning around at the monuments, playing peekaboo and hide-and-seek out there, dancing the twist during pitching changes. It was really disrespectful to Yankee fans. Joe Pepitone hit a home run for the Yankees in the ninth inning, so the Mets won 6–2 instead of 6–1. Still, it was an annoying defeat.

———

For the Yankees, 1963 was another terrific season. They won 104 games, winding up 10½ games ahead of Chicago and recording another pennant. But in the World Series, the Dodgers had too much pitching. They humbled New York, sweeping them in four. Sandy Koufax won two games and Don Drysdale and Johnny Podres each won one.

Ralph Houk was kicked upstairs, becoming Yankee general manager. In came Yogi Berra. In his first year as manager, he steered the Yankees to the 1964 pennant. The team scored 730 runs, allowed just 577, and led the league in attendance with 1,305,838.

DICK GROAT: In 1964, I returned to Yankee Stadium with the Cardinals in the World Series. I didn't like hitting there with a packed house. It was tough with that bleacher background—all the people sitting out there wearing white [or light] shirts that seemed to come right at your eyes, making it very difficult to pick up the pitch.

———————————

JIM BOUTON: The first World Series I pitched in was game three of the 1964 Series at the Stadium. The score was tied 1–1 going into the ninth. There was a pitchers' duel between me and Curt Simmons.

In the bottom of the ninth, the Cardinals brought in Barney Schultz, the knuckleballer, a right-handed pitcher. Mickey, who was the leadoff batter, had been batting right-handed all game against the lefthander Simmons. But now he was coming against Schultz, who was throwing his warm-up pitches, and the ball was coming in about thigh high and dropping down to the knees, dropping down to the ankles. You could see his pitch was really moving well but it was dropping down.

Now, Mickey Mantle had two strokes. When he hit the ball right-handed, he would attack it like he was chopping a tree. It would be a vicious line drive with topspin on it. But when he hit the ball-left handed, it was like a golf stroke. He would hit under the ball.

With Barney throwing his knuckleball, you could see it was coming right into Mickey's wheelhouse, right where he liked to hit the ball.

Mickey, standing at the bat rack, saw it, too. Now, he wasn't one to make announcements, to say, "Watch me. I'm gonna do this." He wasn't that kind of guy. He was just standing there with a bat on his shoulder watching Barney Schultz's knuckleball, and I thought I heard him say, "I'm gonna hit one out of here." Just to himself.

He walked up to home plate. Barney Schultz threw his knuckleball, threw it in there, the ball came in knee high, broke down to the ankles, and Mickey hit a seven iron into the upper deck. The shot went way up, above the facade, and dropped down into the upper deck. And that, of course, was the ball game.

———————————

In the third game of the Series, at the Stadium, Mantle, playing in his final World Series, blasted a leadoff home run in the bottom of the ninth, giving the Yanks a 2–1 win and a 2–1 lead in the fall classic. It also gave The Mick 16 career Series homers, breaking Babe Ruth's record.

The next day Ken Boyer of the Cardinals hit a grand-slam homer, propelling St. Louis to a 4–3 win at the Stadium. On October 12 the teams were tied,

ABOVE: 1963 starting pitchers, (l to r) Whitey Ford, Jim Bouton, Al Downing, Ralph Terry, and Stan Williams

2–2, going into the tenth inning after the Yanks rallied for two runs in the bottom of the ninth. Home run power once again ruled, as Tim McCarver smashed a three-run shot, giving the Cards a 5–2 triumph, saddening the huge Stadium crowd.

An 8–3 Yankee win in St. Louis set up game seven.

Bob Gibson, starting on two days' rest, was heroic. Although he yielded five runs and nine hits, he pitched a complete game as the Cards edged the Yanks, 7–5, to win the world championship. It was such an incredibly tight series. The Yankees outscored St. Louis, 33–32. The Redbirds outhit the New Yorkers, 61–60.

DICK GROAT: It was unique for me beating the Yankees in two World Series with two different teams, the Pirates and then the Cardinals.

Yogi Berra paid the price for the Yankee defeat. He was fired. St. Louis winning manager Johnny Keane would take over for him the following year. By then the team would be owned primarily by CBS, which had purchased 80 percent of the Yankees for $11.2 million.

PAUL DOHERTY: In April 1965, the Yankees introduced a Lowrey organ, to be played pregame and between innings. It was stationed in the press level along the third-base line and was manned by Toby Wright, Yankee organist 1965–1966 and 1971–1977. Eddie Layton, who had been the organist from 1967 to 1970, took over again in 1978 and remained until he retired in 2003.

EDDIE LAYTON: I knew nothing about baseball when I started. But I learned a lot about the game since then.

PAUL DOHERTY: The 1965 season not only featured an organ but also the first of the Yankee promotional days (anything to draw some fans from the Mets at the brand-new Shea Stadium). The first was Bat Day, on Sunday, June 20, when 71,245 came to get bats for their kids and to see the Yankees dump both ends of a doubleheader to Minnesota.

On September 18, 1965, before a crowd of 50,180 that included Joe DiMaggio and Bobby Kennedy, Mickey Mantle Day took center stage at the Stadium.

GARY LEFKOWITZ: Even my father was cheering, albeit grudgingly—Mays was his guy. Bobby Murcer, just called up from the minors, was starting at shortstop for the Yanks.

The whole place was packed to see Mantle play his 2,000th game. Mickey made a speech. The crowd was loud, and the love was just overpowering.

Among the gifts Mickey received were two quarter horses, an American breed bred for short distance sprints; a barbecue grill in the shape of a prairie schooner; and a 100-pound, six-foot kosher salami.

When The Mick stepped into the batter's box in the first inning, Detroit pitcher Joe Sparma walked off the mound to shake his hand.

But there were not many handshakes for the 1965 New York Yankees, a team that suffered through its first losing season in 40 years.

PAUL DOHERTY: CBS and the Yankees worked hard to rebrand the general Stadium atmosphere and the team's image: new friendly

female greeters were hired, new uniforms for the ushers and the grounds crew were created, Stadium staff members were asked to try smiling at the paying customers, and even a new Yankee theme song was written, "Here Come the Yankees." CBS's Columbia Records staff composer Sid Bass created and conducted this catchy number that Yankee organists still play and Yankees fans still hum.

On April, 11, 1966, as a public relations gesture and for the first time in their history, the Yankees opened their lower stands to the final preseason practice free of charge to the public from 12:30 to 2:00 P.M. Bob Sheppard introduced Yankees as they took turns in the batting cage. About five thousand to ten thousand youngsters showed up.

But the "uniformed specials" could not control the fans who turned into a mob. Roger Maris was "pelted by a shower of debris including a baseball wound in black tape. This narrowly missed his head and he refused to go back to the combat area," wrote Leonard Koppett in the *New York Times* the next day.

With 20 minutes remaining, the practice was stopped; players started to rush to the clubhouse. That triggered a stampede out of the stands. Players were mobbed in the outfield, according to

Koppett, "by cap-and-glove grabbers, backpatters and autograph seekers."

In the pandemonium, two bases were stolen, the infield grass was badly scuffed up, and several dozen new baseballs disappeared.

PAUL DOHERTY: This was a significant cultural turning point. Afterwards, fans no longer were allowed to exit by the field at game's end.

Despite the pre–Opening Day debacle, the 1966 Yankee season seemed full of hope—at least on paper. The roster had many prominent names, including Clete Boyer, Horace Clarke, Elston Howard, Mickey Mantle, Roger Maris, Bobby Murcer, Joe Pepitone, Pedro Ramos, Roger Repoz, Bobby Richardson, Roy White, Jim Bouton, Whitey Ford, and Mel Stottlemyre. However, the careers of the really big guns—Howard, Maris, and Mantle—were coming to an end.

On May 7, with the Yankees having lost 16 of their last 20 games, General Manager Ralph Houk fired Johnny Keane and announced that he would manage for the rest of the season.

PEDRO RAMOS: Ralph came in when things weren't going good. He was there for the players. He was there to try and straighten things out.

On Old-Timers' Day, July 23, 1966, Mickey Mantle tied Babe Ruth's record for games played as a Yankee, smacking a grand-slam home run.

LEFT: Bobby Kennedy is on hand for Mickey Mantle Day in 1965
OPPOSITE: The press box during a 1967 game
OVERLEAF: "The Mick"—pulverizing power personified

ROB EDELMAN: That entire '66 season I went to just one Yankee game. It was in June, and the Stadium was nearly empty. Attendance was 10,600, I looked that up later. The Yankees played Baltimore. Three of us were sitting together in a section in the upper deck, the only ones there. In the eighth inning an usher politely told us to move because the section was going to be closed.

Wouldn't you know that five minutes after we moved, Mickey Mantle smacks a home run off Jim Palmer, and the ball lands right where we had been sitting.

SAM MELE: When I managed Minnesota, Billy Martin was my first-base coach and a great friend of mine. All the writers would tell me, "He wants to manage so bad, he'll stab you in the back."

But I defended him as being a damn good coach who would help me win ball games. And if I won ball games, I would keep my job.

We're in Baltimore. I'm eating breakfast, and Billy comes in. He'd always find me at breakfasttime, that son of a gun, because he knew I'd pick up the tab. And he always ordered steak and eggs.

Well, he gets a phone call. This is 1966, and I'm all set to manage the American League All-Star team.

"It's Mickey Mantle," he says. "He wants to talk to you."

I get on the phone—Mantle is my center fielder for the game. He says: "Do you mind if I take the three days off? My legs are killing me."

I call American League president Joe Cronin and replace Mantle with Tommy Agee of the White Sox, a damn good player. We finish our series in Baltimore and get to New York. In the hotel I get a phone call from this guy who is a diehard Mantle fan, and he is cursing me up and down the line.

"How the hell can you pick Tommy Agee over Mantle? When you go on the field tomorrow at Yankee Stadium I'm going to shoot you and Tony Oliva."

"If you shoot Oliva, you might as well shoot me," I tell him. "He's my best all-around player."

Calvin Griffith, our owner, was in the hotel. I called him and I called the Yankees. When I get out of my room, there's all kinds of security. They walk me to the elevator and we go downstairs.

Our whole team gets on the bus. There are cops and FBI guys making sure nothing is happening. We get to the Stadium and the route from the bus to get inside is lined with cops, and outside the clubhouse are more cops.

I call my coaches in and tell them the story and ask if they think I should tell the team about the threats.

They say, "No, no, who the hell knows? It may be just a prank." They start to leave, and I call Billy Martin back. "Now, Bill, you've always wanted to manage. You take my uniform. Put it on. Go to home plate and give out the lineups."

He refused the offer. I can't repeat what he said.

So I go running like a son of a gun to home plate to the umpires and then run back even faster to the dugout. Nothing ever happened, but you never know.

On August 31, 1966, with memories of the good times and the great teams still with him, Bobby Richardson announced that he was calling it a career. He was only 31 years old.

On September 17, 1966, Bobby Richardson Day was staged at the Stadium.

BOBBY RICHARDSON: I played at the right time. Nine of my first 10 years, we won the pennant. The only thing I hated was going into the Stadium or walking out of it—there were always so many young kids there. But you couldn't stop because if you did there was no way you could sign for all of them.

Losing 15 of their last 24 games in 1966, the Yankees won 70 games and lost 89. They finished 26 ½ games out of first, 10th in a 10-team league, the first last-place finish for a Yankee team since the 1912 Highlanders. Yankee Stadium attendance dropped to its lowest level since World War II, 1.2 million, for an average of 13,715 a game. The '66 Yankees scored 611 runs but gave up 612 runs. Mel Stottlemyre went from being a 20-game winner to a 20-game loser, the worst record in the league.

The fire sale began, and the fall from the heights accelerated. Pedro Ramos, a top stopper for two years in a row and a man suffused with Yankee pride, was traded to the Phillies. Roger Maris, Elston Howard, Johnny Blanchard, and Clete Boyer would all, in good time, be traded away.

PAUL DOHERTY: Except for the adding of lights in 1946, the look of Yankee Stadium was essentially the same until the winter of 1966–1967. Then new owner, CBS, spent $1.5 million for minor modifications. A "Telephonic Hall of Fame" was located in Lobby Six, where telephones fea-tured a memorable moment in Yankee history. One could pick up a phone and hear the broadcast of Mantle's 500th home run, the farewell speeches of Babe Ruth and Lou Gehrig, and so on.

A new public address system was put in place. For the first time, Bob Sheppard's cultured voice was able to be heard clearly throughout all of Yankee Stadium as a result of a novel column speaker designed by Paul Veneklasen, a world-renowned acoustician. In dead center field near the 463-foot sign, it resembled a short flagpole stacked tightly with massive J. B. Lansing equipment.

New 463- and 433-foot signs appeared in the power alleys, and in what some called the world's most expensive paint job, 90 tons of paint were used to paint the Stadium's brown concrete exterior and greenish-copper facade white and the green grandstand seats blue.

By the start of 1967, Ballantine Beer's wonderfully lighted red and white signage at the bottom of the big scoreboard had been removed. The sponsor's departure, coupled with declining ratings and a booming syndication market for old TV shows and movies, allowed WPIX to cut the number of Yankee telecasts in half, thereby driving even more fans away from the team.

On Opening Day, April 14, 1967, at the freshly painted Yankee Stadium, Hall-of-Famer-to-be

ABOVE: Yankee Stadium gets a makeover before the 1967 season, going from green and copper to blue and white

Whitey Ford went up against 21-year-old rookie Billy Rohr in his major league debut. An Elston Howard ninth-inning single was the only Yankee hit. They lost 3–0 to the Red Sox.

Eleven days later, on April 25, the Chairman of the Board got his final career win, 11–2, over Chicago at Yankee Stadium. And four weeks later, Ford announced he would be retiring.

———————————

TRACY NIEPORENT: We were at the Stadium on May 14, 1967, when Mantle hit his 500th home run in the seventh inning of a game against Baltimore. It was Bat Day. We were standing on the chairs and holding up our bats. As it turned out, he didn't have that many home runs left in him after that.

———————————

JOE GARAGIOLA (GAME CALL, NBC): *Three balls, two strikes. Mantle waits. Stu Miller is ready. Here's the payoff pitch by Miller to Mantle. Swung on! There she goes! …Mickey Mantle has hit his 500th home run!*

———————————

ROD CAREW: I came in as a player in 1967. All my family and friends came out to Yankee Stadium to see me for the first time. I was hoping I would do a good job. Bob Sheppard announced my name, Rod Ca-rew, as "Rod Cay-rew." You know Bob has this way of pronouncing the names; he must study the names of every player. It was the first time I ever heard my name pronounced that way.

I was born in Panama and grew up in Manhattan, and played across from Yankee Stadium and outside of it for a couple of years on sandlot teams. I always would hear the crowds roar and felt the mystique of the Stadium. Maybe one day, I would think to myself, I'll play there.

I'd never been to a ball game at the Stadium, never was inside until the day the Minnesota Twins invited me to work out with them during my senior year in high school.

They were interested in signing me, but before they did, they wanted to take a look at me and see what kind of a player I was.

They had no uniform that would fit me because I was skinny. Finally they put me into Tony Oliva's shirt. I walked out of the dugout, a nervous kid, so amazed at what I was seeing, thinking of all the memories that Yankee Stadium held, all the great players that had played there. I stepped out onto the field, and the kids began yelling "Tony Alleva," because I had his shirt on.

I started playing catch with a couple of the players. During batting practice, I was hitting the ball good and was enthralled at being able to hit one into the seats. That memory will last a lifetime.

Later, Sam Mele told the coaches to get me out of the batting cage; they didn't want the Yankees to see me.

Playing as a major leaguer, I got to love the park. It was spacious; you saw the ball real well. I really enjoyed hitting in the Stadium. There is a little tilt, like a crown to the infield (which they got rid of after refurbishment), and sometimes I felt like it was a little uphill. But it was great. The grounds crew did a magnificent job. I would go out and look at the monuments, admire Ruth, Gehrig, The Mick, and think, How did this happen to me?

———————————

The Yankees had finished in ninth place in 1967. On April 10, 1968, only 15,744 were present at the Stadium opener between the Yanks and the Angels. Poet Marian Moore tossed out the first ball. She was in top form. So was Phil Rizzuto. And although his idiosyncrasies were in full bloom, so was his broadcasting game.

DON CARNEY: He used to drive me crazy talking about people's birthdays, Italian food or some restaurant, or who got married. Once he announced a funeral. He used to take off the eighth and ninth innings, saying he had to go to the bathroom. And that was it. Gone. One of the greatest turnarounds in the history of baseball was when Rizzuto turned his car around on the George Washington Bridge and came back to the Stadium to do extra innings.

He was afraid of lightning. I used to record giant lightning flashes, and before a storm, I'd get out those tapes and scare him half to death.

———————————

FRED CLAIRE: In 1968, I was covering the Angels for the Long Beach, California, paper and we went into Yankee Stadium for several games. It was like black-and-white television coming to life. I had grown up in a small town in Ohio seeing the Yankees at the Stadium in their annual World Series visits. What set the ballpark apart was the formality of it. It was as if you had walked into a grand, formal, historic place. Bob Fischel was part of that ethos as PR director for the Yankees, always in dark suit and tie, or sport coat, lending him such a prestigious look. And in 1968 the Yankees were not a very good team.

———————————

BOB SHEPPARD: At one time Bob Fischel said to me: "I think it would be nice to recognize the boys and girls, the young people." That was when I began saying: "Ladies and gentlemen, boys and girls." But I did it under force for a short time and then returned to saying just "Ladies and gentlemen."

———————————

MICKEY MANTLE

NEW YORK YANKEES   OUTFIELD

Mickey Mantle Banner Day, the second day honoring Mantle, was held on August 4, 1968. On the September 20, The Mick launched homer number 536, the last of his fabled career. The Red Sox defeated the Yankees, 4-3.

Five days later, on September 25th, in his final appearance at the Stadium, Mickey Mantle slapped a two-out first-inning single off Cleveland's Luis Tiant. It was his last hit.

ROLLIE FINGERS: When I first got to the Stadium in 1969 with Oakland, about two or three of us went to the ballpark early. I didn't go into the clubhouse. I just walked down the runway toward the dugout and looked onto the field.

The experience of pitching your first game there. You stand on the mound. You start thinking of all the guys who stood on that mound, who stood at home plate. And this was the original Yankee Stadium. Funny, things you remember—bleacher seats in 1969 were 75 cents; non-reserved seats were a buck fifty.

June 8, 1969, was all Mickey Mantle. His uniform number 7 was retired. "Ladies and gentlemen, a magnificent Yankee, the great number 7, Mickey Mantle," was the Mel Allen introduction line that brought down the house of 60,096.

"When I walked into this stadium 18 years ago," Mantle told the throng, "I felt much the same way I do right now. I don't have words to describe how I felt then or how I feel now, but I'll tell you one thing, baseball was real good to me, and playing 18 years in Yankee Stadium is the best thing that could ever happen to a ballplayer."

The Mick received a 10-minute standing ovation. Kids paraded around the field with posters in tribute. Mantle and Joe DiMaggio exchanged plaques, which later were placed on the center-field wall close by the monuments for Miller Higgins, Lou Gehrig, and Babe Ruth. When DiMag gave him his plaque, Mantle cracked, "His should be just a little bit higher than mine."

Mantle was driven around the Stadium on a golf cart. "And the guy that was driving me was Danny," he recalled, "one of the grounds crew guys who came up at about the same time I did in '51.

"The last time around the park. That gave me goose pimples. But I didn't cry. I felt like it. Maybe tonight when I go to bed, I'll think about it. I wish that could happen to every man in America. I think the fans know how much I think about them—all over the country. It was the most nervous I've ever been but the biggest thrill."

FRANK RUSSO: My first game at Yankee Stadium was Thurman Munson's first game, August 8, 1969. My dad was a huge Yankee fan and he read in the papers that their number one draft pick had been recalled from the minors. We went to the second game of a twinight doubleheader against Oakland. We walked right up and my dad bought the seats, good seats behind the first-base line.

Munson was definitely a confident guy. He had some swagger to him, which was what I liked. He got his first major-league hit against Catfish Hunter, another single and his first two RBIs in that game. We knew if the Yankees were going to get better in the 1970s, he would help lead the way.

The Yankees drew a little more than a million fans in 1969, 1,067,996, finishing with 80 wins and 81 losses, in fifth place. It was not the best of time to be a fan of the team that played in "The House That Ruth Built." The Bombers began the decade with average attendance of 21,134. They ended it in 1969 with average attendance of 13,350.

JIM BOUTON: After enjoying consecutive winning seasons for years, the Yanks, who had dropped to sixth place in 1965, were out of pennant contention through the remainder of the decade. By 1969 the team, to its ignominy, watched the New York Mets win both the National League pennant and the World Series.

RIGHT: The Mick addresses fans at the retirement ceremony for his number in 1969

CHAPTER

SEVENTIES

It was boom-time baseball for Billy Martin and George Steinbrenner. There were two world championships and lots of sound and fury. Reggie Jackson hammered three home runs on three consecutive pitches in the 1977 World Series. Writers seemed to never be late at the Stadium that decade with so much going on.

YANKEES YEAR BY YEAR 1970–1979	YEAR	POSITION	WON	LOST	PCT.	MANAGER	ATTENDANCE
	1970	**SECOND**	93	69	.574	RALPH HOUK	1,136,879
	1971	**FOURTH**	82	80	.502	RALPH HOUK	1,070,771
	1972	**FOURTH**	79	76	.510	RALPH HOUK	966,328
	1973	**FOURTH**	80	82	.494	RALPH HOUK	1,262,103
	1974 s	**SECOND**	88	73	.549	BILL VIRDON	1,273,075
	1975 s	**THIRD**	83	77	.519	VIRDON/BILLY MARTIN	1,288,048
	1976	**FIRST**	97	62	.610	BILLY MARTIN	2,012,434
	1977*	**FIRST**	100	62	.617	BILLY MARTIN	2,103,092
	1978*	**FIRST**	100	63	.613	MARTIN/BOB LEMON	2,335,871
	1979	**FOURTH**	89	71	.556	LEMON/MARTIN	2,537,765

*WORLD CHAMPIONS

s: YANKEES PLAYED AT SHEA STADIUM

DAN MARENGO: The 1970s were my time at Yankee Stadium. Back in those days, I would take the subway and come out on the el. You could stand on the platform and look at the ballpark, and it was like The Wizard of Oz, with you in black-and-white looking at a world in color. You would walk in from the sidewalk and go in through the tunnel and see the white facade and the blue sky and the green grass and the brown infield. That old Stadium was beautiful. But the surrounding neighborhood of the South Bronx was pretty depressing.

In 1970, Mel Stottlemyre was on the mound for his fourth straight Opening Day start. Gary Peters was the Red Sox pitcher.

BILL LEE: Gary Peters left after five plus innings. They put me in to relieve him, and I got out of a jam there and ended up throwing about four innings. We won the game, 4–3. And I got my first save at the Stadium.

That was when I learned that the Yankees and Yankee Stadium did not intimidate me. I thought the field was a cow pasture and that it rolled a lot. I thought it was very forgiving for left-handed pitchers if you had a good outfield that could run behind you. It was an old-time ballpark; when you walked through the clubhouse into the dugout, it was like walking from a cave or mine shaft into the bright sunlight.

I liked going into Yankee Stadium as an opposing pitcher because it got my adrenaline up. But you had to have a good catcher at that park. There was a long distance between home plate and the backstop.

ROLLIE FINGERS: There was so much space behind home plate that on a passed ball or wild pitch you had to make sure you got all the way in from the mound. There was even a chance a guy could score from second base if your catcher got turned around not knowing where the ball went. On the other hand, it was also nice having the extra space and getting outs through pop-ups.

JONATHAN EIG: My first major league baseball game was about 1970. I was taken there by my dad. I have great memories of all the shadows and the big steel beams. That was where I learned to watch baseball, to keep score. As time went on, I went with my Little League teams. Sitting in the cheap seats, we were where the smokers, the guys who drank all the beer, the raucous guys were. It was like sitting in a cloud of smoke and by the third or fourth inning we'd all be coughing horribly. We had to buy those little malted ice cream cups to soothe our throats.

BILL LEE: This was the stretch when the Yankees were owned by CBS and they had a lot of left-handed hitters. I kind of went through them; I found them so easy to get out.

RON SWOBODA: I got to be a Yankee about halfway through the 1971 season after being traded by the Montreal Expos. The time between 1971 and 1973 was not one of the high points in Yankee history. In fact, it may have been one of the low points. You sensed somehow that there was not a great commitment from CBS to the Yankees.

The clubhouse had cement walls that had been repainted many times. It was architecturally whipped. She was getting to be a tired old lady. I wasn't prepared to be awed. But when I got

to put on the pinstripes and walk through the tunnel and up those steps as a Yankee, I felt this chill; the little short hairs on the back of my neck went up.

TONY FERRARO: I grew up in south Florida and went to the University of Miami where I played second and third base. I had a real good arm and signed a bonus contract with the St. Louis Cardinals. After four years in the minor leagues, I went to spring training with the team, and there I hurt my shoulder.

It just didn't heal so I started working as an actor. Everybody used to tell me, "You gotta go to New York, that's where you gotta be." So I came to New York, where one night I ran into Dick Howser. He knew me from the University of Miami, because he coached Florida State. He asked me if I wanted to work with the Yankees. They needed somebody to pitch batting practice.

I threw over a million pitches to hitters through the decades that I was with the team. I probably have thrown more pitches to more hitters than anybody else in the history of the game. I'm supposed to be in the *Guinness Book of Records.* The only ones who have had longer tenures than me at Yankee Stadium are Bob Sheppard and Pete Sheehy. "Here comes the iron pitcher," Bob'd always say when he saw me.

The Yankees always did everything first class. We would start with a case of new balls. By the time batting practice ended, we'd go through the whole case. And if some were left over, you went up and handed a fan a baseball.

ROLLIE FINGERS: At first, I was mainly a starting pitcher. I didn't become a closer until a ball game in Yankee Stadium. All of a sudden Dick

Williams, our manager, brings me in. I get a save. We won the game, 6–3.

The next day he says, "You're gonna be my closer." It was the end of May, something like that. I thought I was on my way out of base-ball. That moment in Yankee Stadium turned my career around.

On April 18, 1972, the first Opening Day night game was played at the Stadium. The Yankees hung a 2–0 shutout on Milwaukee.

CHRIS CARTER: Mr. Fowler, my friend Mike's father, worked for the printing company that made the Yankee yearbooks. He had the best seats in Yankee Stadium, box seats right behind first base. On a Friday night in August 1972 he gave Mike and me those tickets. They were right on the field. You could lean down and grab the dirt.

Since my birthday was coming up. Mr. Fowler surprised me. Mike and I got to walk out from those seats to the mound and take a picture with Yankee pitcher Fritz Peterson before the game. Talk about a Yankee Stadium memory.

But from some players' perspectives, the envi-ronment at the Stadium in the early 1970s was not as pleasant.

DWIGHT EVANS: When you have Coke bottles go by your head from the third deck and they miss you by six inches, you wonder what kind of people these are. When you have cherry bombs

PAGE 136: Manager Billy Martin kicks up some dirt
RIGHT: Fans at 1972's bat day

thrown at you or into crowds, that's not fun. They used to throw glass balls at me, broken glass wrapped in masking tape. And when it hit, it punctured. They'd throw a penny or a dime from the third deck and when it hit, it put a knot on your head. Think about trying to play in the outfield and having things thrown at you all game long. When people called Yankee Stadium the Bronx Zoo, I agreed.

Even though the majority of the people that come to the Stadium are great, knowledgeable baseball fans, they know what I mean when I talk about the crazy ones. I've had to wear helmets in the outfield many times. It's a wonderful ballpark to play in, yet you have to watch out for things.

———————————

BILL LEE: I once got smoked on the chest with an empty whiskey bottle being bussed from the bullpen to the mound.

———————————

ROLLIE FINGERS: Every time I was in the bullpen at the Stadium, I would tell the guy who drove us to the infield: "Don't start the car up. I'll walk in from center field." By the time the car went from the bullpen to the infield, it looked like a fruit salad. Everything you could imagine was on the windshield. You could hardly even see.

———————————

PAUL DOHERTY: It's a hot summer night in the Bronx. Yankee manager Ralph Houk, head down, strides towards the pitcher's mound to relieve a tired starting pitcher who has gotten himself into some ninth-inning hot water. On the way, he signals with his left hand to coach Jim Hegan in the right-field Yankee bullpen. A burly pitcher, his long brown hair flowing from under his Yankee cap, jumps up from the pen's bench, grabs

his mitt and warm-up jacket, and heads to the waiting bullpen car, a 1972 pinstriped Datsun, "The Official Car of the New York Yankees."

Grabbing a quick chaw of Red Man from a pouch in his jacket, he hops in the car and slams the door behind him. The car goes through the opened navy blue bullpen gate heading down the brown clay of the right-field track toward home.

Up in his tiny press box booth, Toby Wright, Yankee Stadium organist on the scene for 1971 to 1977, picks up the ringing phone. He shuffles through his sheet music and begins playing "Pomp and Circumstance" on his mighty Hammond. Each bar is greeted in the Stadium with louder cheers.

Just before the Datsun comes to a complete stop in front of the Yankees' dugout, the pitcher jumps out, tosses his jacket into a waiting batboy's arms, puts his glove on his right hand, makes sure that chaw of Red Man is behind his right-hand cheek, and jogs with confidence to the mound, where manager Houk and a couple of infielders wait.

Bob Sheppard, poised in the press box in the loge above third base, glances up from the Chesterton poems he's been immersed in and clicks on his gray Electrovox microphone. His cultured baritone interrupts the ponderous organ.

"Your attention please, ladies and gentlemen, coming in to pitch for the Yankees, number 28, Sparky Lyle, number 28!"

———————————

DAN MARENGO: Oh, to hear "Pomp and Circumstance" one more time and see the Sparkler jump from the Yankee car pumped up. How many times did we chant that year: "See you later Danny Cater."

———————————

"What happens," Sparky Lyle asked, "if some guy brings his two kids and wife to the game, and

I come in and all the fanfare is going on and I get my [butt] kicked?" They're going to wonder: "What the hell are they playing this song for that guy for?"

———————————

ROLLIE FINGERS: The Stadium bullpen was a good place to watch a ball game from. Sitting on the bench, you would pop your feet up on the fence. If you were hungry you could always give a kid a baseball and he would go and get you a hot dog.

———————————

RON SWOBODA: All kinds of things went on in the bullpens. Sometimes we would send out the back door for pizza. There were rumors that some young ladies would occasionally slip in through the back door. I was never involved in any of that, but it was entirely possible.

———————————

BILL LEE: The guys who worked at the Stadium, the ones who groomed the area, the ushers, they were the ones to be friendly with. That was how you got your food. You tipped them well and they would bring a pizza, anything.

———————————

RON SWOBODA: The folks who used to sit in the bleachers were interesting. You saw the same people every day. They were mostly guys, a bit older, all huge fans. You kind of wondered what they did. You could stand up next to the fence there in right field and just talk to them.

———————————

BILL LEE: Moe Drabowsky, who played for Baltimore, as the story goes, would get into the Stadium switchboard. Moe called the Queen of England one time. He called China one time. He called the Vatican.

———————————

AUGUST 10, 1972, NEW YORK VS. DETROIT FRANK MESSER (BROADCAST CALL):

Top of the ninth, two outs. Yanks lead 1–0 with Sparky Lyle pitching. Ike Brown, hitting .300.

[Bob Sheppard in the background, under Messer] Your attention please, ladies and gentlemen, batting for Brinkman, number nine, Ike Brown, number nine.

With two home runs and eight runs batted in, Ike Brown will bat for Ed Brinkman . . . . Ike Brown is two for seven in the series.

[The crowd begins to chant "Dee-fense! Dee-fense!"]

The "dee-fense" chant goes up again. The Tigers have the bases loaded.

[Th crowd's rising volume: "Dee-fense! Dee-fense!]

Two outs, Yankees leading 1–0 in the ninth inning. Ike Brown, pawing around at the dirt . . . backs out again. Now moves in and Lyle will work from the full windup. Here's the first pitch to him: down low. Ball one. Dug out of the dirt. Taylor at third, Freehan at second, Horton at first. They lead away. Yankees in front, 1–0. Windup by Lyle, here's his pitch . . . check swing and a strike called. One and one.

[A huge cheer from the crowd.]

Lyle with both feet on the rubber, looks at third, the windup, the one-one pitch. Swing and a miss, strike two.

[A steady, rapidly increasing roar from the crowd.]

One ball, two strikes. Three on, two gone. A one-run lead. What more can you ask? Here comes the pitch to him. HE STRUCK HIM OUT! HE STRUCK HIM OUT! And the ball game is over!

The entire bench charges onto the field and the Yankees have beaten the Tigers 1–0 and have taken three out of four. Bedlam in the Bronx! Nobody's leaving. Nobody! They're standing here cheering their hearts out.

For Steve Kline. For Rob Gardner, for Sparky Lyle, for Bloomberg. For an unknown kid from Mexico named Celerino Sanchez. For well-known-in-New-York Ron Swoboda. . . . For Felipe Alou, for Thurman Munson, John Ellis, Stottlemyre, Peterson, all the rest of 'em. Just delirious Yankee fans again have something to be delirious about!

[The crowd starts chanting: "We're number one! We're number one!"]

The 1972 season ended with the Yankees at 79–76, in fourth place in the American League East. Their attendance was a puny 966,328, the only time that decade that the Yankees would have a season's attendance below 1 million at home.

However, they contended until the middle of September, thanks to the superb relief pitching of Lyle and the solid hitting of Bobby Murcer.

—————

TONY FERRARO: Bobby Murcer used to sit in his chair and rock all the time. A friend of mine was in the furniture business. I asked him, "Can you send me a rocking chair?"

He said, "Yeah. Where do you want me to send it?"

"Send it to Yankee Stadium."

He sends the rocking chair, and we put it in front of Murcer's locker. "I'm getting tired of seeing you rocking in the chair," I told him. "You need a regular rocking chair." Then one day someone sawed the rockers off it. Who do you think that was? Sparky Lyle. He was a great guy for doing pranks. But Murcer had it fixed and before long, he was rocking again. When he was traded to San Francisco in 1975, he took the rocking chair with him.

—————

On January 3, 1973, a group led by George Steinbrenner III purchased the Yankees from CBS for an estimated $10 million, a price called an "astonishing bargain" by some, since the City of New York paid more than $1 million for a parking lot as part of the package.

Opening Day of the first year of Steinbrenner's principal ownership and the last season of the old Yankee Stadium, the Yankees became one of the last major league clubs to convert to nonflannel uniforms made of polyester.

DAN MARENGO: There were autograph sessions in 1973, three Yankees in the outfield giving autographs two hours before the game. I think they only did that for a year. The players didn't seem to be too happy with it. I was a big Munson fan and made sure I got there for his session which was with Gene Michael and Mel Stottlemyre. They sat at a table in left field at field level. You walked down the steps, and they signed what you gave them. I didn't talk to them. Still, it was just so cool.

—————

PAUL DOHERTY: In the Old Timers' Game on August 11, Mickey Mantle batted from the right side against his pal Whitey Ford and hammered his first pitch—a long, but foul, home run to left field. Mel Allen, calling the game on the PA from the field, yelled, "Straighten it out, Mick!"

The next pitch Mantle slugged another towering, but this time straighter drive into the left-field seats.

Mel Allen shouted, "It is going, it is going, it is GONE!"

Mantle, wearing probably his biggest grin in his 22 years at the Stadium, trotted joyously around the bases.

—————

The last game of the 50th anniversary season took place on September 30 before 32,238, capping a season's home attendance of 1,262,103. The widows of Babe Ruth and Lou Gehrig were there. So were Bob and Mary Keaney.

—————

BOB KEANEY: It was the first time my mother and I went to New York City. Two gawking fans from Lynn, Massachusetts, come via Greyhound. Babe Ruth's widow, Claire, was sitting in our general section. We watched her every move.

Hank Aaron was one home run shy of tying Babe's all-time record and was playing his last game of the year in Atlanta, sitting on 713.

Finally, it was announced that Hammering Hank did not nail his 714th home run! Cheers and tears. At that moment, Claire Ruth started to leave the park. Seeing her departing move, my mother and I scurried into the exit runway leading from the stands to the Yankees' locker room. We stood waiting for her to arrive. New York cops accompanied Mrs. Ruth through the walkway. She greeted us with a satisfied smile and an extended hand. We shook her hand and I said, "We love you and the Babe, Mrs. Ruth, and we are glad Aaron didn't hit a home run today."

She replied, "Me too!"

She posed for one picture with us as the police stood by patiently. Then she was hustled off into the Yankees' offices.

DUKE SIMS: As a country boy in Idaho, I would listen to the World Series over the radio in school. It was always the Yankees: the Yankees and the Dodgers, the Yankees and whoever else managed to squeeze in. The Yankees epitomized winning, and I guess that's why I was a Yankee fan.

It was such a great honor to be playing for the team at the end of my career. I had played at the Stadium before, but as an opposing player. In the early '60s, when I was playing for Cleveland and we were in New York at the end of the season, I actually took a cab down the West Side Highway to see Yankee Stadium. But now I was wearing the pinstripes. The Yankees had picked me off waivers from Detroit on the 24th of September.

My first day, I got down to the Stadium around 10 in the morning. I went into the clubhouse; I looked at the lockers and thought of the greats who had played for the team. I had

come up when Maris was there, Mantle, Moose and guys of that era. I thought of them and of Gehrig and Ruth. I didn't know which locker belonged to which player, but I knew I was in the environment.

No one was on the field. I sat down right behind home plate for a few minutes, then did a little tour of the upper deck and the outfield, and then walked straight out to the monuments. It was a very quiet, almost reverential moment in my life.

On August 8, 1972, two years after the Mike Burke–John Lindsay meeting, the Yankees signed a 30-year lease with the City of New York with the proviso that Yankee Stadium be completely modernized in time for the 1976 season. The projected cost for the makeover was $24 million. The actual cost would ultimately approach $100 million.

DUKE SIMS: Now it's September 30, the day of the last game at [the original] Yankee Stadium. I'm sitting with Jerry Moses when Ralph Houk comes over to us and says, "I need a catcher today. George [Steinbrenner] has sent Thurman [Munson] back to Ohio. Which one of you wants to play?"

Neither Jerry nor I said much real quick. We weren't prepared. We didn't think of Thurman not being in the lineup. So Ralph took out a quarter and flipped the coin. I called "heads" and it turned up tails, and that's how I ended up in the lineup and catching for the last game at Yankee Stadium before it closed down.

The funny thing is I didn't realize the impact of that game at the time. I was getting married in November. The Tigers, the club I had just left, were in town, and I had arranged to fly back with the team to Detroit, pick up my car, which

I'd left there, and drive back home to the West Coast to get ready for my wedding.

So I was involved in a totally different mindset. When I hit the last Yankee home run at the Stadium, I ran around the bases thinking that I would be going behind the plate for the next two innings and that there would have to be six more outs by both clubs before the game was over. It never crossed my mind that I might have hit the last home run in "The House That Ruth Built."

It was only at the moment of the final out when I saw the crowd hit the field that I went "Whoa! They want souvenirs." It seemed there were thousands of people, all in a frenzy, tearing up everything, even scooping dirt from the ground. I was right at home plate. If I were smart, I would have grabbed it.

Instead, I went down to the locker room, took my uniform off, went to the shower, got cleaned up, got my bag, got the Tiger bus to the airport, and flew to Detroit. I got into my car not knowing I'd become part of Yankee history. It was only later on when someone pointed out I was the guy who hit the last home run at Yankee Stadium that I realized "Gee, that was me."

PAUL DOHERTY: The Yankees had given all ticket holders a free copy of a special 50th Anniversary Commemorative Record Album. It was narrated by Mel Allen Many actual highlights of the Stadium's 50 years were featured, and a few were re-created. By the end of the game the fans would turn the album into an all-purpose Frisbee.

OPPOSITE: Fans take mementos of the original Yankee Stadium, following the last game before reconstruction begins

The Stadium was chaos, a free-for-all to get souvenirs. People had come not only to see the last game but to take pieces of the Stadium, and they were tearing it apart. Back then, they didn't have that much security.

JOEY COOPERMAN: I took the wooden chair I had been sitting on. Heck, nobody stopped me. People were wandering around with chairs. It was like a riot broke loose. Phil Rizzuto, on the broadcast, was very, very upset that somebody stole second base.

Afterward, a more civilized disposition of artifacts was organized. The bat racks and bullpen steps were donated to the Smithsonian. Babe Ruth's widow received home plate; Lou Gehrig's widow was given first base. George Steinbrenner loaned a group of seats for the audience to the producers of a new television show, "Saturday Night Live." (Never returned, they remain in use to this day.) Those seats that had escaped the free-for-fall following the final game were sold to ex-players and fans.

DAN MARENGO: By the sixth inning of that last game, all you heard was hammers. When the game finally ended, people jumped out of the stands trying to get anything that was not nailed down. They even took stuff that was: second base, sod, signs, advertising paraphernalia, chairs. Using tools my father had brought along, my friend Jerry and I took the chairs we had been sitting on. But we saw people carrying off rows of seats.

PHIL SPERANZA: I went down with three friends and we all bought seats, $13 each, the old wooden seats, all blue, the ones that when fans banged on them, an echo would go through the Stadium. I also picked up a one-piece grounds crew uniform which had the Yankee logo on the back for about $8.

JIM BOUTON: I bought a whole bunch of stuff: pictures, chairs which I have in my basement right now, a stool from the clubhouse—Babe Ruth used to sit on a stool like that.

TRACY NIEPORENT: My brother Drew and I got ourselves a chair. It had iron stanchions and was very heavy. We'd come up to the Stadium by subway and now had to climb that damn el on 161st Street to get back home. When we did, we found a piece of petrified gum underneath the chair. At first, I thought to scrape it off. But then I thought it might have been there when Joe DiMaggio had his 56-game hitting streak.

SETH SWIRSKY: I got one of the seats. It has the original paint on it, that particular blue and the slats in the back. I sit in it in my house now, and I think about whoever sat in this seat over the years.

The excitement that accompanied the last game at the Stadium was hardly a reflection of the 1973 season, which saw three winning and three losing months. The Yankees finished fourth in the American League East for the third straight time. Had they been as good on the road at they were in the Bronx, it would have been a different story. Ralph Houk resigned as manager.

Still, 1973 did mark the end of an era whose time was captured by Bob Sheppard in an elegiac ode:

Farewell, old Yankee Stadium!
You've filled these fifty years
With a treasury of memories
Some laughter, thrills, and tears.
Farewell, old Yankee Stadium!
We'll miss your graceful sweep . . .
The far facade . . . that triple deck . . .
That center field so deep.
Farewell, old Yankee Stadium!
We'll miss you while at Shea;
But we'll be waiting anxiously
For your next Opening Day.

1973 FIRE SALE OF YANKEE STADIUM
Artifacts and mementos were sold off by Invirex of Long Island, the firm hired to dismantle the Stadium.
$30,000: lights purchased by Osaka baseball team of Japan
$10,000: foul poles purchased by Osaka baseball team of Japan
$500: box seats, enlarged photos of Babe Ruth on Babe Ruth Day, and clubhouse stool purchased by Jim Bouton
$300: sign "Gate A"
$200: huge picture of a young Joe DiMaggio
$150: photo of Dan Larsen making the last pitch of his perfect game
$100: turnstiles
$75: locker room scale
$50: an old duffel bag that belonged to Joe Pepitone
$20: box seats
$10: groundskeeper's uniform
$5: trays of hot dog vendors
$3: men's lavatory "In" sign
$3: a sheet of World Series tickets, unused from 1972
50 cents: sign: "Scout Admission—50 Cents"
Total proceeds from the sale were $300,000.

On April 6, 1974, the Yankees played their first home game outside of Yankee Stadium since 1922. They began the first of two seasons at Shea Stadium.

TRACY NIEPORENT: I went to Opening Day for the Yankees at Shea Stadium, and that was a surreal experience. On the top of the scoreboard where there was always a Mets logo, they had the Yankee logo. We went to that game for the novelty of it more than anything else.

BILL VIRDON: I am the only one to manage the Yankees not in Yankee Stadium. I replaced Ralph Houk as manager for 1974 and 1975. Then Billy Martin replaced me on August 1, 1975. I was so busy I never even went to Yankee Stadium to watch any of the demolition or construction.

PAUL DOHERTY: Back on August 17, 1970, Yankee president Mike Burke and Mayor John Lindsay had met prior to the Yankees-Mets Mayor's Trophy Game in Burke's Stadium office. The subject of Yankee Stadium and its current condition came up.

Burke cited the Stadium's age, 47, and the accelerating decline of the surrounding neighborhood. Lindsay was not a baseball fan. But he recalled how much the departure of the Dodgers hurt Brooklyn, and he was smart enough a politician to realize the Yankees leaving the Bronx would further devastate that borough. He tells Burke the city built Shea Stadium for the Mets and perhaps it could invest the same amount of money in refurbishing Yankee Stadium and the surrounding neighborhood. The seeds that led to the refurbishment of Yankee Stadium were planted that evening.

Presiding over the demolition and resizing of Yankee Stadium from a ballpark of 70,000 seats to one with a capacity of 57,545 was Jay Schwall, owner of Invirex, a Long Island–based company. Nearly 90 employees were involved, including about 14 iron-workers, 35 to 40 house wreckers, 8 crane or roller operators, security personnel, and half a dozen supervisory staff. The "new" Stadium was built by NAB-Tern and supervised by Walsh Construction.

Several more rows of box seats were added. Old 18-inch wooden seats were replaced by 22-inch plastic seats. A new upper concourse was built above where the old one had existed. Old exits were closed in by new seating. A smaller "loge/middle tier" section was built, creating room for a larger press box and 16 luxury boxes. A new system of suspension cables was installed in the upper deck, expanded by about 15 rows. The lower deck in right became essentially covered by the upper deck.

JAY SCHWALL: I didn't think the Stadium was falling apart. But they had a worry that the upper deck, which was made of wood, would catch on fire. We took out roughly 60 percent of the structure. It was just down to bare concrete and steel.

At first they were selling the players' jockstraps. They had their names on them so they'd know whose each was when they came back from the laundry. But that was stopped because of sanitary reasons.

Stuff from the radio and TV booths were sent on trucks to a company in Pennsylvania. The informational signs—sections, ejection, etc.—were sold. Somebody bought the lights for a couple of dollars apiece and sold them to Little League fields. There were World Series tickets for games that were never played because they

RIGHT: Scenes from the mid-seventies reconstruction

ABOVE: The reconstructed Yankee Stadium, close to completion
RIGHT: Opening Day at the new Stadium, April 5, 1976

had to have them printed up just in case. We sold those off as souvenirs.

In a sealed room under the stands we found a safe with a number of personal papers, invoices, and leather-bound corporate books from the Dan Topping era. All of that somehow disappeared.

We had round-the-clock security so we didn't have any people scavenging through our Dumpsters at night, and hired trucks that hauled everything away.

We threw a lot of stuff away. Probably a million dollars' worth. None of it meant anything to me. Nostalgia was starting, but we just did not have the time. We were under a lot of pressure to get the job complete. All I ended up with was the old golf cart that was shaped like a baseball hat. One thing I was sorry that I didn't save was a huge urinal that had been there from the beginning. They said it was built that big for Babe Ruth.

The most noticeable difference resulting from the renovation was the removal of the 118 steel columns, supports for each tier of the Stadium's grandstand. The Stadium's roof was gone, including the distinctive 15-foot facade that circled its interior.

PAUL DOHERTY: The facade had been transported on flatbed trucks and sold for scrap to a man in Albany. But a duplicate was made and installed atop the new scoreboard which ran across a new wall stretching from center to right field, blocking out most of the views from the 161st Street station of the IRT subway and the roofs of nearby apartment houses. You felt much more connected in the old place.

The 560-foot-long electronic scoreboard had baseball's first "telescreen." Built by Conrac, it featured instant replays in what was then state-of-the-art "nine shades of gray."

There were no longer seats in the middle portion of the bleachers. Instead it became a dark mass of seats (which could be used for other events) known as "the black," a site batters could focus on without being blinded by a sea of white shirts gleaming in the sun. Eighteen different players have since hit balls into the black a total of 24 times.

Sight lines were improved through the upper decks by cantilevering and lowering the playing field almost seven feet while increasing the slope of the lower stands. Several more rows of box seats were added.

A 138-foot-tall replica of a Louisville Slugger baseball bat was installed near the stadium entrance. The Stadium Club was now bilevel, with room for 500. There was also a 300-seat public cafeteria, a 100-seat Yankee dining room, 50 public restrooms on four levels, more elevators, and three escalator towers at each entrance, ending the long, steep climbs to the third level for most fans.

The three-foot-high outfield fences were no more. The plaques and monuments were moved out of fair territory and into their own "park" behind fences. There was a new and wide pedestrian plaza and parking garages that could hold almost 7,000 cars—a concession to the suburban crowd the Yankees sought to attract even more than before.

Outfield dimensions changed. "Death Valley" was reduced from 457 feet from 417 feet. Left- and center-field fences were drawn in but were still pokes of 430 feet and 417 feet respectively. Home plate was moved forward by about 10 feet, but several rows of seats in the right- and left-field corners were removed, so that distances down the lines increased slightly. Bullpens were moved from gaps between the bleachers and the grandstands in right and left fields.

———————————

WHITEY FORD: I hated it when we went to Shea and was so happy to come back. We all thought the refurbished Stadium was very nice. They cleaned the place up, did the dressing rooms over; there were mirrors and electric outlets in the lockers.

———————————

JON MILLER: There's something different about the architecture in the new, refurbished Yankee Stadium that's never been duplicated in another ballpark. The upper deck is much closer to the field of play than any of the other new ballparks with the cantilevered effect. The trade-off of not having the support poles and the obstructed views is that the upper decks are pushed back further. But for whatever reason, the upper deck is much closer to the ball field.

You associate great players and great teams with Yankee Stadium. You think of Babe Ruth and Roger Maris and Mickey Mantle and how far the bleachers are in center field and left center, and you realize guys used to have to hit the ball into those bleachers to get a home run. So the footprint of the old Yankee Stadium in many ways is still there.

JIM BOUTON: For me, it was heartbreaking to see them tear the ballpark apart, to take the upper facade off the outside and inside the Stadium, to take out the poles. The old lower facade was beautiful and classic, and then they jammed it into the top of this modern cantilevered thing.

They made it ugly inside, too. They dropped the ceiling so that it wasn't like you were underneath the Stadium anymore. It had been so interesting to look up and see the pipes and vents. They painted all the lockers blue, making them look cheap and tacky. It was like a Disney-fied version of Yankee Stadium.

They had already ruined the exterior design of the ballpark and then they completed the job when they tore it down. I was a sportscaster at that time. I went out there and did three or four stories the whole week long while they were demolishing the ballpark.

Everyone talked about what a sad thing it was to see that facade coming down. The people in charge, the ones who were doing those terrible things, had no sense of class or style or history or reverence for the game.

———————————

"When I first came to Yankee Stadium," Mickey Mantle said, "I used to feel like the ghosts of Babe Ruth and Lou Gehrig were walking around in there. After the remodeling, I didn't feel that the ghosts were there anymore. It just wasn't the same."

On April 15, 1976, the refurbished Yankee Stadium—dubbed "The House That Lindsay Rebuilt," in recognition of the expensive renovations instigated by Mayor Lindsay—opened before 52,613. It was the largest Opening Day crowd in 30 years.

Yogi Berra, Mickey Mantle, Joe DiMaggio, and the widows of Babe Ruth and Lou Gehrig were part of the scene. Ceremonies honored the 1923 team, and Bob Shawkey, 85, the winning pitcher in the 1923 opener, tossed out the first ball.

BOBBY RICHARDSON: Since I was a former Yankee and a man of prayer, Mr. Steinbrenner asked me to deliver the prayer. I was coaching at Clemson at the time, but I understood that Mr. Steinbrenner felt Bishop Sheen or Billy Graham would have been too denominational.

———————————

Change was everywhere at Yankee Stadium in 1976, but one thing that had not changed was the Yankee–Red Sox rivalry. It was center stage on May 20, 1976, as Lou Piniella barreled into Boston's Carlton Fisk at home plate. Pushing and shoving followed as both teams flailed about on the field.

———————————

BILL LEE: We always had scraps. Munson. Fisk. Gene Michael.

That May day, Lou Piniella was at third base, and a ball was hit to right field. Dwight Evans threw Piniella out at the plate by quite a bit. Fisk bobbled the ball, and Piniella tried to wrestle it from his body. Fisk came down on Piniella and stuck him with the ball with his bare hand. It looked like a right-handed punch.

All hell broke loose. The Yankees rushed out of their dugout.

I found out later from [Graig] Nettles that the Yankees actually had a vendetta against me and that there was a separate group of guys that pulled me off the pile, threw me on the ground, and beat the living snot out of me.

I got up and realized I had a numb arm, a broken collarbone. I realized I wasn't going to be able to pitch for a while and that's when I went after Nettles and tried to hit him with a left lead. But I didn't have a left arm. Nettles came over the top and hit me with a right, and I went down over the top of the pile. My arm was never the same after that.

RIGHT: Red Sox and Yankees brawl in a 1976 game

Yankee Stadium attendance in 1976 went over the 2 million mark for the first time since 1950 as Billy Martin rode his troops to a 97–62 mark and a 10 1/2-game finish ahead of the Orioles in the American League East. On October 12, 1976, the first championship series game was played at Yankee Stadium. The Bombers and the Royals had split the first two games in Kansas City. The Yanks beat K.C., 5–3, then lost game four at home, 7–4, to set up the deciding fifth game.

It was typical New York City 1970s baseball on a raw, misty Thursday night. Chris Chambliss came to bat for the Yanks. The score was tied.

PAUL DOHERTY: In the top of the ninth, a very controversial call went against the Royals. The fans started throwing stuff between innings because they were nutty Yankee fans who started celebrating and causing trouble early, knowing this was going to be a "sudden death" finish. They rattled the K.C. pitcher and forced Bob Sheppard to make a "Please do not litter the field . . ." announcement.

"I never went up to the plate thinking about power too much because that would ruin my swing," Chambliss said. "I was just thinking about hitting the ball hard."

KEITH JACKSON, REGGIE JACKSON, HOWARD COSELL (ABC-TV):

Reggie Jackson: Chambliss is so hot he's got his shirt unbuttoned. He's in heat.
Keith Jackson: Mark Littell delivers: there's a high drive hit to right-center field.
Howard Cosell: That's gone!
Keith Jackson: It issss GONE!
Howard Cosell: Chris Chambliss has won the American League pennant for the New York Yankees. A thrilling, dramatic game with overtones of that great sixth game of the World Series a year ago—and the seventh game, too! What a way for the American League season to end. A spunky young Kansas City team. Look at them mob Chris Chambliss! What a season he has had! What a series he has had!

BILL WHITE (WMCA RADIO):

And here's the first pitch. Hit DEEP to right field! That ball is up against the wall—IT's GONNNNEEE! A home run for Chris Chambliss and this championship series is over! Look at those fans out on the field. Somebody picked up second base. Somebody just knocked Chambliss down. He's making it to third. These fans are all over the field trying to let—and the cops are out trying to let Chambliss score. And Chambliss running through the crowd. HEY! He did NOT touch home plate! Chambliss hasn't touched home plate yet! Fans are out on the field. Fans are all over the field. Chambliss had to work his way all the way around the field from second base after he touched first. Fans out on the field pulled second base up. Somebody pulled third base up. They're down there now trying to take up home plate.

And Chambliss still has not touched home plate. And the ball game, I think, is over—

PHIL RIZZUTO (WPIX-TV):

He hits one deep to right center. That ball is OUTTA HERE! The Yankees win the pennant! Holy cow! Chris Chambliss on one swing. And the Yankees win the American League pennant.

Unbelievable! What a finish! As dramatic a finish as you'd ever want to see!

And on the scoreboard they're flashing "We're Number One" and I wanna tell you the safest place to be is up here in the booth.

Chambliss watched the ball vanish over the right-center field fence. Throwing his arms into the air, the burly Yankee did a little victory dance heading down the line to first base.

"The fans ran on the field," Chambliss said. "I was in the middle of a mass of people. I had a little trouble touching the bases."

"By the time Chris got to third base," Thurman Munson, now Yankee captain, recalled, "all hope of reaching the plate was gone. He never did make it."

BOB SHEPPARD: The game was over. The Yankees had won. Ten thousand people, as if they were shot out of a cannon, ran out on the field. I just folded my arms and let them do it.

There was such a mob that crowded the field that Chambliss was delayed several minutes before finally touching the plate. The New York Yankees "officially" had the 30th pennant they had sought for the past dozen years.

"The Chambliss home run was the highlight of our season," said former Yankee second baseman Willie Randolph. "We celebrated that night and flew all the way to Cincinnati for a game the next day."

SPARKY ANDERSON: My "Big Red Machine" was the defending world champs in 1976. I didn't worry managing in the World Series against the Yankees with those guys.

A couple of friends asked: "What do you think?"

I said "Four." And I stuck up four fingers, meaning "We sweep!"

You are not awed by the Stadium but you are awed by the setting and the people who played there. The Yankees retired more numbers. With the Yankees you could go on forever naming names of so many great ones who played in that house. When I sat in the visiting manager's office, in the dugout, I thought a lot about the magic of the place. When I went out to the monuments, that moved me.

We took the first two games against the Yankees in Cincinnati, 5–1, 4–3. And the World Series moved to New York for the next two. It was the most media I was ever exposed to in one place. But I liked the media there. They knew the game.

_____

On October 21 before 56,700 at the Stadium, a Johnny Bench home run gave the Reds a 3–1 lead in the fourth inning.

_____

SPARKY ANDERSON: In game four, after Johnny Bench hit his second homer, I yelled out to coach Alex Grammas: "I got news for ya, Sugar Bear. We are going to be world champions again."

We beat 'em four straight.

_____

JOE GARAGIOLA (GAME CALL, NBC): _This could be it, George Foster, Geronimo, Foster makes the catch, that's it. The Cincinnati Reds win the World Series in four straight, it was a sweep. The final score, Cincinnati 7, the New York Yankees 2!_

BRAD TURNOW: My first game was late 1970s. I was just a young kid and my mom and dad took me from our home in Hillsdale, New Jersey. Back then the Bronx was a little bit of a scary place. A year before, my uncle and his friend had gone to Yankee Stadium. On the way back to his car after the game, a guy tried to get his watch. He would not give it up. There was a struggle. He got stabbed outside the ballpark by McCombs Dam.

_____

"With so much money having been expended by the City of New York on a 'new' Yankee Stadium, with the South Bronx a dangerous and decaying neighborhood, a backlash set in," according to an article in _New York_ magazine. "Yankee Stadium stands on the edge of the neighborhood like a master's house in a concrete plantation."

_____

LEIGH MONTVILLE: When I was covering the Red Sox back in the 1970s and early '80s, they always talked about what a tough neighborhood it was around Yankee Stadium. You would leave the hotel in midtown Manhattan, get on a bus. As you went through Harlem, it would get real quiet. It felt like you were driving through trouble. And then you'd get to this place that was an oasis. Yankee Stadium.

You'd get finished with a game and by the time you got through writing your story it would be midnight, maybe one, even two in the morning. You would go out, and there would be all these kids playing basketball and you'd watch them play for a while.

You couldn't get a regular cab. You had to get one of those gypsy cabs.

You'd get in a car that looked like it had been driven by Mel Gibson in _Mad Max_. The guy would drive some way that you never went before, banging and clanging over these back

roads. Then, all of a sudden, you'd be back at your hotel. Surreal.

_____

MIKE KILKENNY: I started out as a vendor working in the upper deck. I was 15 and small for my age so I was assigned peanuts and ice cream. A lot of my bigger friends were forced to wear the "bug juice" tank on their backs. Tough work having to negotiate the steep aisles of the upper deck.

As I got more seniority, I moved to the lower confines of the Stadium, where there would always be a higher concentration of fans. The most desirable area to work was usually out of the third-base area. Due to the configuration of the ballpark, this was the "sun field," so the fans were always thirstier in that area.

When you reached age 18, you were eligible to sell beer and that was the ultimate opportunity to maximize your income (we got good commission in those days).

There was a lot of competition as to who was the best hustler, and the better hustlers were known to move 30–35 cases during a hot, sweltering night game, or a long doubleheader. We paid a lot of attention to who was pitching. Some could wrap things up in a couple of hours; others would usually go three.

One occasion, a section of Tiger fans gave me a little something extra to basically be their bartender for the entire game, planting myself in their aisle. Working at the Stadium basically paid my way through college.

_____

The Stadium vendor crew numbered 250 in 1977. Before the Opening Day game, all of them were seated close together in the right-field stands for a meeting and a pep talk. Sal Luigi, the field manager, addressed them in what can only be described as classic Brooklynese: "O.K., guys, let's stay together. This is a family deal. Yiz wanna make a buck? I'll see yiz make a buck. Let's get to our areas and keep the stuff moving."

The vendors took up positions, and so did the New York Yankees against Milwaukee that 7th of April before 43,785. An All-Star was at every position: Catfish Hunter, Thurman Munson, Chris Chambliss, Willie Randolph, Bucky Dent, Graig Nettles, Roy White, Mickey Rivers, Reggie Jackson. The Yankees won 3–0. Catfish coasted for seven innings. Sparky Lyle finished things up. And the Yanks were off and running with the first of what would be their 100 wins that season.

During the off-season Steinbrenner had signed Reggie Jackson and Don Gullett as free agents. The acquisition of the controversial Jackson and his $3-million contract would add another element to the soap opera atmosphere at the Stadium. Steinbrenner–Martin–Jackson would be grist for all the gossipmongers, making for never a dull day at "The House That Ruth Built."

May 28, 1977 was "Jacket Day," and 54,881 were on hand to watch Ron Guidry go against the White Sox. The paying customers enjoyed their jackets but not "Gator's" performance. He was not in his usual form, giving up six hits in 3 1/3 innings. Chicago won, 9–4.

On June 24, 1977, a 6–5 New York victory before 54,940 ended a seven-game Boston winning streak. Roy White's two-out, two-run homer in the bottom of the ninth tied the game, 5–5. An eleventh-inning Reggie Jackson bases-loaded single clinched the Yankees' 6–5 victory. Sparky Lyle was the winning pitcher.

The fun-loving but sometime acerbic Sparky Lyle, plus manager Billy Martin, outfielder Reggie Jackson, second baseman Willie Randolph, third baseman Graig Nettles, and catcher Thurman Munson were part of the Yankee contingent at Yankee Stadium on July 19, 1977 for the All-Star Game before 56,583 and a national TV audience. The National League won, 7–5.

DAN MARENGO: I had a seat behind home plate in the upper deck. I knew the press always made a big deal about the feud between Munson and Fisk. I looked down and the two guys were around the batting cage enjoying a conversation with each other, smiling. What do you believe?

"I was a young kid in that All-Star Game, in front of my hometown fans, my family, playing in the game with guys I had grown up idolizing, like Reggie Jackson and Rod Carew," said Willie Randolph.

ROD CAREW: To play in the All-Star Game with my mom in the stands watching was such a thrill. Just being in Yankee Stadium was incentive to want to do well. The fans are special people. They'll root for you if they like you. I think they knew I was from New York so they gave me a good ovation that day and every time I played there.

DENNIS ECKERSLEY: I was like 22 years old. Before the game, Billy Martin—who was a nut but I loved him—told me I was going to pitch the fourth through sixth innings. Well, our starter, Jim Palmer, couldn't get out of the third. They lit him up. I came in a little earlier and pitched two scoreless innings.

The "Bronx Zoo" was a decidedly apt moniker for the Yankees of 1977. Yet, as manic and moody as some of the players, George Steinbrenner seemed a perfect complement to them as well as to his generally agitated manager. It was always on-the-edge time at Yankee Stadium.

PHIL RIZZUTO: The writers were never late that year because something was always going on. A lot of egos were vying for headlines.

As July moved into August the Yankees were playing .500 ball, but they finished the season with a kick, winning 40 of their final 53 games.

In September, just days after a humbling 19–3 loss to the expansion Blue Jays, the Yankees took two of three in a showdown series with Boston at the Stadium. That pushed the Bosox back 3 1/2 games. New York went on from there to win its second straight division title. Then they defeated K.C. in the ALCS.

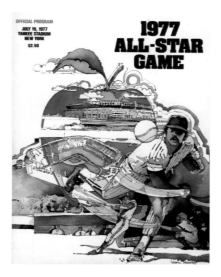

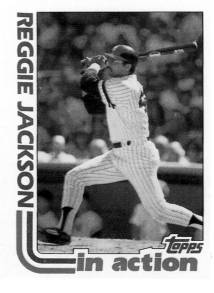

PREVIOUS SPREAD: Reggie Jackson hits his third home run in as many at-bats during the 1977 World Series
ABOVE: Jackson doffs his cap to an elated crowd
OPPOSITE: Martin and Jackson revel in the moment after Reggie hits three homers in game six of the 1977 Fall Classic

FRED CLAIRE: I was on the scene at Yankee Stadium as director of public relations for the Los Angeles Dodgers for the World Series of 1977, 1978, and 1981. It was Tommy Lasorda's first [full] year as manager in 1977, and a lot of the young players that had come up with the Dodgers were now matured. We had home-run hitters. We had power.

Yankee Stadium was the setting for the first two games. In game one, on October 11, Don Gullet matched up Don Sutton of L.A. before 56,668. The game moved through the tenth and eleventh innings tied 3–3. In the bottom of the twelfth, Willie Randolph doubled off Rick Rhoden, the fifth Dodger hurler. Munson was walked intentionally. Paul Blair, who had been in the game since the ninth inning, when he replaced Reggie Jackson for defense, slapped an outside pitch to right. Randolph scored the Yankee winning run to end the almost 3½-hour contest and give the Yankees first blood in the Series.

On October 18 the Yankees and the Dodgers faced off in game six at Yankee Stadium, with the home team a win away from its first world championship in 15 years. The temperature at game time was a brisk 51 degrees, and the announced attendance was 56,407.

It was truly the game of games for Reginald Martinez Jackson. In batting practice, he had been all over the ball.

TONY FERRARO: There was zip in his bat, pitches high, low, strikes, balls, he was right on it with power.

Willie Randolph joked: "Save some of those for the game."

"No problem," Jackson said. "There are more where those came from."

First time up, Jackson walked on four pitches from L.A.'s Burt Hooton. Next time up, fourth inning, Jackson sent the knuckleballer's first pitch into the lower bleacher seats in right field, formerly "Ruthville." A two-run homer. Circling the bases, Reggie mouthed, "Hi, Mom," twice to TV cameras.

Fifth inning, Jackson versus Elias Sosa. First pitch, a laser shot to right-center field. Second two-run home run. The Yankees led 7–3.

Yankee Stadium was heating up. Feet were stomping. Hands were clapping. Voices were chanting "Reggie! Reggie! Reggie!" And the rocking, stomping, and chanting kept intensifying.

"All I had to do was show up at the plate," Jackson remembered. "They were going to cheer me even if I struck out."

Knuckleballer Charlie Hough faced Reggie in the eighth inning. First pitch, home run deep into the "black seats" in right-center field.

HOWARD COSELL (ABC-TV):
Oh, what a blow! What a way to top it off. Forget about who the Most Valuable Player is in the World Series! How this man has responded to pressure! Oh, what a beam on his face. How can you blame him? He's answered the whole WORLD! After all the furor, after all the hassling, it comes down to this!

ROSS PORTER: (CBS RADIO NETWORK):
Jackson, with four runs batted in, sends a fly ball to center field and deep! That's going to be way back! And that's going to be gone! Reggie Jackson has hit his third home run of the game!

"I felt like Superman," said Reggie afterward. "If they had tied it up and we played eight more extra innings, I'd have hit three more home runs on the first pitch that night. Nothing can top this. Who in hell's ever going to hit three home runs in a deciding World

REGGIE JACKSON'S

THREE HOME RUNS ON
THREE CONSECUTIVE SWINGS

GAME	DATE	INNING	PITCHER
6	OCTOBER 18	4th	**BURT HOOTON**
6	OCTOBER 18	5th	**ELIAS SOSA**
6	OCTOBER 18	8th	**CHARLIE HOUGH**

Series game? Babe Ruth, Hank Aaron, Joe DiMaggio. At least I was with them for one night."

Jackson's three homers paced the 8–4 Yankee clinching victory.

They called him "Mr. October" for his feats and "Mr. Obnoxious" for his arrogance.

The 1978 season began, and Reggie was still hot. At the Yankee home opener on April 13, 1978, Reggie Candy Bar Day, Jackson smashed a first-inning three-run homer.

TONY FERRARO: The fans went crazy. It was his first at-bat of the season after the three home runs in the World Series the year before. They threw all kinds of stuff on the field, including his candy bars. The game had to be delayed. Bob Sheppard had to tell people to stay off the field and conduct themselves properly.

"Ladies and gentlemen," Sheppard said, "we ask for your cooperation to avoid delay in this game or any game during the season. Please remember that the delay of the game is caused by the throwing of objects on the field, which necessitates the clearing of the field before the game can resume. We appreciate your cooperation from this point on. Thank you."

CHRIS PAVIA: It was '78 and the Yankees were very good again, and my family had banners in the windows of our house and pictures of Yankee players. I was about six years old and went to the Stadium with my parents. They put me out on the first row of the upper deck right on top of the railing. It was terrifying looking down on the field from that height. We had to go down to the office and ask for a seat change. They gave it to us.

As years went on I loved to get to the Stadium early and listen to Eddie Layton on the organ. I loved hearing "New York, New York," "Yankee Doodle," and the Latin rhythms he played. I got to know Eddie and learned he was playing a Hammond Colonade organ, a very rare instrument. It had a tremendously distinct sound.

That was Yankee Stadium. All those years, people came to the Stadium and heard Eddie Layton on the organ. It added character to the ballpark. Now rock music has become prevalent. At other parks it's not a problem. But at Yankee Stadium?

One time Eddie Layton was playing the disco song "The Hustle" while Reggie Jackson stepped into the batter's box. Eddie got so much into the song that he never looked down on the field. Reggie stepped out of the box and looked up. The umpires looked up. Eddie kept playing. So Reggie threw the bat down and started doing the hustle right at home plate.

PAUL MOLITOR: In 1978, I was on the team bus going from the old Sheraton on 57th Street in Manhattan through Harlem on the way to the Stadium. Having never been to New York before, it was an eye-opener for me. Here I was a 21-year-old kid, trying to take everything in.

It was something to be there playing against guys I had watched for many years, men like Munson and Nettles and Reggie. I was down in the Instructional League in Arizona in '77 when Reggie hit the three home runs, and being a huge baseball fan, I had seen many Stadium games on television. I was kind of awestruck at playing my first game in the Stadium.

I came up to bat in the ninth inning against Sparky Lyle. I had never faced him before and noticed before I got in the batter's box that

Graig Nettles went in and kind of looked at me and said something to Lyle. Then he ran back to third base and Lyle threw me his first pitch. He kind of hung me a slider. I hit a home run.

I ran around the bases, and there goes Nettles to the pitcher's mound, saying something else to Lyle. Later I found out the first time he went out there, Nettles said, "Watch out. This guy likes to bunt." The second time he said, "That was the longest bunt I have ever seen." My home run tied the game. But we lost, with Thurman Munson getting the game-winning hit. Still, it was a memorable day for me.

DENNIS ECKERSLEY: When I became a member of the Red Sox in 1978, Yankee Stadium took on a different meaning for me. It was one thing to come in with Cleveland. It was another to come in with the Red Sox. Oh, my God! It was a madhouse each time we came in there. It was baseball turned up a notch with all that noise and hype.

Being in the bullpen back then was nasty. The fans get pretty violent out there. It was the most intimidating ballpark to come in and relieve from.

STEPHEN BORELLI: My dad started taking me to the Stadium in the late '70s. He could call up a night or two before and get seats right behind home plate under the net. It seemed easier to get tickets then. This was around the time fans started clapping with two strikes when Ron Guidry was on the mound.

RIGHT: Bobby Murcer scores—barely—in a 1979 game against the Red Sox

"Gator" was set to take the mound at the Stadium on June 17, 1978, sporting a perfect 10–0 won-and-lost record. Yet players on the California Angels' bench felt he didn't seem to have good stuff going into the game. The slender hurler had bad-mouthed himself to Sparky Lyle before the game: "I've got nothing tonight."

Nothing was what his opponents had. Guidry fanned two in the first inning. He had nine K's after four innings, 11 after five. "Louisiana Lightning" was honed in.

Later Guidry explained: "I wasn't trying to strike out guys. I was throwing fastballs right down the middle. They couldn't hit them. And the crowd started to get into it."

The crowd was into it from the first inning; they got more into it as the game moved along. Guidry had 14 K's after six innings, 15 after seven, 16 after eight innings.

"He was so dominating that it wasn't even funny," said Willie Randolph, who played second base behind Guidry. "It was like he was cheating. He grunted on every pitch. He had that slider. I can still see Thurman putting down slider, slider, slider."

The strikeout record for a single game was 19. Guidry got numbers 17 and 18 in the ninth. Don Baylor, who had fanned in his last two at-bats, came up. "I wasn't going to be number 19," Baylor said. He singled, but was forced at second base by a Ron Jackson grounder, ending the game. "Gator" had the record for the most strikeouts in a game by a southpaw. He went on to post a record of 25–3, with 274 strikeouts, and a 1.74 earned run average, and to win the Cy Young Award.

Just a month after the "Ron Guidry Show," the Billy Martin–Reggie Jackson tag team event took center stage on July 17. The Yankees were tied with the Royals in the tenth. Ignoring Martin's instructions, Jackson failed in a bunt attempt, popping up. In the eleventh, the Yanks lost the game, 9–7. They were swept in the series by K.C.,

and fell 14 games behind the first-place Red Sox. A vengeful and in his phrase "pissed off" Billy Martin suspended Reggie Jackson for five games without pay.

On Old-Timers' Day, July 29, 1978, Bob Sheppard told the full-house crowd that the manager of the Yankees through 1979 would be Bob Lemon. Then he stunned the throng, announcing, "The manager of the Yankees for the 1980 season and hopefully for many years after that will be number one, Billy Martin."

All of this incredibly took place just five days after Martin resigned under pressure as manager, and 12 days after he had suspended Jackson.

The 1978 Yankees, managed that season by Martin (94 games), Dick Howser (one game), and Bob Lemon (68 games) would draw 2,335,871. They would defeat the Red Sox in what became the historic one-game play-off at Fenway Park, aided by Bucky Dent's pop-fly home run, and defeat the Dodgers in the World Series.

**BILL WHITE
(GAME CALL, OCTOBER 17, 1978):**
Popped up behind the plate! Coming back. Munson! Throws the mask away! He's there. It's all over—the Yankees charge out on the field. They mob Goose Gossage. The Yankees have won their second straight world championship.

PAUL DOHERTY: The Yankees introduced Dandy, their first team mascot, in July 1979. A young Bronx guy, Rick Ford, was in the Dandy costume. He estimated that he lost an average of five pounds per day in that hot outfit. The pinstriped character was designed by Bonnie Erickson of Harrison/Erickson in New York City (now known as Acme Mascots). Never appearing on the field, Dandy walked the nosebleed areas in the stands.

The world of baseball and especially that of the Yankees was stunned at the news that Thurman Munson, the first Yankee captain since Gehrig, was killed on August 2, 1979, when his twin-engine jet plane crashed shy of a runway in Canton, Ohio. On the field for the first game since the tragedy, the Yankees left the catcher's position unoccupied. Backup catcher Jerry Narron stayed on the dugout's first step for the singing of the national anthem, then went out to his position. For the rest of the season, the Yankees would follow the same procedure. Munson's locker, with the number 15 on it, has remained untouched.

FRANK RUSSO: I was at the first game at the Stadium played after Munson's death, pretty beat up because the night before I had gotten into a fight with a bunch of Red Sox fans in a bar. They were celebrating the fact that Thurman had died. I was hit in the face with a pool cue. I had a broken nose, black eyes, and there I was crying my eyes out.

It was a sad year, 1979, a sad ending to an eventful decade. Munson's death, physical scuffles and emotional crises, injuries to key players, a terribly overbearing owner, replacement in midseason of Billy Martin as manager by Bob Lemon, the fourth-place finish in the American League East, 13½ games back, that broke the string of three straight World Series appearances. There was, however, one big bright spot. The Yankees paced the league in attendance: 2,537,765 — their best in history to that point in time.

OPPOSITE: Thurman Munson on deck
RIGHT: Graig Nettles reflects after Munson is killed in a 1979 plane crash

CHAPTER

EIGHTIES

In 1980, Dick Howser, 44, became the new man in charge, the 24th manager in the history of the franchise. And he was up to the challenge, guiding the Yanks through an incredible bounce-back season. Howser's accomplishment, however, was not without its price. All season long, George Steinbrenner would place calls to the manager's office before or after games. Howser would pick up the phone, and explain: "I'm busy," and hang up on the Boss. Meeting with players, coaches, and reporters was Howser's priority.

	YEAR	POSITION	WON	LOST	PCT.	MANAGER	ATTENDANCE
	1980	**FIRST***	103	59	.630	DICK HOWSER	2,627,417
	1981	**THIRD**	59	48	.551	GENE MICHAEL, BOB LEMON	1,614,353
	1982	**FIFTH**	79	83	.488	LEMON, MICHAEL, CLYDE KING	2,041,219
	1983	**THIRD**	91	71	.562	BILLY MARTIN	2,257,976
	1984	**THIRD**	87	75	.537	YOGI BERRA	1,821,815
	1985	**SECOND**	97	64	.602	BERRA, MARTIN	2,214,587
	1986	**SEVENTH**	90	72	.556	LOU PINIELLA	2,268,030
	1987	**FOURTH**	89	73	.549	LOU PINIELLA	2,427,672
	1988	**FIFTH**	85	76	.528	MARTIN, PINIELLA	2,633,701
	1989	**FIFTH**	74	87	.460	DALLAS GREEN, BUCKY DENT	2,170,485

YANKEES YEAR BY YEAR 1980 – 1989

*LOST TO KANSAS CITY IN ALCS

In 1980, Yankee fans showed up in droves—2,627,417, a new American League home attendance record, and 2,461,240 on the road, crashing the 5-million figure for combined home and road.

A powerhouse veteran team whose average age was 31.4, a team with nine players smacking at least 10 homers, a team with a deep bench as well as an All-Star double-play combo in Bucky Dent and Willie Randolph, the 1980 New York Yankees scored 820 runs while allowing 662. The heart of the pitching staff was stopper Goose Gossage with 33 saves, 22-game winner Tommy John, and 17-game winner Ron Guidry.

At the 1980 Old-Timers' Day, to the delight of the assembled, Oakland manager Billy Martin donned his Yankee uniform once again.

PAUL DOHERTY: For the first time, an actual New York Yankees Old-Timers' Day was filmed for a major motion picture: *It's My Turn*, starring Michael Douglas and Jill Clayburgh. It utilized emcee Frank Messer and several of the old-timers.

Frank Sinatra had recorded Kander and Ebbs' "New York, New York" in 1979. At some point in 1980, after Sinatra's *Trilogy* album was released, the Yankees began playing the song after home wins. It soon became a tradition.

MICHAEL BOLTON: Because I know musical history, it made perfect sense that at the end of a game at Yankee Stadium, you would hear Sinatra and "New York, New York." Sinatra is in our psyches and memory cells the way a lot of Yankee Stadium is a part of our DNA.

At the Stadium, Baltimore swept three from the Bombers from August 8–10 and went on to take six of eight games that month. The Yankee lead was cut to 2 1/2 games. But a Yankee home stand beginning on August 28 saw them win 10 of 11 games, 28 of 37 from that date until the season ended. That was what the Yanks needed to finish first in the American League East, with a record of 103–59.

Kansas City, the team the Yankees had put away three times in the 1970s, was the competition in the American League Championship Series, then a best-of-five series.

Kansas City won the first two games at home. In the second game with the Royals ahead 3–2 in the eighth inning and two out, Yankee third-base coach Mike Ferraro sent Willie Randolph home on a Bob Watson double. Willie Wilson, in left field, overthrew his cutoff man. George Brett, however, backed up the throw and cut Randolph down at home plate.

Live national TV caught George Steinbrenner leaping out of his seat, screaming what seemed to be profanities. Despite Steinbrenner's rage, Howser defied the Boss and would not fire Ferraro. He stood by his friend and coach.

PAUL DOHERTY: Willie Randolph has gone on record saying that it wasn't Ferraro's fault. He was heading for home no matter what signal he received from Ferraro.

The series shifted to Yankee Stadium for game three, and New York carried a 2–1 lead into the top of the seventh inning before 56,588 on October 10. There were two outs. Speedy Willie Wilson was on second base for the Royals.

Dick Howser did not hesitate. Pulling Tommy John, he brought in hard-throwing Goose Gossage. U. L. Washington singled, sending Wilson to third.

"Beating the Yankees," George Brett said, "had become the biggest obstacle in our lives. Walking

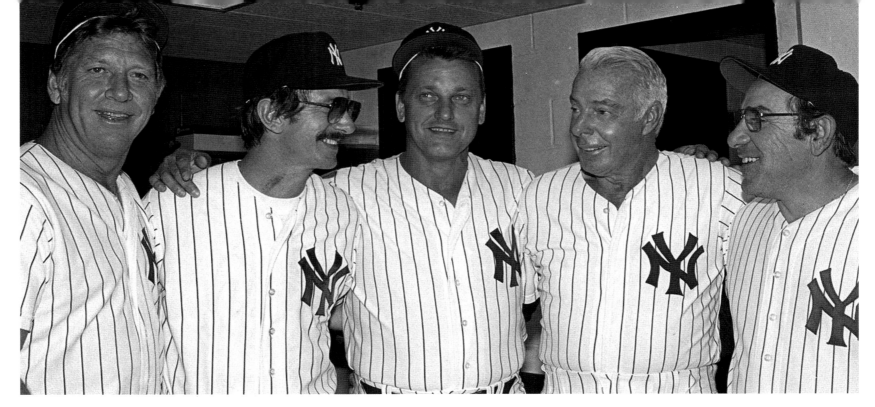

up to home plate, I could hear the roar of the crowd, the anticipation. But once I got in that batter's box I never heard a thing. Hitting the ball, I didn't feel any reverberation in my hands."

Into the upper deck went the three-run shot. Around the bases went Brett. Fans were stunned and distraught. The Yanks lost the game, 4–2. Their season was over.

And so was Dick Howser's time as Yankee skipper despite his having won 103 games in his rookie season, piloting a team that set attendance records, and making a great deal of money for the franchise. The Boss canned him as manager. And the Boss had Ferraro switched in 1981 to be the first-base coach.

On Opening Day, April 9, 1981, a record crowd of 55,123 was at "The House That Ruth Built" along with new manager Gene Michael. Bob Sheppard delivered a tribute to Elston Howard, who had died the previous December. "Elston Howard . . . set an outstanding example for all of us. Elston was a gentleman. A gentleman of great character who always stood ready to help a youngster, a teammate, or a friend. This is our greatest loss."

The Yanks torched Texas, 10–3. Bobby Murcer hit a grand-slam home run. Bucky Dent also homered. Dave Winfield, who had signed an eye-popping (for that era) 10-year, free-agent contract over the previous winter for $21 million, walked twice and collected two hits.

This was the season of a two-month bitter players' strike that began on June 12. In the American League, it resulted in the winner of the first half of the season (before the strike) champion Eastern Division New York Yankees playing the second-half champion Milwaukee Brewers. The Western Division Oakland Athletics, winners of the first half, played Kansas City, the second-half champion.

PAUL MOLITOR: That was the first time Milwaukee got into the playoffs. It was my first taste of playoff baseball, and playoff baseball in New York, in October, at Yankee Stadium, takes on a whole different feel. It's played at an elevated level. As a young and visiting player at the Stadium, it was a challenge to keep my composure.

The Yankees and the Brewers split the first four games setting up a decisive fifth game. On October 11, against Milwaukee at the Stadium, Reggie Jackson, Oscar Gamble, and Rick Cerone all homered, pushing the Yankees to a 7–3 victory. It was the fifth division title in six years for New York. Four days later the Yankees notched their 33rd pennant, trimming the A's, 4–0, for a three-game sweep.

The 1981 World Series was Yankees versus Dodgers, the third matchup between the two storied franchises in five years. A 9–2 win at Yankee Stadium in game six gave the world championship to Los Angeles.

**KEITH JACKSON
(GAME CALL, ABC-TV):**
Watson hits it high in the air for the center fielder Ken Landreaux. This should do it—and the Dodgers are the 1981 champions of baseball.

LEFT: Ron Guidry getting set to do what he does best
ABOVE: Goose Gossage follows through

PRESS RELEASE

I want to sincerely apologize to the people of New York and to the fans of the New York Yankees everywhere for the performance of the Yankee team in the World Series. I also want to assure you that we will be at work immediately to prepare for 1982.

—GEORGE STEINBRENNER

FRED CLAIRE: Steinbrenner's apology came in the form of a release, which he passed out after we won the Series. I though it was strange. The Yankees had given all they could to win. There was really no need to apologize for an all-out effort by your team.

The Boss did much more than apologize. He kicked ass and rolled heads. He demeaned Dave Winfield, who had only one hit in 21 at-bats in the Series. Having signed him to a huge contract, Steinbrenner was furious at "Winny," dubbing him "Mr. May," a sarcastic reference to Winfield's peak performance in May and poor performance in the fall classic.

On January 22, 1982, Reggie Jackson, irritated by Steinbrenner put-downs, signed as a free agent with the California Angels.

The commencement of the 1982 season at the Stadium was a hard time coming and as far as Yankee fans were concerned, largely not worth waiting for. Bob Lemon, who had managed the final 25 games in 1981, lasted through only 14 games in 1982.

On April 6, almost a foot of snow canceled Opening Day against Texas and the next game, too. It was April 11 before the ballpark was finally in shape for playing baseball. In recognition of how hard the grounds crew worked to make the field ready, crew chief Jimmy Esposito was given the honor of throwing out the first ball. The Yankees lost both games

ABOVE: Fans line up for the 1981 World Series
OPPOSITE: Willie Randolph homers in the 1981 World Series
OVERLEAF: Dave Winfield looks for the call during a 1981 game against the A's

of an Easter Sunday doubleheader to Chicago. But at least their season was finally under way.

The roster had what Yogi Berra would call "deep depth," with a pitching staff featuring southpaws Ron Guidry, Tommy John, and Dave Righetti. Goose Gossage was a flame-throwing stopper. Still, even with all that talent, the Yankees could not get it going. In June they were 9 1/2 games out.

On August 3, the White Sox took two from the Yankees at the Stadium, and the Boss fired Gene Michael, who had replaced Bob Lemon, supplanting him with Clyde King.

All season long Steinbrenner kept his circus jumping, seeking quick fixes. Beyond a trio of managers, he went through a merry-go-round of three hitting coaches, five pitching coaches, and 47 players. The chaos and the musical chairs did not make

for an environment that suited a winning ball club.

The 1982 Yankees were not a winning club. They ended the season in fifth place, 16 games behind Milwaukee. They would not return to postseason play for the next 13 years. From that season until 1991, with George Steinbrenner having his say and having his way, the Stadium would become a mix and match of players and pilots. Highlighting the mayhem of the era were eleven managerial changes, including the hiring and firing of Billy Martin six times. "They know what the bottom line is," Steinbrenner said.

––––––––––––––

PHILLIP DEMERSKY: My father was a police officer, and in the early '80s, he used to be able to get us into the Stadium and out on the field before the games. It was an unbelievable thrill, like we were part of the team. I got to go down to the dugout and sit next to Bucky Dent, have him sign a ball for me. I was in the locker room when Willie Randolph just got out of the shower and was standing around, getting himself toweled off.

One of the Stadium's groundskeepers was a friend of a police officer who had been in the Academy with my father, and when they relaid the sod in front of Yankee Stadium, he passed us some. We had a small lawn, maybe ten by ten, but it was made of the sod that had lain in front of Yankee Stadium.

––––––––––––––

PAUL DOHERTY: Just in time for Opening Day 1983, the Yankees installed their first big-screen DiamondVision TV in right-center field, and that radically changed the fans' Stadium experience. The 1976 black-and-white replay board in center field was converted into a combination scoreboard and message board.

Now the Yankees could deliver a contemporary Stadium "show" more akin to watching MTV. Rock music began cutting into the playing time of the organ.

Between the TV commercials, the prerecorded music, and a wave of more aggressive

cross-branded promotions and giveaways, from Surf laundry detergent to commemorative pins to Milk Duds chewy caramels to honorary batboys and batgirls to the Teenage Mutant Ninja Turtles appearances, it was hardly your dad's Yankee Stadium anymore.

But it had been quite a while since the time-honored and dignified ambience, the summertime pace and casual quiet of major league Bronx baseball had defined the Stadium scene.

One banished element of Yankee Stadium life, however, returned in 1983. The word on the street was "Billy's back." Many Yankee fans rejoiced, although one scribe quipped: "May the Lord have mercy on the big guys, wherever they are." The scribe knew of what he wrote, for "Billy the Kid" spared no one—big guys, little guys, whoever.

"Billy Ball" was on parade again, as was "out of control" Billy Martin. His Yankees were mediocre out of the gate, nine wins and 11 losses in April. By mid-May, the team was lodged in sixth place.

One of the reasons that George had brought back Billy was the Yankee owner's claim that he

"put cans in seats." But there were fewer of them. In 16 home dates the team had drawn 356,777, down from 411,515 the previous season.

Tension characterized the clubhouse. At times, lineups for games would not be posted until just a few minutes before the team was set to take the field. Martin ignored coach Roy White. Dave Winfield ignored Martin.

Down was Martin. Up was Martin. He was cussing one umpire, kicking dirt on another, suspended for three days and then a couple more. Martin undermanaged; Martin overmanaged.

BOBBY MURCER: A lot of managers were afraid to make certain unorthodox moves. They were afraid of the heat of the second-guessers. Billy was not.

Drinking more and enjoying it less, he was abrasive, often closed off in the manager's office, alienating everyone around him. He made appointments with media people and failed to keep them. An earnest author showed up for a long-scheduled

appointment only to have Martin tell him, "You got the day wrong. You better learn how to do your job."

Coach Don Zimmer announced he would not return in 1984 if Billy came back. Goose Gossage, Steve Kemp, and Ken Griffey all went on record that they would not be back in '84 if the little manager was still there busting chops.

But the story of the 1983 season at Yankee Stadium was not all Billy Martin, although he probably would have wanted it written that way. On a very hot Fourth of July, a holiday crowd of 41,077 was at the big ballyard. Yankee hats were atop the heads of many fans, a promotion that day for the game against the Boston Red Sox. Dave Righetti, 24, was on the mound for the home team.

FRANK MESSER (GAME CALL, WABC RADIO):
The Yankees lead, 4–0. Glenn Hoffman is at second base, two outs, in the top of the ninth inning. And Dave Righetti on the threshold of making history here at Yankee Stadium. He sets, the kick, and the pitch . . . HE STRUCK HIM OUT! RIGHETTI HAS PITCHED A NO-HITTER! DAVE RIGHETTI HAS PITCHED A NO-HITTER!

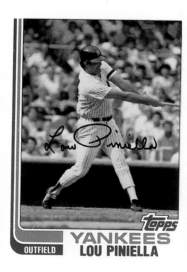

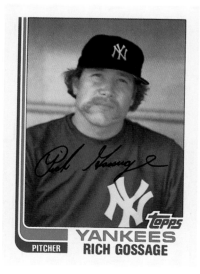

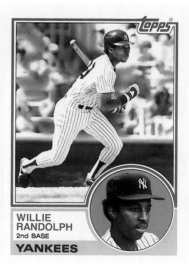

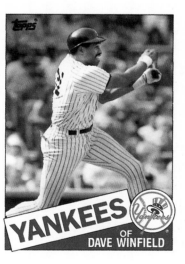

Wade Boggs, no slouch there, was the man who made the final out. It was the first Yankee Stadium no-hitter by a lefthander, the first no-hitter by a Yankee hurler since 1956, and the sixth regular-season no-hitter in Yankee history. That gem by the man they affectionately called "Rags" was a highlight of 1983. Righetti had fanned nine, walked four, and used his hard slider to get out after out.

On July 24, as the Yanks got ready to play the Royals at the Stadium, upside prevailed as the New Yorkers were positioned to take over first place.

Normalcy ruled the day, until the top of the ninth, as the Royals came to bat trailing, 4–3. With two outs, Goose Gossage faced George Brett. The Kansas City superstar hit a two-run homer into the right-field stands. Crossing the plate, going into his dugout, Brett spied Billy Martin in animated conversation with rookie home plate umpire Tim McClelland.

"I was feeling pretty good about myself after hitting the homer," Brett said. "Somebody said they were checking the pine tar, and I said, 'If they call me out for using too much pine tar, I'm going to kill one of those SOBs.'"

Asking for and receiving Brett's bat, McClelland conferenced the other umps and then thrust his arm in the air, signaling that Brett was out. Enraged, the Kansas City star charged out of the dugout.

"Brett ran out there like he was going to kill McClelland," Righetti said.

FRANK MESSER (GAME CALL, WPIX):
"He's out! Look at this! He is out, and having to be forcibly restrained from hitting plate umpire Tim McClelland. And the Yankees have won the ball game, 4 to 3!"

Bringing forth rule 1.10(c): "a bat may not be covered by such a substance more than 18 inches from the tip of the handle," McClelland ruled that Brett's bat had "heavy pine tar" 19 to 20 inches from the tip of the handle, lighter tar for another three or four inches. Brett's homer was nullified.

That was when berserk behavior took over. Brett led the charge and was ejected. Royals pitcher Gaylord Perry grabbed the bat from McClelland, and tossed it to Hal McRae, who gave it to pitcher Steve Renko, who ran halfway up the tunnel to the visiting team's clubhouse before Stadium security guards got him and impounded the bat.

The Royals protested. The Yankees headed off to Texas after the game, where they won three games and took over first place in the American League East for the first time that 1983 season.

Some time passed. American League president Lee MacPhail overruled McClelland's decision, saying "Games should be won and lost on the playing field not through technicalities of the rules." The contest was declared "suspended."

The game was scheduled for completion on August 18. The last four outs would be a "continuation." At first the Yankees announced they would charge regular admission for the game's resumption. Then they said they would not. No matter—around 1,200 diehard or curious or fans with nothing better to do showed up to watch the bizarre scenario play out.

Jerry Mumphrey, who had come into the game for defensive purposes for the Yankees, had been traded away. So Ron Guidry played center field for the final out in the top of the ninth. Left-handed first baseman Don Mattingly played second base. New York's George Frazier struck out Hal McRae for the third out. In the bottom of the ninth, Royals' reliever Dan Quisenberry got the Yankees in order. The "continuation" took 9 minutes and 41 seconds. And the saga of the "pine tar game" became another curious happening in Yankee Stadium history.

The talent was there for the 1983 Yankees but so was the tension. It was a team that loved playing at Yankee Stadium, where it posted a 51–30 won-lost record. But their road record was 40–41, and one of the main reasons that they finished in third place.

On December 16th, with 1983 drawing to a close, the principal owner of the Yankees announced,

"I'm shifting people around. Nobody is leaving. I'm doing what's best for everybody's interests, not just mine's and Billy's, but for the team's, too."

The headline in the *New York Daily News* announced: "Hello, Yogi! Berra Replaces Martin as Yankee Manager."

The fifty-five-year-old Martin was kept on as an official member of the Yankee family; "kicked upstairs" was the euphemism. When asked if Martin might one day be back as manager, the Boss responded, "Nothing is sure but death and taxes."

Speedy Rickey Henderson was at the top of the batting order in 1984. Power came from Don Baylor and Dave Winfield. Don Mattingly, in his first full season, was always an offensive threat. With these stars and others, the Bronx Bombers had the weapons.

Old-Timers' Day on July 22 was a time of special poignancy. Homage was paid to the late first black Yankee, Elston Howard, and to Roger Maris, who had cancer and would die the next year. Numbers 32 for Howard and 9 for Maris were retired. Plaques were established honoring them in Monument Park, which was installed during the rebuilding of Yankee Stadium between 1973 and 1976.

Another Yankee icon had his time in the spotlight. Lou Piniella Day was celebrated at the Stadium on August 4. "Sweet Lou" had hung up his spikes a little less than two months before.

Throughout that season, Dave Winfield and Don Mattingly went head to head in a battle for the American League batting title and the affection of Yankee fans. On June 25 Winfield notched five singles and four RBIs, capping a Yankee victory over the Tigers. A truly professional hitter, he had three five-hit days in June. But he was the outsider who was booed at Yankee Stadium, while Don Mattingly was the home-grown talent, the favorite who was cheered at the Bronx ballpark.

OVERLEAF: Don Mattingly watches his ball sail over the fence in a 1981 game

"Donnie and I were at different points in our careers," explained Winfield. "He was a young kid who had a lot of support from the public."

On the last day of the season, Mattingly went four for five, while Winfield managed one hit in four at-bats. "Donnie Baseball" won the batting title with a .343 average. Winfield finished second in the league, at .340.

The Yankees, a terrific team at Yankee Stadium in 1984 (51–30), were, once more, less than stellar on the road (36–45) and wound up 17 games behind Detroit in third place, with 87 wins and 75 losses.

After 16 games of the 1985 season, Yogi Berra was out. Steinbrenner, coldness personified, did not even give the Yankee great the news personally. He sent Clyde King as the messenger.

Billy Martin was in—for the fourth time. The prideful Yogi vowed never to set foot in Yankee Stadium again—at least as long as Steinbrenner was the principal owner of the Yankees.

"I keep hearing about this guy and that guy being unhappy," Steinbrenner said. "Well, if they're not happy, let them get jobs as cabdrivers, firemen, or policemen in New York City. Then they'll see what it's like to work for a living."

On August 4, 1985, Tom Seaver, then with the White Sox, came to Yankee Stadium honed in to win his 300th major league game. Coincidentally, that also was Phil Rizzuto Day. Paired that day, the duo would be partnered in the Yankee broadcast booth later on.

BILL GALLO: It was a *Daily News* promotion. With the help of a cow trainer, I brought a cow from center field to home plate, where Rizzuto, who had just been given a set of golf clubs, stood with a golf club in his hand. I handed Phil the cow. It stepped on his foot. The golf club flew

out of his hand, and he went ass-up into the air. It was almost like a cartoon. And of course, he shouted, "Holy cow!"

PHIL RIZZUTO: That big thing stepped right on my shoe and pushed me backwards, like a karate move. That thing really hurt.

Despite the pain, Rizzuto had a good day. So did "Tom Terrific" Seaver.

RUSS COHEN: I was a Mets fan and also a big Tom Seaver fan. I planned my life around his starts. On August 4, 1985, Seaver came to Yankee Stadium as a member of the White Sox, going for number 300. Naturally I went, and I wore my Mets hat; I wore it everywhere. All through the game, I heard those rants behind me, people saying he's all washed up.

But Seaver pitched the White Sox to a 4–1 six-hit victory over the Yankees, becoming the 17th pitcher to win 300 games.

PAUL MOLITOR: In mid-September at the Stadium during a very heated division race, I was in with my Toronto team. They played the Canadian national anthem before the game, and to my amazement, the fans booed. It was a cheap shot, something I never expected from Yankee fans.

But the following evening, Bob Sheppard reminded the fans: "They [Canada] came to the aid of Americans held in hostage . . . proving to the world that they are true allies and friends of America." It was class, Bob Sheppard class.

They played the Canadian national anthem, and the crowd cheered wildly.

On August 14, 1985, the longest-serving Yankee, Pete Sheehy, who had been so much a part of the scene from the time he was 17 years old in 1927, died. Equipment manager for the team, Sheehy had seen it all, including 21 world championships. The clubhouse at the Stadium is named for him. A dugout plaque reads: "Pete Sheehy, 1927–85, Keeper of the Pinstripes."

In 1985, terrific at home again (58–22) but not so terrific on the road, the Bombers finished third once more. On September 22 Martin battled with pitcher Ed Whitson. The hyper manager got the worst of it: the Yankee hurler broke one of his arms. Almost predictably, Billy Martin was fired for the fourth time. Lou Piniella was put in place as manager for 1986.

PHILLIP DEMERSKY: My grandmother was a die-hard Yankee fan who had followed the game from the time of DiMaggio and Rizzuto (she loved Rizzuto). To the day she passed away at the age of 83, she was watching Yankee games on TV. But she'd never been to Yankee Stadium until I took her to a Kansas City Royals game sometime in the late '80s. Back then, you could still bring food into the Stadium, and there she was with her sandwiches and everything else. She was Old World Italian and made sure we all had something to eat.

Everything old was new again at the Stadium in 1986. Officially Martin was out, but he always found a way to be around the Yankee scene. Lou Piniella, who had been honored with a day the previous

August, was in. He would direct the fortunes of the home team in 1986, 1987, and most of 1988.

Billy Martin's uniform number, 1, was retired August 10, 1986, and a plaque for him was put up in Monument Park. It reads: *"There has never been a greater competitor than Billy."* Always ready with something to say, the once and seemingly forever Yankee manager told the huge Stadium crowd: "I may not have been the greatest Yankee to put on the uniform, but I am the proudest." A Yankee broadcaster by then (and perennial manager-to-be), Martin was still part of the Stadium scene.

But even more so was "Sweet Lou," who steered his team to a 90–72 record in '86, five games behind Boston in the American League East.

The Yankees were close and could have been closer if not for poor performance at Yankee Stadium, 41 wins and 39 losses, and a backbreaking stretch of eight straight home losses in June. On the road, this time around the Bombers were the cream of the crop in the American League, playing at a .598 clip.

Perhaps in response to the increasingly raucous atmosphere at the Stadium, a "Family Section" was created in 1988, costing $11 a ticket. And on May 13 and 14, the Yankees hosted the Walt Disney World Series pregame show, honoring America and its favorite pastime, baseball. Mickey, Minnie, Goofy, and Pluto starred in an elaborate event on the playing field.

On August 2, 1987, Whitey Ford and Lefty Gomez were honored by the Yankees with plaques in Monument Park. It was a season where Lou Piniella did all he could. He employed a then team record 48 players that year, including 15 different starting pitchers. He cajoled and coaxed. In the end, none of this seemed to help. The Yankees, 89–73, finished fourth in the American League Eastern Division.

George Steinbrenner was making moves again—it seemed he never stopped. The 1988 sea-son began with Lou Piniella as general manager. And for the fifth time, Billy Martin was back in the saddle as manager.

But Billy did not last long in his fifth go-around even though he was getting results on the field. The Yankees were 40–28, just a couple of games out of first place, when the ax fell on him on June 23. He had brought it on himself, with weird and antisocial behavior on and off the field. Piniella returned as manager and had the Yankees in the pennant race almost to the end. And the Yankees established a new franchise home attendance record of 2,633,701.

Three days later, following a Yankee-Indian game, the Stadium hosted the Beach Boys in a concert that held special appeal to Baby Boomer fans and players alike.

JEFF IDELSON: On Old-Timers' Day 1989, Joe DiMaggio came into the locker room. He looked around and turned to our clubhouse guy: "I want to meet the Yankee center fielder," he said.

So Nick brings him over to Roberto Kelly, who was in his first full year with the team. Joe looks in his locker and sees a Wayne Tolleson bat, a Steve Balboni bat, and a Don Mattingly bat.

He says to Kelly: "How come you don't have your own bats?"

Roberto says: "I had some bats at the beginning of the season, but I've gone through them. So I'm using bats from some of my teammates."

Joe goes out on the field and throws out the ceremonial first pitch. Then he goes up to George's suite.

George says, "Great to see you."

Joe says, "How can the Yankee center fielder not have his own bats?"

Within a week, Roberto had three cases of bats.

Rich Marazzi began in a unique role at Yankee Stadium in 1989. A rules writer for *Yankees Magazine,* Marazzi would umpire for the next 16 years at Old-Timers' games.

RICH MARAZZI: Being on the field, being in the dugout in the pregame introduction, and sitting next to many of the great players was always a thrill. We dressed the last few years with the old-timers. So I would be lockered next to people like Dooley Womack, Tom Lasorda, Hank Bauer, Bill Skowron, Jocko Conlan—the legendary umpire with his patented bow tie, Ray Kelly, who was Babe Ruth's mascot, Tracy Stallard.

I asked Stallard: "What does it mean to you to be known as the pitcher who gave up the 61st home run to Maris?"

And he said, "If I hadn't done that I wouldn't be here today."

The 1980s was a time of frenetic activity for the Yankees of New York. Yet despite all the comings and goings at the Stadium, all the new locker assignments, all the new uniforms handed out, all the title changes, all the executive office games of musical chairs, they won more games than any other team in major league baseball in that decade.

The arithmetic, however, only added up to general mediocrity on the playing field. All that money spent, all that turmoil, not much payoff.

OVERLEAF: Young Yankee fans vent their frustration toward The Boss

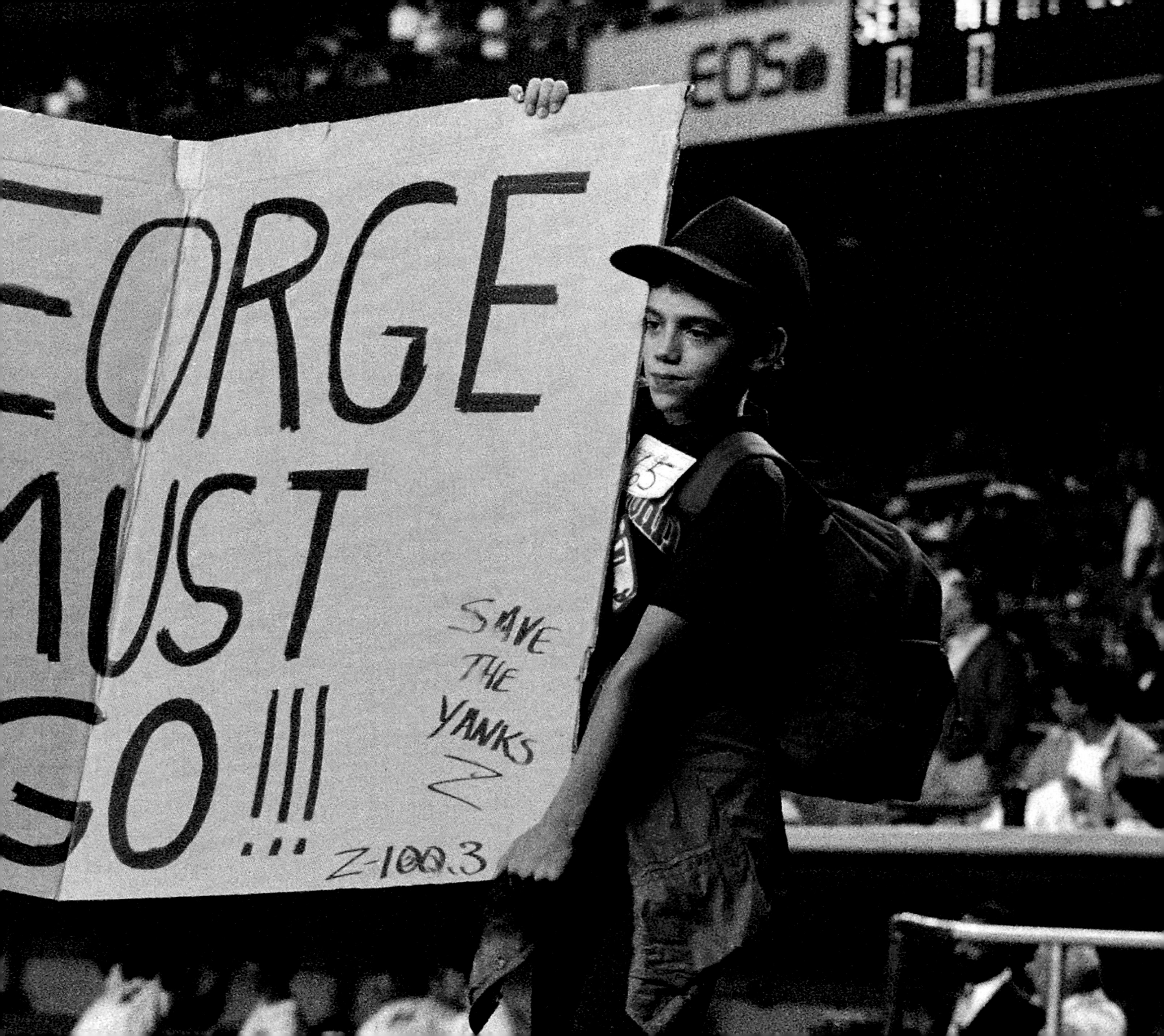

EORGE
MUST
GO!!!
SAVE
THE
YANKS
Z
Z-100.3

CHAPTER

NINETIES

It was a poignant moment at the season opener in 1990 when the son of Billy Martin threw out the first ball before a crowd of 50,114. The feisty player and manager, so long a member of the Yankee family, had been killed in a car crash the previous Christmas Day.

	YEAR	POSITION	WON	LOST	PCT.	MANAGER	ATTENDANCE
YANKEES YEAR BY YEAR 1990 – 1999	1990	**SEVENTH**	67	95	.414	BUCKY DENT/STUMP MERRILL	2,006,436
	1991	**FIFTH**	71	91	.438	STUMP MERRILL	1,863,733
	1992†	**FOURTH**	76	86	.469	BUCK SHOWALTER	1,748,737
	1993	**SECOND**	88	74	.543	BUCK SHOWALTER	2,416,942
	1994≠	**FIRST**	70	43	.619	BUCK SHOWALTER	1,675,556
	1995§	**SECOND**	79	65	.549	BUCK SHOWALTER	1,705,263
	1996*	**FIRST**	92	70	.568	JOE TORRE	2,250,877
	1997	**SECOND**	96	66	.593	JOE TORRE	2,580,325
	1998*	**FIRST**	114	48	.704	JOE TORRE	2,955,193
	1999*	**FIRST**	98	64	.605	JOE TORRE	3,292,763

*WORLD CHAMPIONS   ≠NO POSTSEASON DUE TO PLAYERS' STRIKE
†TIED WITH CLEVELAND   §WON WILD CARD PLAYOFF BERTH BY ONE GAME OVER SEATTLE AND
CALIFORNIA; LOST TO SEATTLE IN ALDS

Bucky Dent was there, too, in his role as manager. But on June 6, with the Yankees in seventh place at 18–31, Dent—like others before him—got the ax. Carl "Stump" Merrill, his replacement, up from the Columbus farm team, had been a highly successful minor league manager, albeit one lacking glitz.

"Here we have a fellow who doesn't come with a whole lot of glamour," said George Steinbrenner. "For the first five years I knew him I kept calling him 'Lump.' He was madder than hell."

Merrill may have lacked star quality, but no one would have ever accused Billy Joel of that; it was on display at the Stadium that night in June when the superstar performed.

DENNIS R. ARFA: Billy wanted to play Yankee Stadium, but the local promoters were going, "Oh, you'll never get it. You're wasting your time."

We had a relationship with the Nederlanders, the Broadway moguls who are also partial owners of the Yankees. Jimmy Nederlander Jr. was key; he was instrumental in getting us to have conversations with George Steinbrenner. George and I spoke several times. It went on for months.

Then George heard a rumor that Paul McCartney was going to play Shea Stadium. And when he heard that, he said to Jimmy Jr., "Get me that piano kid." That's exactly how it turned. We got the Stadium because, for a given moment, George wanted to outdo the Mets.

When Billy broke into "Piano Man," I was on the field, and I just turned around and looked into the stands and looked up, and it was like being in touch with the ultimate dream.

On July 17, two who had made their names in football were on the field at Yankee Stadium. Bo Jackson of the Royals smashed three consecutive homers against the Yankees. Then in the sixth inning, diving for a liner hit by Deion Sanders, Jackson separated his shoulder, and the fleet Yankee raced for an inside-the-park home run.

Back when he assumed principal ownership of the New York Yankees on January 3, 1973, Steinbrenner had said, "We plan absentee ownership as far as running the ball. I've got enough headaches with my shipping company."

As things turned out, however, he was anything but hands off—that is, until July 30, 1990, when he was forced to surrender control of the Yankees. He was banned from baseball for life by Baseball Commissioner Fay Vincent for alleged payments he made to a gambler in New York City seeking to gain damaging information on outfielder Dave Winfield.

When the news of the banning reached the fans that day in Yankee Stadium, they chanted, "No more George." They had had enough of the Boss for a while.

Denied access to his spacious office at Yankee Stadium where a favorite pillow proclaimed "Give me a bastard with talent," Steinbrenner in exile was "the Big Eye in the Sky," the man who wasn't there but who really was watching things play out through the 1990 season.

His presence or absence seemed to make little difference to the 1990 team, whose season was largely a disaster. There were some high points, such as the time during an August 2 game when rookie first baseman Kevin Maas hammered his 10th home run in just 77 at-bats, the fastest any player had reached that mark. The Stadium's short right-field porch seemed tailor-made for the southpaw swinger, and Maas finished 1990 with 21 home runs in only 254 at-bats. But he was the exception for that squad rather than the rule—the team finished dead last in batting average, a pathetic .241.

The 1990 Yankees had but one starting pitcher who won more than seven games, nine-game winner Tim Leary. But he also lost 19 before Stump Merrill showed some pity and took him out of the rotation. When the season mercifully came to a close, the Yanks wound up 21 games behind Boston in the American League East, the first time during Steinbrenner's time that his team finished in last place. One had to go back to 1913 to find a Yankee team with a lower winning percentage. Only the Yankees of 1908 and 1912 lost more games. Ironically, the Stadium box office registers just kept on ringing. The Bombers drew a healthy 2,006,436 to the big park in the Bronx.

A survivor, "Stump" Merrill lasted through 1991 as field boss of the Yankees. Among the dubious and memorable moments of the season was the 479-foot homer Seattle's Jay Buhner hammered over the left-field bullpen, the shelling of Oakland outfielder Jose Canseco by Yankee fans who pelted him with assorted objects, such as an inflatable doll, a cabbage head, and a transistor radio, among others, and the honoring of Joe DiMaggio on the 50th anniversary of his 56-game hitting streak.

RICH MARAZZI: During the pregame introductions, players were brought out to the first- and third-base lines, and I, as one of the four umpires working the Old-Timers' game, was called out to the home plate area. I remained there through the introductions. When the national anthem ended, I walked over to DiMaggio.

"Joe, thanks for the memories," I said.

Whenever DiMaggio saw me with a press tag around my neck, he was tentative. But whenever he saw me in my umpire's uniform, he would put his hand out to me like we were old buddies. And that's what he did this day.

I met my childhood heroes—Ned Garver, Mickey Mantle, Mike Garcia—the former top pitcher. I always wanted to meet Mike. I found him in a locker stall, giving himself dialysis

treatment. He was half the size he was when he pitched. I had a nice interview with him.

I umpired second base most of the time but did get to umpire the plate three times. I made sure my son would warm me up during the week so my arm would not turn on me when I had to throw the ball back to the pitcher.

The 1991 Yankees finished with a 71–91 record, in fifth place, 20 games behind the Toronto Blue Jays. The team results were less pathetic than in the '90 season, but still underwhelming. Attendance at the Stadium dropped to 1,863,733, placing the Yankees 11 out of 14 American League teams. Average attendance per game was just 23,009.

By 1992, Stump Merrill was gone, replaced by 36-year-old Buck Showalter. He had progressed from "Eye in the Sky" to third-base coach to hitting coach to manager. The losing ways continued for the fourth season in a row. Ten games below .500, the Yanks finished 20 games behind first-place Toronto in the American League East, but there was some incremental progress—for the first time since 1987, they finished (tied) in fourth place.

JEFF IDELSON: In November of 1992, Roberto Kelly was traded for Paul O'Neill, who came up to the Stadium for a press conference. There was snow on the ground. We gave him his uniform and his number 21, and we stood out there right outside the dugout waiting for some photos to be taken. Paul took about four or five steps out towards the first-base coach's box and stood there just looking at right field.

I went over to him. "What's going on?"

Paul had a tear in his eye and he said, "I just cannot believe that I am going to get to play right field in Yankee Stadium."

The 1993 season began with Paul O'Neill on the scene. After many appeals, a contrite Boss would also return to the scene in the Bronx, back from exile, having been reinstated by Commissioner Fay Vincent. Winning baseball would also be back on parade at Yankee Stadium.

On August 14, controversial old-timer Reggie Jackson, who had left as a free agent on less than amicable terms, came back to thrill the fans. His number, 44, was retired on his "day." Jackson and Steinbrenner had reconciled, and when Jackson went into the Baseball Hall of Fame in 1993, he decided to wear a Yankee cap on his plaque.

On September 4, in the waning weeks of a season that was a tight race for the pennant, Jim Abbott, whom the Yankees had obtained in a trade the previous December, took the mound against Cleveland. Abbott, born without a right hand, had more than made his way through competitive baseball, graduating from the University of Michigan in 1989 to the starting rotation of the Angels.

The solidly built southpaw had his ups and downs in 1993. Just six days before the September 4 match, the Indians had roughed him up. But on this day, he twirled a 4–0 no-hitter.

"I remember," said Abbott, "it was a cloudy day. A day game, the kind of game I like to throw. The no-hitter was the highlight of my career."

Frankie Albohn, head Yankee Stadium groundskeeper, also was missing a hand. The day after the no-hitter, he presented Abbott with the pitching rubber, signed by all the Yankees.

That 1993 season the Yanks shared first place 18 different times, but they could never get Toronto out of the way. Ultimately they finished seven games behind the Blue Jays, in second place, with an 88–74 record and home attendance of 2,416,942, their best since 1989.

Now it was 1994, and suddenly everything was coming up roses. Opening Day attendance at the Stadium was a jam-packed 56,706.

PAGE 180: David Wells celebrates his perfect game
PREVIOUS SPREAD: The scene around the Stadium in the nineties
ABOVE: Ubiquitous Yankee fan Freddy

Yankee fans bragged about Paul O'Neill, the best hitter in the league, and about Jimmy Key, their best pitcher. The Yanks went on to have the best record in the American League, and the fans at the Stadium were big-time into winning and cheering on the home team.

MICHAEL WISE: My first game at the Stadium writing for the *New York Times* was in the summer of 1994, a late July or early August game. I remember walking down a cramped corridor to the field.

Now, for many a sportswriter, this is a routine thing. But I had no job six months earlier. My former paper had gone out of business. I was seriously contemplating a change in careers when the sports editor of the *Times* asked if I could write a freelance story for them.

Within two months, I was hired full-time, and one of my jobs was to do backup baseball coverage. I was now working for the *Times* and typing my story in the same press box where Red Smith wrote. I was working alongside the *Times's* Dave Anderson. The final out of my

game working at Yankee Stadium, speakers blared the familiar "New York, New York."

I looked beyond center field. I had paid off all my bills the day before with my *New York Times* bonus. I was sitting in the greatest cathedral for baseball in the world, listening to Frank Sinatra, working for the most prestigious paper. Life was very good.

Life was good for the Yankees, too. On August 12 they were in first place by 6 ½ games in the American League East. Then the season was shut down by a players' strike.

There was no action at any major league ballpark for the duration of the 232-day strike. Nine hundred thirty-eight games were canceled; there was no postseason. The last time something like this had happened was in 1904, when the World Series was canceled.

Settlement of the strike dragged into 1995 and resulted in a 144-game schedule. The new season began for the Yankees on April 26. Just 6,300 fans had showed up at the Yanks' preopening workout. Opening Day drew just 50,245, the smallest at the Stadium in five years. It was a sign of attendance woes to come. The Yanks would wind up drawing 1,705,263 in 1995, their lowest attendance since 1981.

PAUL DOHERTY: This low attendance was a baseballwide reaction to the strike of '94. It took a bit to get people back. By the time the strike hit, the Yankees were already drawing very well. Their attendance was at 1,600,000 plus. But fans were very ticked off in 1995, even against the Yankees, and it showed at the Stadium.

LEFT: Jim Abbott following his incredible 1993 no-hitter
TOP RIGHT: Fans react to impending 1994 strike
BOTTOM RIGHT: Doc Gooden and teammates celebrate his no-hitter.

Most experts thought the Yankees could win the American League East in 1995. The Red Sox, however, broke from the gate. With 38 games of the season in the books, Boston had a double-digit lead on New York. The rivalry between the Yanks and the Bosox was a tradition that had lasted a long time.

So, it seemed, had Mickey Mantle. At age 63, he died of cancer on August 13. "He was a presence in our lives," Bob Costas said, "a fragile hero to whom we had an emotional attachment so strong and lasting that it defied logic."

EDDIE LAYTON: When I became the Yankee organist, I got to know Mickey Mantle very well. He would always ask me to play "Over the Rainbow." It was my favorite song, but— as I told him over and over again—I can't play it at Yankee Stadium because it's a ballad. The day after he passed away, however, I did play it. And there was not a dry eye in the Stadium.

Bob Sheppard told the crowd, "Today is a sad moment. We have lost one of our own, one of the greatest baseball players of all time, Mickey Mantle."

The man whose first game as the Yankee public address announcer had coincided with the Mantle's first game as a Yankee player asked for a moment of silence. Then on DiamondVision, time came back in a rush from black-and-white to color, Mickey Mantle running the bases, making the catches, blasting the home runs, batting left-handed, batting right-handed, underscoring Casey Stengel's remark "He was fairly amazin' in several respects."

On August 25, a monument to the late Mickey Mantle was dedicated, the first in 47 years. Its inscription read, "A great teammate. A magnificent Yankee who left a legacy of unequaled courage."

The Yankees finished the truncated season seven games behind the Red Sox in the American League East; a strong spurt, however, down the stretch, 26 wins in 33 games, got them into the playoffs as the first American League wild-card team.

The Seattle Mariners were the competition in the American League Division Series. The Yankees won the first game. The second game, on October 4, 1995, was a seven-hour marathon. Going into the bottom of the fifteenth inning, the score was tied, 5–5, and the rain was coming down in sheets.

Tim Belcher was on the mound for the Mariners. Pat Kelly walked. Backup catcher and first baseman Jim Leyritz made contact with a pitch on the outside corner of the plate and drove the ball toward the right-field wall. The two-run opposite-field home run gave

PREVIOUS SPREAD: Fan Jeff Maier affects the fate of the 1996 playoffs; Yankees celebrate their team's 23rd world championship

ABOVE: Torre and Steinbrenner after 1996 World Series triumph

OPPOSITE: Bernie Williams, a perennial fan favorite

the Yankees a 7–5 win. Leyritz's dramatic home run notwithstanding, the Yankees went on to lose the next three games and were knocked out of the playoffs.

In the Stadium tunnel after the second game, Belcher, very upset at being tagged with the home run, cursed and threatened a cameraman who walked along with him.

The team had not been in postseason play since 1981. Buck Showalter had gotten them in and had a plus .500 record as Yankee manager for 312 games, and had lasted four seasons, making his the longest managerial tenure of the Steinbrenner era.

But now the Boss needed more. The Boss needed change. He dumped Showalter.

"The media was against it," Steinbrenner said of his new hire Joe Torre. "'He never won anywhere,'" they said. "But he was a New Yorker and mentally tough." In 1996, 22-year-old Derek Jeter, who had appeared in 15 games in 1995, was now the starting shortstop for the Yankees. And in place as the manager was Joe Torre, 55 years old, the 20th manager in Steinbrenner's time. The image of him sitting on

the bench in the dugout at Yankee Stadium conferring with coach Don Zimmer would linger in the mind's eye of many.

A new routine at home games debuted that year as well. After the top of the fifth inning, the grounds crew would take a break from grooming the infield and lead the crowd in dance to the upbeat strains of "Y.M.C.A."—a 1978 song by the Village People.

PAUL DOHERTY: It was influenced by a similar dance being performed by the grounds crew with the Tampa Yankees. Yet another loss of Yankee dignity.

"When I first got the job," Joe Torre said, " I felt a little strange putting on the uniform because of all the tradition that went with being a part of this organization."

George Steinbrenner had taken a chance on Joe Torre. He also took a chance that season on Dwight Gooden, whose battles with drugs and alcohol had made him pay a price.

With his father in the hospital in Tampa awaiting double bypass surgery on Tuesday, May 14, "Dr. K." took the mound against Seattle before 20,786. Pushing himself inning after inning, Gooden had a no-hitter still alive in the top of the ninth. Runners were on first and second base. A wild pitch to Jay Buhner moved them up. Gooden then struck out Buhner. Two out. A swerving curve to Paul Sorrento. A high pop to Jeter. A no-hitter!

Celebration time at Yankee Stadium. Gooden was carried off the field on the shoulders of his Yankee teammates. "The Doctor is in the House" was the message on the center-field scoreboard. Outside, the Major Deegan Expressway signboard lit up in neon: "Oh, My Gooden-ness!"

Darryl Strawberry also was part of the Yankee scene that 1996 season. He and Gooden, two for-

mer Met phenoms, contributed a good deal to the Yankees' cause, one that saw them finish first in the American League East, going 92–70.

JON MILLER: I always felt that especially since 1996 when the Yankees got good again, the crowd at the Stadium was the best at any ballpark. It's almost like Yankee fans consider themselves part of the scene, part of the organization. They go beyond just coming to the ballpark and enjoying the game. Today you'll hear the chanting at any ballpark, but it all started at Yankee Stadium.

I remember a game with Baltimore in 1996 when Reuben Sierra came up and the whole Stadium started doing this chant: "Reuben" clap, clap, "Reuben" clap, clap. Thirty-five thousand, thirty-eight thousand—whatever the crowd was that night—they were all doing it.

At the time the Orioles were ahead 2–1 and there were two men on base. I paused between pitches to let the chant come through on the air. The next pitch comes in, and Reuben hits a three-run homer over the 399 sign in left-center field—a pretty good poke. The crowd goes nuts as he's rounding the bases. And as he gets to third, the chant "Reuben, Reuben" gets louder and bigger. I've never heard that at any ballpark at any time.

Broadcasting from Yankee Stadium, I noticed how it always seemed much noisier than any other ballpark. The sound system was louder. The crowd was louder.

I've seen whole sections go "hip, hip" and jump up and throw their arms in the air. At times it will carry through the entire Stadium. And there are the "bleacher creatures"

in right field. After the first pitch is delivered in the first inning, they'll chant the names of players, starting with the center fielder, and they won't stop until a player, by waving or pointing, acknowledges the "creatures."

And there is something else about Yankee Stadium: the significant role of the fans. The fans want the Yankees to win. They'll torment the visiting players, make them uncomfortable, make them lose their concentration, try to intimidate them. But they'll cheer the opposition, too. They are such a part of the scene there.

But for me the thing that lingers is how great the fans are, how unique they make the

experience. It starts right at the beginning of every game when the Yankees take the field, and the fans in the bleachers have a cheer for every player, and each guy tips his cap to them. That doesn't happen anywhere else.

DAN MCCOURT: We spent the night outside the Stadium before both the Division Series and the Championship Series hoping to be able to purchase tickets. You had to pay with cash and there we were walking around with thousands of dollars, something you would not usually do too often in the Bronx. But I am a diehard.

The Yankees defeated the Texas Rangers in the American League Division Series, then came up against Baltimore in the American League Championship Series.

Game one against Baltimore was at the Stadium, an environment where many odd happenings had taken place through the decades—especially in October. This night there would be another one for the books.

The Yankees trailed 4–3 in the eighth. Rookie of the Year Derek Jeter batted against the Orioles' hard-throwing relief pitcher Armando Benitez.

The swing—and the ball headed out toward the right-field stands. Right fielder Tony Tarasco, on the ball from the sound of the bat, headed back to the wall, and waited.

So did twelve-year-old Jeff Maier. From the stands, he stretched out over the wall with his black baseball glove and caught the ball. Right-field umpire Rich Garcia ruled that there was no interference by Maier, that Jeter's shot was a home run, tying the game, 4–4.

Despite the television replay showing interference, despite Baltimore's protests, the Yankees went on to win the game on an 11th-inning home run by Bernie Williams. The controversial 5–4 triumph sent the Yankees on their way to getting by Baltimore in five games.

Half a dozen days passed before the Yankees were finally able to face off against the Atlanta Braves in the World Series. Rain delays and a long series with the Cardinals pushed the start of the fall classic to October 20 at the big yard in the Bronx.

Pregame ceremonies resonated with the tradition, magic, and aura of the Stadium. Opera legend Robert Merrill sang the national anthem. Joe DiMaggio tossed out the first ball.

But rust showed on the Yankees; momentum was there for the Braves. They routed New York, 12–1. Then Atlanta did it again the next night, winning 4–0. But the Yankees won the next three games in Atlanta.

Game six took place on October 26 before a packed and rowdy house. It was the 100th World Series game played at Yankee Stadium. Behind Jimmy Key, the Yankees edged the Braves, 3–2, and won their 23rd world championship.

JOE BUCK (FOX):
Another chance to the left side, Hayes waits. The Yankees are champions of baseball!

JOHN STERLING (WABC RADIO):
They have surmounted every challenge, they have climbed every mountain.

The Yankees had also taken the hearts of so many baseball fans, especially in New York City. In the greatest ticker-tape parade since "Lucky Lindbergh's" in 1927, the Bronx Bombers were saluted all the way down the Canyon of Heroes in lower Manhattan. From Battery Park to City Hall, more than 3 1/2 million lined Broadway in tribute to the world champions.

The time of Joe Torre was off and running. And though one Yankee's time started, another's ended on January 22, 1997, when Don Mattingly announced his retirement at a Yankee Stadium news conference. He would be given a plaque and his

ABOVE: In 1997, Yankees play their first interleague regular-season game versus their crosstown rivals
RIGHT: (clockwise from top left) Mariano Rivera and Joe Girardi, Orlando "El Duque" Hernandez, Jorge Posada, and Paul O'Neill

number, 23, retired later in the season. Although Donnie Baseball's retirement was made "official" in 1997, his career actually came to an end after the 1995 season. In 1997 Mattingly would join the Yankees as a spring training instructor and become a coach in 2003.

On June 16, 1997, the Yankees played host to the Mets in the first regular-season interleague game between the two New York teams. The three games at the Stadium attracted 168,719, further intensifying the New York–New York rivalry and starting a new version of the old "Subway Series."

Overall, 1997 wound up as a disappointing season for the defending champions, who finished 96–66, a couple of games back of the Orioles. Winning the wild card, they then lost to Cleveland in the American League Division Series.

It was a downer, but that was the way 1997 played out. The 1998 season would turn out to be another story, one of rare accomplishments and the emergence of one of the greatest baseball teams in the history of the franchise.

The season got off to a slugging start on the April 10, when 56,717 fans set a record for Opening Day attendance at the refurbished Stadium, and behind a Tino Martinez homer, double, and five RBIs, the Bronx Bombers outslugged the A's, 17–13. The combined 30 runs scored by the teams established a new Stadium record.

Just five days later, a 500-pound steel joint fell from the Stadium's upper deck. Fortunately, no one was injured. The Yankees played a home game at Shea Stadium in the afternoon against the Angels while repairs were being made at Yankee Stadium.

Beanie Baby giveaway day at Yankee Stadium was a dark and gray Sunday, May 17. Quite a few in the paying crowd showed up mainly to collect the stuffed toy.

SUSAN TUCKER: I had bought tickets for myself, my nine-year-old nephew, and his friend for the game that was canceled when the Stadium was closed because of the joint falling. Instead I took them to Beanie Baby giveaway day. It seemed there were millions of kids there.

PHILLIP DEMERSKY: We had tickets for Beanie Baby day, my girlfriend—now my wife, her little niece, who was about three at the time, and myself. The little girl was very into those Beanie Babies. We got her one and watched the game for an inning or two when my girlfriend said, "Why don't we take Vanessa to the Bronx Zoo?"

I'm thinking okay. The kid got her Beanie Baby. She doesn't really like baseball.

So we left and spent the rest of the day at the zoo.

Later, when I get home, I get a call from a friend: "I can't believe you were at the Stadium today," he says. "I can't believe you saw the perfect game." I thought he was joking, hung up, and called a second friend. It was true. We came in for the Beanie Baby and missed the perfect game.

The crowd numbered 49,820. The competition was Minnesota. The Yankee starter was David Wells, possessor of a 5.23 ERA and a reputation for doing things his way and giving offense when none was due.

Three days shy of his 35th birthday, Wells had it going right from the start. Through six innings, the burly hurler was pitching a perfect game.

In the seventh, fellow hurler David Cone, sitting next to Wells on the bench, said: "It is time to break out the knuckleball."

PAUL MOLITOR: It was my last season. They put a Beanie in the locker of each of the visiting

players. Emotion escalated inning to inning. The crowd backed David every time he took the mound. Fourth, fifth, sixth. I got my last chance in the seventh with two outs. I worked the count to 3–1. He threw a pitch that was kind of close. It was called a strike. Count 3–2 and then I swung at the same pitch and struck out. It was a big out for Wells. I could tell I was a big hurdle for him to overcome.

"I knew what was going on," Wells said. "I was hoping the fans would kind of shush a little bit. They were making me nervous."

The Yankees had a 4–0 lead as Wells came out to pitch the ninth inning. The fans gave him a standing ovation.

Twins infielder Jon Shave flew out to right. Wells fanned Javier Valentin. Then Pat Meares flied out to right.

Wells pumped his left fist twice at the ground. Swarmed over by his teammates, he was carried off the field. The stout veteran had pitched only the 14th regular-season perfect game in baseball history, and the first ever hurled by a Yankee.

"What happened?" asked Billy Crystal, who wandered into the Yankee clubhouse after the game. "I got here late."

JIM BOUTON: When I returned to the Stadium for Old-Timers' Day on July 25, 1998, it was the first time I'd been back there in 28 years. My book _Ball Four_ had been published in 1970, and at the time, while I thought it would ruffle some feathers, I never dreamed it would lead to my not being invited to Old-Timers' Days nor that the reaction would last as long as it did. After all, the book was not a tell-all but one that revealed the players as human beings and made them more likable.

By the time I returned to Yankee Stadium, the book had gone through several editions and achieved its reputation as one that turned a lot of people onto baseball. All the negative things that had come out when the book was first talked about before it actually hit the stands had been completely washed away by the good reviews and the response of fans. I have no idea who originally put the ban on me.

My return was a very emotional time because it was more than just going back. It followed by a year the death of my daughter Laurie, and it was her death that inspired my son Michael to write a letter to the *New York Times* saying that they should invite me back, let bygones be bygones. The final line of the letter was "My dad could use all the hugs he could get right now."

Since that first return, I've appeared at several Old-Timers' Games. And once in a while when friends come in from out of town and want to go to ball games, I'll take them to Yankee Stadium.

On September 27, the Yankee Clipper made his final appearance at Yankee Stadium, on Joe DiMaggio Day. After being driven around Yankee Stadium in a convertible, the great DiMag was presented with replicas of his nine World Series rings that had been stolen from his hotel room decades before.

George Steinbrenner, hyperbolic even for him, said, "Joe DiMaggio is a national institution, and he is a living symbol of the pride, class, and dignity which are synonymous with the Yankee pinstripes."

Also synonymous with Yankee pinstripes was winning, and that's what the powerful and talented team from the Bronx did in 1998. By the end of July, the Yanks were making a shambles of the American League East Division race—going up fifteen games over the Red Sox, winding up with a regular-season record of 114–48, a winning per-

centage of .704, and finishing the year 22 games ahead of Boston.

The Yanks got by Texas, three games to two in the ALDS, won the ALCS against Cleveland in six, and were primed for San Diego in the World Series. The first two games, won by the Yankees, were played at the Stadium.

JON MILLER: Tony Gwynn of the Padres had come out early to really soak it in before the workouts began, to go out to Monument Park and read all the inscriptions, to look at the ballpark from different angles.

And Tony had said he was so much looking forward to hearing his name introduced in the starting lineups before the game. I thought that was really cool. For Tony, it was almost like a

religious experience, one of the great moments of his career, playing in a World Series at Yankee Stadium and he wanted to savor every aspect of it.

I remember Ken Caminiti, a huge star that year who hit 40 home runs and won the MVP award in the National League, also felt that being at the Stadium was a special experience. Ken said that when he was introduced by Bob Sheppard and trotted out to the third-base line with his teammates in the pregame ceremony before game one, it looked like the fans in the upper deck were right over him, and he allowed how that was a little intimidating.

ABOVE: Roger Clemens' first game as a Yankee
OVERLEAF: Derek Jeter's defensive prowess on display

It was the team that was intimidating. The Yankees made swift work of the Padres, sweeping four games to win another world championship.

On Opening Day, April 9, 1999, after 14 years of self-exile, Lawrence Peter "Yogi" Berra was back home. His pride had been ruffled when George Steinbrenner fired him as manager after 16 games in 1985. The Boss had finally apologized. The enmity ended there for Yogi. Now the former All-Star catcher would even be accorded the privilege of sitting in the owner's box.

"I was always a Yankees fan," Berra said. " I rooted for them. I watched them on TV. I was happy to come in today. I'm glad it's over with. It's good to be back.

There to throw out the first ball in his return, Yogi was called "a great leader and a man of conviction" by Bob Sheppard. As Yogi walked slowly out of the Yankees dugout, the full house gave him a rollicking welcome. It was as if he never had left.

But the Yankee Clipper had left. He passed away in Hollywood, Florida, at age 84 on March 8, 1999. His mark on the franchise was everlasting. April 25 was Joe DiMaggio Day at Yankee Stadium. A monument honoring the late Yankee Clipper, the fifth one in Yankee Stadium history, was unveiled in Monument Park.

It reads in part:

JOSEPH PAUL DIMAGGIO
"THE YANKEE CLIPPER"
1914–1999
RECOGNIZED AS BASEBALL'S
"GREATEST LIVING PLAYER"

and concludes:

"AN AMERICAN ICON. HE HAS PASSED BUT
WILL NEVER BE FORGOTTEN."

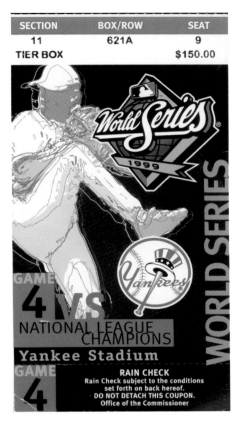

In front of DiMaggio's locker, Bernie Williams joined Paul Simon in a duet of "Mrs. Robinson," the song that wistfully summed an earlier time and the sense of loss felt by all this day in its poignant lyric "Where have you gone, Joe DiMaggio?"

The Yanks eased past Toronto, 4–3, improving their record to 15–5 in the young season, a season when DiMaggio's number 5 would be on the left sleeves of all Yankee uniforms.

On June 1 Derek Jeter rapped out two hits, stretching his string of getting on base to 50 straight games. Paul O'Neill slugged a two-run homer. The Yankees trounced Cleveland, 11–5.

July 18 was Yogi Berra Day. The spotlight was back on the Yankee icon. It would turn out to be a very special day. There were 41,930 on hand to witness a loving tribute to one of the all-time Yankee greats. Number 8 enjoyed picking up his gifts, especially a trip to Italy and an audience with the pope. Don Larsen threw out the first pitch to his old batterymate.

And then David Cone stole the show.

Against Montreal, inning after inning, he was perfect. In the eighth inning, Jose Vidro grounded the ball sharply up the middle. It looked like it was going through for a hit. But moving to his right, deftly backhanding the ball, second baseman Chuck Knoblauch threw Vidro out.

"When Knoblauch made the great play," Cone said later, " I decided there was some kind of Yankee aura. Maybe this was my day."

The ninth inning started. Most of the large crowd remained standing. One out. Two outs. Then he popped up Orlando Cabrera. His Yankee teammates swarmed all over the happy hurler, lifting him onto their shoulders. The Yankees had a 6–0 win, and David Cone had pitched a perfect game.

"You probably," Cone said later, "have a better chance of winning the lottery than this happening. The last three innings, that's when you really think about it. You can't help feel the emotion of the crowd. I felt my heart thumping through my uniform. It makes you stop and think about the Yankee magic and the mystique of this ballpark."

PHIL SPERANZA: That day was double the pleasure. It was Yogi Berra Day, the Cone perfect game. So much electricity in the Stadium. A little rain delay in the third inning, but it was worth it. I can swear that was the only time I was there and didn't see anybody leave.

Red Sox fans got some happiness seeing a couple of winning games played by their team at Yankee Stadium in September. On the 10th, Pedro Martinez fanned 17, the most strikeouts against a Yankee team ever. He tossed a one-hitter, trimming the home team, 3–1. A homer by Chili Davis was the only Yankee hit. Two days later, Boston beat the Yankees, 4–1, completing its first three-game sweep at the Stadium since 1986.

But those losses were small blips in a sensational season for the 1999 New York Yankees, who would get by the Red Sox in the American League Championship Series. Then on October 27, 1999, behind Roger Clemens, the Yanks recorded their 25th world championship, finishing off a sweep of Atlanta. It was their third World Series title in four seasons, making their postseason record over the past two years 22–3.

For hours after the game in the Yankee Stadium clubhouse, the champagne flowed and was splashed amid shouts of triumph. There were embraces, and even tears were part of the scene. Reggie Jackson and Dave Winfield chatted. Yogi Berra hugged Derek Jeter. Mariano Rivera was congratulated by Whitey Ford. A lot of the old stories were told again. The old ballpark in the Bronx truly had a time of it following that last game of the 20th century.

NBC's Jim Gray asked George Steinbrenner, "How long can this go on?"

"Forever!" replied the principal owner.

OPPOSITE: Joe Girardi and David Cone celebrate a perfect game

CHAPTER

21ST CENTURY

The greatest baseball team of the 20th century began the 21st century and their 77th season at Yankee Stadium with a tip of the cap to tradition and history with Bob Sheppard Day. In 2000, more than 3 million fans came to see the Yankees, who won another championship that year, this time beating their crosstown rivals in a Subway Series.

YEAR	POSITION	WON	LOST	PCT.	MANAGER	ATTENDANCE
2000*	**FIRST**	87	74	.540	JOE TORRE	3,227,657
2001	**FIRST**	95	65	.594	JOE TORRE	3,264,552
2002	**FIRST**	103	58	.640	JOE TORRE	3,461,644
2003	**FIRST**	101	61	.623	JOE TORRE	3,465,600
2004	**FIRST**	101	61	.623	JOE TORRE	3,775,292
2005	**T-FIRST**	95	67	.586	JOE TORRE	4,090,440
2006	**FIRST**	97	65	.599	JOE TORRE	4,200,518
2007	**SECOND**	94	68	.580	JOE TORRE	4,271,083

YANKEES YEAR BY YEAR 2000 – 2007

*WORLD CHAMPIONS

BOB SHEPPARD: The Yankees called me to give me the news that they were going to hold a Bob Sheppard Day. And frankly I was speechless. That rare honor, started in 1932, had been reserved for Ruth, Gehrig, DiMaggio, Mantle, Berra, and a select few others, not for the public address announcer.

The day arrived: May 7, 2000. The Stadium was packed. My family, including my wife, Mary, was there. I delivered the lineups from out of doors for the first time since September 30, 1973.

That I should have a plaque out in Monument Park in center field. It was an incredible, memorable moment in my life.

My saddest moments have been the eulogies that I had to write for those who died and had been Yankees in their time.

They'll say, "We lost Thurman Munson. Write something about it before the anthem is played." And I'll sit down and write something briefly and I hope touchingly. And deliver it sincerely.

I go to Yankee Stadium two hours before game time and check the lineups. At one

o'clock or seven o'clock, I get a signal from the sound man and he says, "Mr. Sheppard, the lineups." And that starts it.

I know every name and uniform number and work diligently to pronounce each name correctly. My favorite name to pronounce? Mickey Mantle. For many reasons. It is a great name for a baseball player and for a speech professor to say. "Mickey Mantle"—it has alliteration. It has the good quality of "M" and "N" and "T" and "L." It runs very nicely.

BROOKS ROBINSON: Doing Baltimore's games on television from '78 to '93, I made a lot of trips to Yankee Stadium and got to know Bob Sheppard. "Bro-oks Rob-in-son" is how he said my name.

PAUL DOHERTY: Bob would pronounce it "Brooks RobINson." However, if Frank Robinson was also in the lineup with Brooks (which he usually was from 1966 to 1971) Sheppard may have pronounced it, "BROOKS RobINson" to differentiate it from "Frank RobINson." That's the sort of careful attention Bob paid so the fans could differentiate between the players who shared the same last names.

ROLLIE FINGERS: He pronounced my name "RAW-lee Fin-gers." It was great to hear your name on the loudspeaker there—that's for sure.

BOB SHEPPARD: For years and years, nobody knew my face and I could walk around the Stadium with 50,000 people and never be recognized. But after a few television shows and movies, such as Billy Crystal's *61**, wherein my voice was heard, I became better known.

On July 8, 2000, the Yankees and Mets met in an unusual day and night doubleheader. Game one was at Shea Stadium, and the second game was scheduled for Yankee Stadium.

In the second inning, Roger Clemens beaned Mets catcher Mike Piazza, sending him to the ground with a concussion and onto the disabled list. That turned up the heat in an already heated New York–New York baseball rivalry.

Clemens–Piazza was topic A for fans of both teams as the Yankees and the Mets met for the first time ever in the World Series. It was the first Subway Series in New York City since 1956. Billy Joel sang the national anthem before game one, on October 21 at Yankee Stadium, and Don Larsen threw out the first pitch. The Yankees won in 12 innings, 4–3. The next day, Robert Merrill sang the national anthem, and Phil Rizzuto and Whitey Ford threw out the first pitches.

Roger Clemens started game two. With what happened earlier in the season between him and Piazza, the media buildup made the mood at Yankee Stadium electric with anticipation as to what would happen when they faced each other.

Clemens versus Piazza. Two quick inside strikes on the Mets' catcher. The next pitch was also inside—backing Piazza off the plate. The noise level rose throughout the Stadium.

Clemens threw again and Piazza fouled off the ball, shattering his bat. The ball skipped into the Yankee dugout. Piazza, unaware of where the ball had gone, began to run down the first-base line. Clemens picked up a piece of the shattered bat and threw it, it seemed, at Piazza. The wood almost made contact with an angered Piazza, who headed slowly toward Clemens.

GARY COHEN (GAME CALL, WFAN): *Broken bat, foul ball off to the right side. And the barrel of the bat came out to Clemens and he picked it up and threw it back at Piazza! I don't know what Clemens had in mind!!*

PAGE 200: Opening Day of the Stadium's final season
ABOVE: Opposing managers, Bobby Valentine and Joe Torre, before the 2000 Series
OPPOSITE: The Mike Piazza–Roger Clemens incident

RUSS COHEN: Met fans screamed that Clemens threw at Piazza. Yankee fans screamed that he didn't. People were pretty charged up. There was a moment when I looked at my wife and thought I hope nothing happens here. Tempers were going in the bleachers. But nothing did happen.

The Yankee and Met benches cleared. There was some cursing, some milling about, some posturing. No fighting. Later, Piazza said he approached Clemens. "I kept asking him, 'What's your problem? What is your problem?' I didn't get a response. I didn't know what to think."

Clemens later said he was "fielding" the broken bat, which he had mistaken for the baseball.

The umpires ruled that there was no intent by Clemens to hit Piazza, and the game continued. Piazza grounded out.

Clemens and the Yankees ruled that night. The Rocket wound up hurling eight scoreless innings. The Mets did rally for five runs in the ninth inning against the Yankee bullpen but came up just short. The Bombers were 6–5 winners and moved on to win the Series in five. The Yankees joined the 1972–1974 Oakland Athletics as the first team to be World Series victors three straight years.

The burly Clemens would be one of the big Yankee stories throughout 2001. He was salaried at $10.3 million, the third-highest on a Yankee payroll for the season of $109,791,893. On August 15 he became the first hurler in 32 years to post a 16–1 record. Then, on September 5, the Rocket won his fifth straight, setting a Yankee record and becoming baseball's first 19–1 pitcher in 89 years.

New Baseball Hall of Famer Dave Winfield, who had enjoyed his time in the spotlight, was honored at the Stadium on August 18, 2001; however, his number was not retired.

In one of those ironies of baseball, Mike Mussina took the mound on September 2 against David Cone, who had pitched a perfect game for the Yankees and who now toiled for their hated rivals the Red Sox. Through eight innings, the Moose was doing what Cone had done two years before—

ABOVE: Mike Mussina
OPPOSITE: Paul O'Neill

pitching a perfect game. No hits, no walks. Just a lot of tension in this game at Fenway Park.

Top of the ninth, Mussina and the Yanks clung to a 1–0 lead. Troy O'Leary, hitting for Shea Hillenbrand, smacked a liner that Clay Bellinger, playing first base, dove for. The toss to Mussina. One out.

Later Mussina said, "I thought maybe this time it was going to happen, considering that I thought that ball was through for sure."

Mussina then fanned Lou Merloni. Carl Everett pinch-hit for Joe Oliver. He was all that stood in the way of the perfect game. The moody vet fouled off the first serve. He swung at and missed the second pitch. The third pitch was a ball. Everett lifted the fourth pitch, a high fastball, to left-center. Running at full speed, Chuck Knoblauch and Bernie Williams did their best to try to catch it. But the ball dropped in—a base hit.

Trot Nixon grounded out to end the game. And Mussina, with the one-hitter and the win, pumped his fist less than forcefully. His teammates ran onto the field, celebrating what he had done.

"I've never been part of a no-hitter before as an opponent," Everett said. "It was very satisfying to get the hit. It was very satisfying to hit the high fastball."

"It was just a phenomenal game," said Mussina. "I was disappointed, I'm still disappointed. But the perfect game just wasn't meant to be."

BILL NOWLIN: We traveled to the Heart of the Beast, the Evil Empire. Two Red Sox fans. Innocents abroad.

We'd heard stories for years: "Don't wear a Red Sox cap or you might get stabbed outside after the game."

"Don't park your car anywhere nearby if you have Mass plates. You're just asking for trouble."

We drove in from Boston for a Friday night game, running a few hours later than we'd planned. It was about an hour and a half before game time. We got off the Deegan, down the 161st Street/River Avenue ramp, and right to a parking lot in the shadow of the Stadium.

The first, pleasant surprise: parking only cost $8.00, not the $20.00 it might have set us back in Boston. It would have been $6.00 round-trip on the D train or the number 4 train, if we'd gone downtown and taken the subway back up, as we'd planned.

Kids were playing catch in the parking lot, with ball and gloves. A few clusters of fans were tailgating. There was a casualness to the scene, not one of guardedness.

There were vendors, clearly unlicensed, working the lot selling T-shirts that said "BOSTON SUCKS!" A lot of fans had their Yankees "NY" caps, but the gear these vendors were selling were a little too crude to be sold in the Yankee clubhouse shops or by the licensed vendors who had their carts on the plaza or sidewalks around the Stadium.

But the tickets we'd been told would be waiting for us weren't there. And this was a sold-out series. Oh, jeez. We tried window N, window V, the guest window, customer service, the press gate, then made the rounds a second time. No luck.

"Be careful," warned the woman at the customer service window when I said it looked like we were going to be reduced to buying on the street. Signs warned it was illegal to resell tickets within 1,000 feet of Yankee Stadium and to be wary of counterfeits. We'd already been offered $8.00 bleacher tickets for $40.00 each. Bleacher tickets for $8.00?! You can get into a game here for $8.00? Back in Boston, the cheapest bleacher seat was $18.00 (though most of them cost $20.00—the cheaper seats are in the very distant top rows).

A little closer to the Stadium, under the tracks, we found three or four sellers and bargained one down to $100 for two. No great bargain, but we were in—and they weren't counterfeit, either.

Upper-deck seats, way up high, a long way from the field. A towering pop-up, and you could be looking down on it.

Tight game. Sox couldn't score. They lost 3–2. An obviously subpar Pedro Martinez, in his last appearance of a very disappointing 2001 campaign, had given up the three-spot early in the game—the second inning, in fact. Boston never did catch up.

Boston never caught up during the whole series, going down September 7, 3–2; September 8, 9–2; and September 9, 7–2.

DAN MCCOURT: On September 10, the Yankees were scheduled to play a makeup game with the Red Sox. It was supposed to be a seven-o'clock start. It poured and then it stopped and then it started again. They held up the game. It was really raining. At 10 o'clock and after two hours of no rain, the game was called because of wet grounds.

We had tickets for the game the next night, September 11: Yankees vs. White Sox.

Within 90 minutes of the horrific terrorist attacks on the World Trade Center, Yankee Stadium was evacuated.

MICHAEL BOLTON: The most powerful memory I have of singing at Yankee Stadium was before the first game played after 9/11. That was on September 18.

Thousands of people were there. The security was massive. The attack was still very, very fresh in everyone's consciousness. It was so dense; the air was so heavy. We were all overcome with the enormity of what happened. There were tearful people, a lot of tough guys with eyes welled up. They let an eagle loose; it flew around the Stadium and back to the arm of the handler.

I am a Connecticut boy, but New York has always been so much a part of me, and that, combined with the icon Yankee Stadium has been for me since I was a child and in view of what had transpired, I was choked up, full.

I did a number of songs that night. But the one that remains with me is "Lean on Me." I sang it early on, together with the Harlem Boys' Choir in honor of the police and firemen. I had already walked up to some policemen and thanked them for what they had done. They were quick to respond in appreciation, but they said it was bizarre that it took 9/11 for people to come up to them and thank them for what they do all the time.

JON MILLER: I was in New York for most of October in 2001, and it seemed everyone was touched by the attack on the World Trade Center somehow. Either they had worked there and survived, or were late going to work that day, or had a relative or friend or neighbor who worked there. Emotions in the city were raw.

After September 11, everything at Yankee Stadium seemed so much more vivid. The policeman Daniel Rodriguez would sing the national anthem wearing his police uniform. There would be such ovations. So much emotion

would cascade through the ballpark. I remember hearing the Irish tenor Ronan Tynan sing "God Bless America," and the whole stadium sang along with him.

In the wake of the terrorist attacks, all major league baseball stadiums played "God Bless America" during the seventh-inning stretch for the remainder of the 2001 season. But by 2002, many teams no longer played it at every game; the song was showcased only in postseason and Sunday games. The Yankees are the only baseball team that has continued to play "God Bless America" at all home games. Most of the time, it is the old Kate Smith recording, but on occasion Ronan Tynan will perform the song as part of the seventh-inning stretch.

In 2001, the World Series did not start until Saturday, October 27, the latest start date ever. The Yanks, facing the Diamondbacks, became the first club to appear in four straight World Series since the Bronx Bombers of 1961–1964.

RICH MARAZZI: First game after 9/11 going from my car in the parking lot to the Yankee clubhouse I was photo ID'd four times. In the press box there were about as many policemen as there were writers.

BRAD TURNOW: October 30: game three. My fiancée, Tara, now my wife, and I were sent four blocks in one direction and four blocks in another direction. Three and one-half hours to get to our seats in the bleachers—which to me is where all the real Yankee fans go—and we got there with just five minutes to spare.

We had to go through metal detectors. They went through everything. You could not bring anything into that game except for what you had

in your pocket. There was security everywhere. There were cops everywhere, undercover cops, police on horseback, soldiers, big machine guns.

JON MILLER: Broadcasting in Baltimore, I'd seen presidents come to the old Memorial Stadium and then the new Camden Yards. I'd seen Presidents Reagan, Bush Sr., and Clinton throw out the first ball. But I will never forget the night of October 30, 2001, when President Bush came out at Yankee Stadium.

With the other presidents, there would always be a crowd: reporters, photographers, Secret Service agents.

But this night, when Bob Sheppard said, "And please welcome the president of the United States," the president came out of the Yankee dugout all alone. He walked to the mound and threw the pitch from the top of the mound like he was a player. It was a strike. And Bob Sheppard said, "Thank you, Mr. President."

What an ovation! There was such a sense among the fans that night.

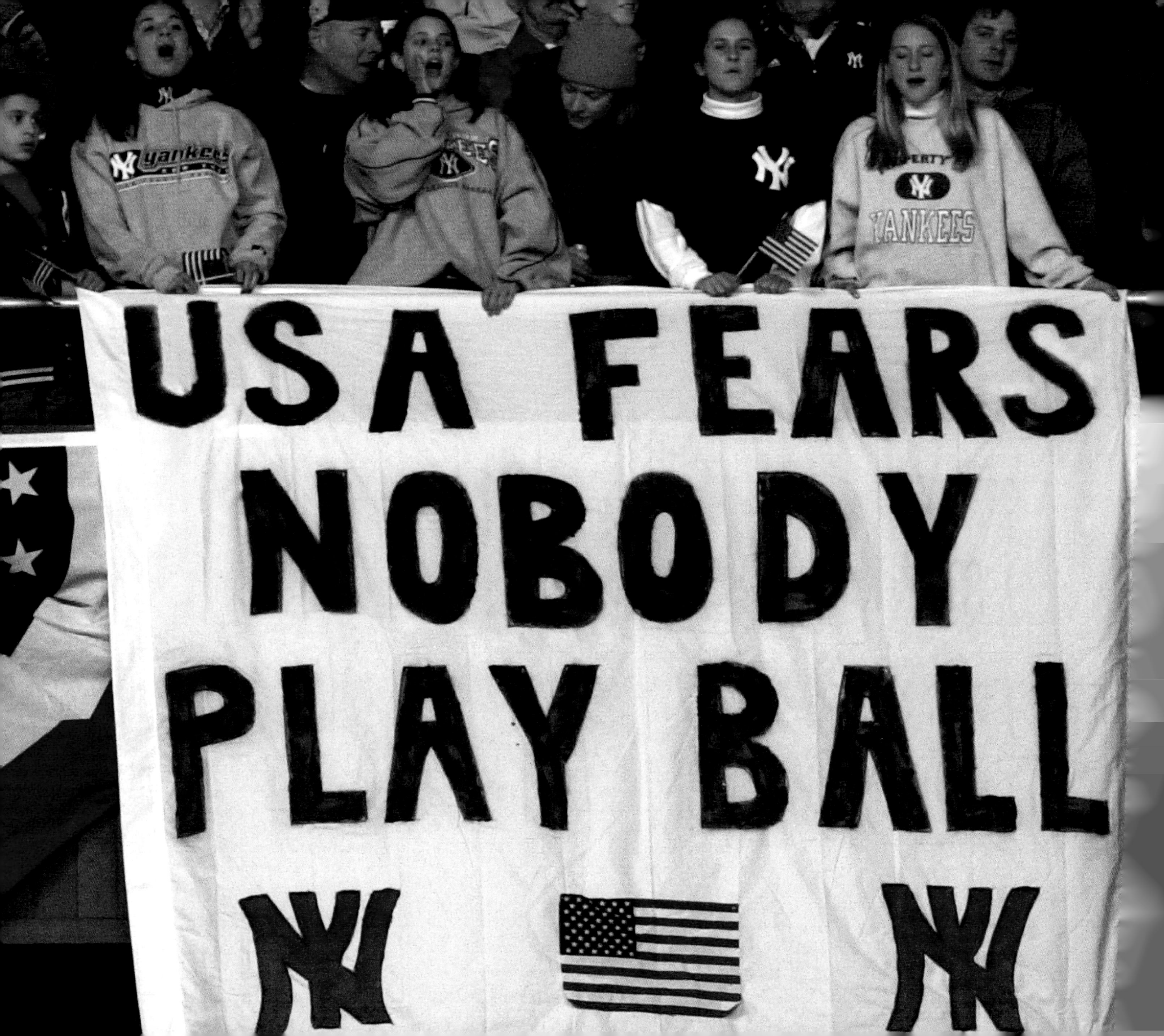
USA FEARS
NOBODY
PLAY BALL
YANKEES

BRAD TURNOW: Our commander in chief, bareheaded and wearing a light gray-blue NYFD jacket (apparently covering a bulletproof vest), had thrown a perfect pitch. He waved to the crowd. They roared and cheered as the F-15's flew overhead.

There were 55,820 people at the Stadium that chilly night. You had the coats, the hats. People were bundled up. I wore my 1998 championship New York Yankees jacket and my Yankee cap.

We had come back from Arizona down two games to none in the World Series. Spirits were a little down, but Jorge Posada got them up, quickly hitting the home run in the second inning. You could feel the Stadium shake.

Roger Clemens was a little tenuous early on. He had some problems with the splitter. Balls were going into the dirt. Top of the fourth, Arizona tied it. Clemens finally handed the game to Mariano Rivera in the eighth inning.

It was Number 18, Scott Brosius, who had the big hit. A single in the sixth putting the Yanks up 2–1.

When Rivera came out of the bullpen to pitch the eighth, the place went nuts. And when he got the final out in the ninth, the place shook again. Yankees won it, 2–1.

The next night was Halloween. Derek Jeter came to bat in the bottom of the tenth. There were two outs. October became history.

The scoreboard messaged: "Welcome to November baseball." At 12:04 A.M., Jeter slammed Byung-Hyun Kim's 3–2 pitch for a walk-off home run into the right-field stands. The Yankees had a 4–3 victory.

LEFT: Baseball returns to the Stadium after 9/11
ABOVE: President Bush throws out the ceremonial first pitch during the 2001 World Series

MICHAEL KAY (GAME CALL, CBS RADIO): *Swung on and drilled to right field, going back Sanders, on the track, at the wall. SEE YA! SEE YA! SEE YA! A home run for Derek Jeter! He is Mr. November! Oh, what a home run by Derek Jeter!*

November 1, Series tied at two games each, another sellout crowd, another game that seemed made for the legend and lore of the Stadium. It was Mike Mussina for the Yankees against Miguel Batista. The odds seemed to favor the home team. But with eight innings in the books, the home team was down 2–0.

"It borders on the surreal here in the Bronx," said Joe Buck on national television.

Throughout the game, knowing that Paul O'Neill was retiring and that this was his final appearance as a player at the Stadium, fans gave him a send-off that intensified in the top of the ninth:

"Paul-O'Ne-ill [clap, clap, clap-clap-clap], Paul-O'Ne-ill [clap, clap, clap-clap-clap]."

MICHAEL WISE: I'm sitting in the upper deck between first base and the right-field fence. One row below is Bob Lipsyte, one of my former colleagues who wrote one of the most sophisticated, smart columns in the country. Now, Lipsyte is a sensible, genteel, thoughtful guy. Not your average Yankee fanatic.

So it's in the middle of the game and the Yankees look dead in the water, about to fall behind three games to two, with the last two in Arizona. At some point, this drunk, young yahoo next to me—who means well, but is just plied with beer—keeps losing his balance, almost falling into Lipsyte.

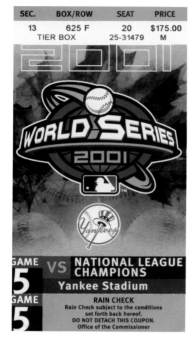

Lipsyte, who was with his wife, was getting agitated and eventually warned the kid. I asked him if he wanted to have him thrown out; he said he would take care of it if it got worse. Well, lo and behold, some wild play sends the kid pitching forward—into Lipsyte's row, almost in his lap. Lipsyte grabs the kid by his shirt collar, threatens him with violence, throws him back into my row, where he gets his bearings and keeps apologizing over and over.

Bottom of the ninth. Bedlam paraded through the Stadium. The Yankees were down to their last three outs, trailing 2–0.

The "goat" of the night before, the Arizona closer, took the mound again. Byung-Hyun Kim pitched to Posada. The Yankee catcher doubled to the left-field corner. Shane Spencer grounded out. Chuck Knoblauch struck out.

The Yankees were down to their final out. Up came Scott Brosius. It would be his last career at-bat at Yankee Stadium. The count was 1–0. It was 14 minutes before midnight. The swing, a long drive. Everybody knew it was a home run. The Stadium shook. An emotional Brosius, his arm raised into the air, cruised around the bases. On his knees at the pitchers' mound, Kim used his glove to cover his head. Extra innings.

MICHAEL WISE: Brosius connecting for a two-out home run sends Yankee Stadium into a tizzy—and an old curmudgeon sports columnist and a young drunk kid into each other's arms.

"You know they have to be thinking, 'I can't believe this is happening.' Not one night, but two nights in a row," Yankee pitcher Mike Mussina said.

"It seemed like the whole situation was set again and it happened again," said Brosius later.

It took the Yankees four hours and 15 minutes, but they prevailed. In the twelfth inning, Alfonso Soriano singled in Chuck Knoblauch, and the Yanks had another come-from-behind dramatic triumph.

The people of the City of New York, still stunned and shaken after 9/11, had something to cheer about.

SUSAN TUCKER: I got a ticket for that November 1 game through a broker. It cost $250. My seat was an auxiliary one, field level, underneath, against the wall behind home plate—one of the temporary seats, folding chairs in the walkway.

It turned out to be the greatest seat I could have gotten. I have MS, so I don't walk very well. The broker did not know this. My getting that seat was total happenstance.

The entire experience was extraordinary. Our winning the game that way, Frank Sinatra singing "New York, New York." I had been to many comebacks at Yankee Stadium. But because of 9/11, nothing can match that one. So what if the Diamondbacks went on to win the World Series in seven games?

The American League champion Yankees began their hundredth season in New York City in 2002. And what a wonderful season it would be, with the Bronx Bombers winning win 103 games and finishing 10 1/2 games ahead of the Red Sox in the American League East.

On July 6, the old hero Reginald Martinez Jackson was honored with a plaque on Old-Timers' Day that reads: "One of the most colorful and exciting players of his era" and "a prolific hitter who thrived in pressure situations." It was a memorable time for Reggie and his fans. Present that day

OPPOSITE: Exultant heroes of the 2001 World Series, Derek Jeter and Scott Brosius

were players previously honored with a plaque: Phil Rizzuto, Yogi Berra, Whitey Ford, and Don Mattingly. Ron Guidry, a longtime teammate of Jackson's who also was present, would be honored with a Monument Park plaque in 2003. Willie Mays, Hank Aaron, and Ernie Banks attended the ceremony, on Jackson's invitation.

JON MILLER: The Giants played the Yankees at the Stadium in an interleague series in 2002. Since they used to play right across the river in the Polo Grounds, they were, in effect, going back to their roots. So was the managing general partner, Peter McGowan, who had grown up in New York, was a Giants fan, and often saw his team play there.

This was the first time Barry Bonds had ever played at the Stadium. Here he was, the guy who had just set the record for the most home runs in a season. His father used to play for the Yankees and would tell him about Yankee Stadium.

It was the best that interleague play can offer. It had all the hallmarks of a World Series between two teams who never play much against each other.

Barry Bonds was hitting against a lefthander in one of the games, and he crushed one at least halfway or more into the upper deck, above one of those walkways. It was one of the longest home runs anyone had ever seen at the new Yankee Stadium. And the Yankee fans cheered him.

The man they called the Rocket was cheered by Yankee fans on September 3, when the Yankees faced off against the archrival Red Sox, who they led by 6 1/2 games in the standings.

Joe Torre, however, was antsy because his team had lost three in a row, including game one of this three-game series at the Stadium to the Bosox.

"I don't care how good your team is," Torre said. "There's always that little uneasy feeling when you lose a few games in a row."

On this mild September day Torre told Clemens, "Roger, we need you today."

The 40-year-old pitcher came through. He struck out the side in the first inning, finished with 10 K's, and yielded just four hits and one walk in 7 1/3 innings.

Notching his 102nd career double-digit-strike-out game, the third most of all-time, Clemens won for the 19th time in 20 decisions at Yankee Stadium, where his .767 winning percentage bettered all New York pitchers with at least 30 wins. The Yankees won that day and the next, widening their lead to 8 1/2 games, triggering another late-season collapse for Boston.

On September 11, 2002, at a 50–minute pre-game ceremony marking the first anniversary of the World Trade Center attack, a monument honoring those who died was unveiled in Monument Park.

The Yankees drew 3,465,807 to the big ball park in the Bronx, where they played sensational base-ball winning 52 and losing just 28 times that season. Overall, they won 103 and lost 58.

Unfortunately, the euphoria of that 2002 campaign was destroyed in the playoffs. Coming up against wild-card Anaheim in the American League Division Series, they went down to the Angels in four. It was the first time since 1997 that Joe Torre's team exited the playoffs so early.

That December two big-ticket free agents showed up at the Stadium, fortification for the Bombers for 2003. Japanese slugger Hideki Matsui signed for three years and $21 million. Roger Clemens agreed to a $10.1 million, one-year contract.

Opening Day 2003 was delayed by 24 hours because of the threat of big snow. When the game was played, on April 8, Yankee fans got their first look at Matsui. Showing the power that earned him the nickname "Godzilla" in Japan, he became the first Yankee to bash a grand-slam home run in his first game at the Stadium. He also showed that his left-handed stroke was tailor-made for the ballpark. The Yanks got off to an 18–3 start through April 23, their best start in franchise history.

Sporting a combined 12–0 record, their starting rotation had bragging rights to the top major league season-opening mark in half a century.

June was a month for records and milestones at the Stadium. On June 3, Derek Jeter was named team captain. Eight days later, six Houston Astro pitchers—Roy Oswalt, Pete Monro, Kirk Saarloos, Brad Lidge, Octavio Dotel, and Billy Wagner—combined to no-hit the Yankees, 8–0, setting a new major league record for the most pitchers combining on a no-hitter.

June 13—a cool, drizzly night—was the Roger Clemens show as the pitcher faced the St. Louis Cardinals in interleague play. The SRO crowd of 55,214 was into the action from the start. So was Clemens. Fanning the side in the first inning, he was one away from 4,000 career strikeouts.

That distinction came to him, in the second inning, courtesy of Cardinal shortstop Edgar Renteria, who struck out on a 3–2 pitch. Flashbulbs popped all over the Stadium, accentuating and preserving the time. The scoreboard in center field lit up "4,000." Leaving his catcher's position, Jorge Posada shuffled to the mound, shook Clemens's hand, and gave him the ball.

Hurling 6 1/3 innings, allowing two runs, and striking out 10, the Rocket became the 21st pitcher to win 300 games. The Yanks won the game, 5–2.

"To have these two milestones that I was able to attain on the same night here, it couldn't have worked out any better," said Clemens. "Four thousand and 300 put me with some [of the] great men that have ever stepped on that mound. I'm real fortunate that I had the opportunity to do it here in this Stadium and in this uniform."

If Clemens was paying off for the Yankees, so was the other December signee. On a day-night doubleheader with the Mets on June 28, Hideki Matsui slugged a grand slam in game one at the Stadium and was on base in nine out of his 10 at-bats in the second fray, at Shea. The Yankees won both games.

Winning 101 games and finishing a half a dozen games ahead of the Red Sox, the Yankees breezed by Minnesota in the ALDS. Boston was waiting for them in the American League Championship Series. Like a pair of heavyweight fighters, the rivals fought it out, bringing the series to a decisive seventh game at the Stadium on October 16.

It was Pedro Martinez for Boston, Roger Clemens for New York before 56,279 in 61-degree weather.

If the Red Sox could win this night they would go to the World Series and possibly win it for the first time in 85 years. And there were many Red Sox fans at the Stadium to cheer the Olde Towne team on.

BOB SULLIVAN: I grew up in Boston. Yankee Stadium was always enemy territory. There were times when my girlfriend and I would be behind or in front of some lout who would carry on over our wearing our Sox caps. It can get menacing at the Stadium for Red Sox fans.

I went to all games of the 2003–2004 ALCS's, blogging for Time.com. I wanted to do it from the stands and not the press box.

In '03 our tickets were out in the center-field bleachers, where you spend most of the game on your feet. It's just the way the section works out there during the playoffs. It's not quite as dangerous in the postseason because people who have those tickets are serious baseball fans. Nevertheless, whoever I went with on a given night, we basically stayed anonymous as Sox fans.

To the delight of Sox fans and the dismay of Yankee rooters, Clemens was racked for four runs in three-plus innings. Mike Mussina, in the first career relief appearance, followed Clemens. Then Jeff Nelson and David Wells relieved.

Pedro Martinez coasted along. A David Ortiz homer in the top of the eighth made it 5–2, Boston. It seemed with his pitch count over 100, with Red Sox relievers at the ready, Pedro was done. But he wasn't. Grady Little, the Sox pilot, sent him out for the bottom of the eighth. He got Nick Johnson to pop up. The Stadium was loud and tense.

"The Curse of the Bambino" was there for the breaking by the Sox. All Boston needed was five more outs to get into the World Series.

But Derek Jeter doubled to right.

Bernie Williams singled.

Jeter scored.

Hideki Matsui was next.

Little exited the Sox dugout. He had a righty, Mike Timlin, and a lefty, Alan Embree, ready in the bullpen. Little and Martinez stood on the mound and talked. The Boston manager patted down his star pitcher with encouragement and went back to the dugout.

BOB SULLIVAN: We were standing up when Grady left the mound. I turned to my wife. I was very upset. I said "He's not taking Pedro out. I can't believe this."

With two strikes on him, Matsui pulled an inside fastball down the right-field line. It bounced into the stands for a ground-rule double. Jorge Posada stepped in. Williams took a lead at third and Matsui at second. Martinez's pitch count was 118.

On a 2–2 count Posada lifted the ball over second base. It wasn't much of a poke, but it dropped in, the fourth straight one-out hit for New York. Williams scored. Matsui scored. The game was tied, 5–5.

Little was out of the Boston dugout; Martinez was out of the game. Allan Embree and Mike Timlin

held off the Yankees. Mariano Rivera, in his longest appearance in seven seasons stifled the Red Sox in the ninth, tenth, and eleventh innings.

Bottom of the eleventh inning. Boston knuckle-baller Tim Wakefield against Aaron Boone. Having been benched for not hitting, Boone had come into the game as a pinch runner in the eighth inning. Now he was leading off in his first at-bat of the game. An adrenaline rush swept across the Stadium.

It was 16 minutes past midnight, Friday morning. Wakefield pitched. Inside, below Boone's hands. He swung. The ball jumped off his bat and went deep over the left-field wall.

There were those who said Yankee Stadium shook and moved. The noise level was ear-splitting. Jubilant Yankees raced out of the dugout and bullpen onto the field.

Rounding third, Boone jumped into the arms of teammates waiting at home plate. Mariano Rivera was lifted onto the shoulders of his teammates.

"All I wanted was to get on base, to make contact. I knew it was out. I finally put a good swing on it," Boone said later.

It was another triumph for the "Evil Empire," its fifth pennant in six seasons, its 39th American League pennant.

"I don't know about a curse, but I believe we have some ghosts in this stadium that have helped us out," Derek Jeter said. "We've just had some magical stuff that has happened to us tonight."

BOB SULLIVAN: The Yankee win was a stunner. I certainly hate the Yankees, of course, although I don't hate everything about the Yankees. Aesthetically, I love the Stadium; I love it when it's rocking. But Frank Sinatra's recording of "New York, New York" seemed louder than usual that night. I'm a kind of baseball traditionalist, so the idea of being in "The House That Ruth Built" is just fine with me. I don't like what Steinbrenner's gang puts on with the noise. I don't think you need the electronic amplification to make a ball game great.

In the clubhouse, his uniform soaked by champagne, his face caked in shaving cream, his teammates shouting his name, the man of the moment, Aaron Boone, spoke:

"When I joined the Yankees, this is the kind of thing I wanted to be part of. The perfect ending. You always emulate these moments in your back-yard. I still can't put them into words. I'm floating. Just to have had this opportunity—it's humbling. This game humbles you all the time in good ways and bad ways."

Afterward Grady Little explained, "Pedro wanted to stay in there. He wanted to get the job done just as he has many times for us all season long and he's the man we all wanted on the mound."

Theo Epstein, Boston GM, was philosophical and prophetic. "You can dwell on what happened and wake up in the middle of the night screaming, 'Five more outs!' but I'm not going to do that. There's a choice. You can sit and dwell in perpetuity or have it inspire you to work harder and get it done next year. When we do win it, that will make it all the sweeter."

The Friday *Boston Herald* front-page headline screamed, "Damn Yankees!"

The *New York Daily News* banner headline blared, "Boone Town!"

New York Post headlines blared: "Curse Lives as Aaron Homer Sends Yankees to Series" and "KA-BOONE!"

The highly upbeat and odds-on favorite New York Yankees were pitted against the underdog Florida Marlins in the World Series. For most experts, it was no contest. Some were even talking of a Yankee sweep. It was no sweep. It went six games, ending on October 25, with Josh Beckett shutting down the Yankees, 2–0, making for the first time since 1981 that New York was eliminated from postseason at the Stadium.

JOE BUCK (GAME CALL, FOX):
Trying to win it all again. Posada, slow roller, right side. Beckett picks it up, tags Posada, and the Florida Marlins are world champions! The Marlins have shocked the Yankees. Stunned New York. And this improbable team, improbable ride. They end up on top, winning in six games over the Yankees.

After the Series, Eddie Layton, who'd played the Stadium organ for 29 seasons, retired. Another longtime tradition would end in 2004 but not before many chills, thrills, and unforgettable Stadium games.

One of the plays in the 2004 season that is very well remembered involved Derek Jeter, who has always had a feel for the dramatic. It was July 1, and another Red Sox–Yankee matchup was into extra innings. This time, top of the twelfth inning. With the score tied 3–3 and two outs, Red Sox base runners were taking leads off second and third base.

Trot Nixon popped the ball up. It drifted down the left-field line, seemingly headed for no-man's-land. But Jeter, breaking from his shortstop position, running all out, made an acrobatic, over-the-shoulder, one-handed catch right by the left-field seats. His momentum sent him into the seats. With his chin bloodied, cheek red and swollen, and shoulder bruised, Jeter was rushed out of the Stadium to the hospital.

"The stomach, the heart, there was no quitting," said Joe Torre. "Jeter, of course, scared the hell out of everybody. Hopefully, he'll be all right."

Jeter was all right. So were the Yankees. With their captain en route to the hospital, they rallied with two outs in the bottom of the thirteenth to nip the Sox 5–4 and finish a three-game sweep. Their lead over Boston had increased to 8½ games.

But if Jeter's gem was a high point of the season, a low point was reached on August 31, when, before

ABOVE: A signature moment for Jeter, showing how he plays full out all the time
OVERLEAF: Scenes from the 2003 and 2004 American League Championship Series against the Red Sox

51,777, the Yankees were booed from the start to the end of their worst defeat in history, a 22–0 smoking at the hands of the Cleveland Indians. Watching his team suffer this humiliating defeat, George Steinbrenner quickly exited the Stadium, refusing to answer questions.

The nightmare trouncing gave the Yanks five straight home losses for the first time since May 2003. Their big American League East lead over Boston was shrinking. Their season was starting to look like 1978 in reverse.

But the Yankees turned things around big time, finishing 2004 with a 101–61 won lost record, three games ahead of the Red Sox in the standings. On September 30, Bernie Williams's walk-off homer against the Twins in the ALDS gave the Yankees their seventh straight American League East title.

Then it was Boston–New York in the American League Championship Series. The longtime rivals split the first six games, with the Yankees winning the first three, and the Sox coming back to tie things up.

It was down to a one-game, winner-take-all, go-to-the-World-Series contest on October 30 at Yankee Stadium. Seemingly every baseball fan in the United States was honed in on the contest, which pitted Derek Lowe for Boston against Kevin Brown for New York. With riot police guarding the foul lines at the Stadium, Bucky Dent threw out the first ball.

Boston struck first as David Ortiz popped a two-run first-inning homer. Then Boston struck again—a grand slam for Johnny Damon in the second. And again—another Damon dinger in the fourth. The Yanks were trailing 8–1.

BOB SULLIVAN: I was in the upper deck behind first base, the nosebleed section, but pretty good seats. I had thought we had a good chance to win with Kevin Brown on the mound. But what happened was the Sox got such a big lead so quickly, that it got out of control up there. The cops spent the whole game marching up and down the aisles pulling out people who were drunk, surly, looking for a fight.

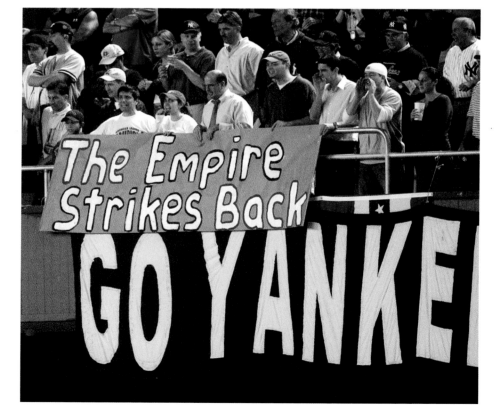

A brief Yankee rally in the eighth off Pedro Martinez, who had entered the game as a relief pitcher in the seventh, gave some zealot Yankee fans hope they could keep the "curse" alive.

They taunted the Red Sox star pitcher—"Who's Your Da-Dee?" But the taunting only seemed to add fuel to the Bosox fire. Two more runs came in. The score was 10–3.

At 12:01 A.M., Boston had its eleventh American League pennant, and the Red Sox had become the first team in history to win a seven-game series after losing the first three games. Moreover, it was the first time in 100 years that Boston had defeated New York to claim the American League title.

Former Massachusetts governor Michael Dukakis had been watching the game with his wife, Kitty. Like other Sox fans, life had taught him not to take anything for granted.

MICHAEL DUKAKIS: When they were leading 10–3 with two outs in the ninth inning, I turned to Kitty. "You know, they could lose," I said to her.

But they didn't.

BOB SULLIVAN: So many people had gotten thrown out, and so many people had left early, that the upper deck had turned weirdly into these little enclaves of Red Sox fans. We were the only ones who wanted to stay. We all put our Red Sox caps on and started cheering for Boston.

By the time Trot Nixon was running around saluting everyone, it seemed like there were only Sox fans around. A half hour after the game ended, you realized just how many Red Sox fans had gotten into the Stadium that night. It was weird. We owned Yankee Stadium. It was almost as if Steinbrenner had rented Yankee Stadium out to us.

There have been so many strange times for Red Sox fans in the Stadium, but that was certainly the oddest. In defiance, Steinbrenner kept playing the "New York, New York" theme over and over again. But we couldn't hear it. We didn't care what they played. We were taking pictures of the rugby scrum of the Red Sox players out on the field, the big pile.

The one nice thing about the Yankees was that they didn't kick us out of their yard but let us hang around to feel the moment.

Alex Rodriguez, who along with Matsui and Gary Sheffield batted .571 in the first three games of the series but just .136 in the four losses, was honest in defeat. "Is it embarrassing? Yeah, I'm embarrassed right now. Obviously being up 3–0 makes it more frustrating. Obviously, it's crushing. We have no excuses. They beat our asses, that's it. It's frustrating because we felt coming into tonight that the winner of this game was going to win the World Series."

A-Rod was right about that. The Red Sox defeated the Cardinals. And for all the months that followed, Boston fans were like glow worms, basking in the accomplishment that had so long eluded them.

The 2005 season started slowly for the Yankees, so slowly that they went 10–14 in April, good enough—or rather bad enough—for a last-place tie with Tampa Bay. Some loyalists despaired; they had not seen their team do so poorly since the late 1980s. But the thrill of being at the Stadium was not diminished.

SETH SWIRSKY: I got incredible tickets, front row, off the netting. So I took my son Julian, who was ten years old then, and my parents. It's late August. We're playing Toronto. A foul ball

OPPOSITE: Alex Rodriguez putting a charge into it—another home run
ABOVE: A-Rod heads home after hitting the 500th home run of his career

in the fourth inning is squibbed to Gary Sheffield in the on-deck circle. He picks up the ball and slowly, as if it was in slow motion, walks over to my son—whose eyes are so wide—and hands him the ball.

Ten minutes later my cell phone is ringing. My dad's cell phone is ringing. My mom's cell phone is ringing. Everybody around the country had seen it on television. That night we turned on the TV and watched the replay, and we hear Michael Kay say, "This is incredible. Sheffield just made a new friend."

I collect a lot of things. But that ball is one of the great family memories. Three generations at Yankee Stadium.

The Yankees spent a good part of the 2005 season chasing the Red Sox for the division title. They clinched it on the second-to-last game of the season against Boston. Both teams actually wound up with identical 95–67 records, but the Yanks had the head-to-head advantage.

The home-field edge helped: they won 53 at the Stadium and lost only 28. Drawing an average of

50,499, Yankee attendance in 2005 was a new major league attendance mark—4,090,440—breaking the 4-million mark for the first time in their history and the 4,057,947 set by Toronto at SkyDome in 1993.

In the 2005 American League Division Series, the Angels defeated the Yankees in five games in the first round of the postseason for the second time in four years. Alex Rodriguez, the American League MVP, had a miserable series, hitting .133 with no home runs and no RBIs.

Joe Torre, despite rumors to the contrary, was still on the scene as head man of the Yankees as the 2006 season began. But none of the coaches from his original staff were. Their payroll was down to $194,663,079 from $208,306,817 the previous season. General Manager Brian Cashman was under orders to cut costs. The 40% luxury tax was a key factor for the economy moves.

Nevertheless, Steinbrenner's team remained the highest-paid in all of baseball. Still smarting from being eliminated in the 2005 playoffs but favored to win the 2006 World Series, they got set for Opening Day 2006.

On May 16th, they overcame a nine-run deficit for the third time in their franchise history (the largest deficit they ever surmounted), nipping the Texas Rangers, 14–13, on a bottom-of-the-ninth-inning walk-off home run by Jorge Posada.

But on the Fourth of July, George Steinbrenner's 76th birthday, the Yanks were blown out by Cleveland 19–1. It seemed the Indians specialized in whopping the Yanks on their home field.

July 16 was a marker moment for ace reliever Mariano Rivera, who got his 400th save. Entering the game against the White Sox in the bottom of the eighth inning with two men on, no outs, and the Yankees up by two runs, "Mo" was in top form. He popped up Juan Uribe. Scott Podsednik grounded into a double play.

In the ninth inning, the first two hitters reached base against Rivera. But Mo induced another

double play and then fanned Paul Konerko to seal the victory, the seventh out of eight games for the Yanks since their devastating loss to Cleveland 12 days earlier.

"It's good," said the slender and serious Rivera. "It's special. It's amazing, amazing to even think about it."

The save put him along with Lee Smith, Trevor Hoffman, and John Franco as the only members of the 400 club. "Super Mariano," however, had saved all his games playing for one franchise.

"For a guy who has pitched as a closer for less than 10 years, and to have been as consistent as he has been, to get there as quickly as he did, it's just remarkable," noted Joe Torre.

"It seems like year after year he just gets the job done," Jason Giambi added. "You get that feeling when he comes out and the song (Metallica's "Enter Sandman") starts playing, that the game is over."

Five days after Mariano Rivera achieved his milestone at the Stadium, A-Rod became the youngest player ever to record 450 home runs. He hammered the shot, which also was his 2,000th career hit, a few days before he turned 31.

"Four hundred fifty is something I'm proud of and 2,000 at the same time—it's kind of unique," Rodriguez said.

The threats, the posturing, the grandiose schemes had been heard for a long time. Through the decades, the Yankees always seemed to be looking around for a new home. From time to time, a site in Manhattan would be brought up; some place in northern New Jersey would be suggested. But nothing came of it.

Nothing came of it until August 16, 2005, the 58th anniversary of Babe Ruth's death, when ground was broken for a new Yankee Stadium—next door to "The House That Ruth Built."

George Steinbrenner, Commissioner of Baseball Bud Selig, New York governor George Pataki, and New York City mayor Michael Bloomberg donned

Yankee hard hats at the site and dug down a bit into the earth.

"It's a pleasure to give this to you people," Steinbrenner said. "Enjoy the new Stadium. I hope it's wonderful."

"The 'ghosts' of Octobers past," Joe Torre said, "will be invited to take limos and vans over to the new Yankee Stadium."

"I think it's a great day," Derek Jeter said. "There's a lot of history here. There were a lot of good memories here. Now we'll try to take that over across the street."

"You always hear stories about the history of the Yankees," Mariano Rivera said, "but it's never like when you're living it. I had an opportunity to be a part of it and live it. Hopefully when they open, I'll be here. I think it's something great for the city and the fans."

"We decided we want to stay in the Bronx," Steinbrenner said. "We want to do the job here. We wanted to do something for the people who've always supported this team. Babe Ruth didn't run on this grass. Mickey Mantle and Joe DiMaggio didn't run on this grass because the Stadium was totally redone [in the mid 70s]. The only thing they may have used that are still there are the urinals and the lockers in the locker rooms."

ROGER KAHN: Yankee Stadium has not been the classic ballpark, "The House That Ruth Built," since it was remodeled in the 1970s. The old Yankee Stadium was one imposing structure, but I when it comes to this one, I don't think we are losing something of great architectural note. We are getting rid

of an architectural mishmash. Sometimes new is better.

JIM BOUTON: To tear down Yankee Stadium, to tear down the field, the locker room, the building where Babe Ruth played and build a duplicate of it across the street is a sacrilege, an outrage, a national disgrace.

And it's just for money. They're not putting in more seats; they're putting in fewer seats. And the ticket prices will be higher. It was hard enough for people to go to games in the old days. Now they can never go to a game.

I don't think a dime of public money should go into a ballpark. These baseball owners make enough money; they can build their own ballparks. It will be looked upon as an awful time

only one-for-eleven through the first three games, was batted eighth, the lowest he had hit in 10 seasons. It didn't help. He went nothing-for-three. The Yankees lost, 8–3, and were knocked out in the first round of the playoffs for the second straight year.

Yankee aficionados were stunned and smarting. George Steinbrenner, speaking through his mouthpiece, public relations guru Howard Rubenstein, was verbose: "I am deeply disappointed at our being eliminated so early in the playoffs. This result is absolutely not acceptable to me nor to our great and loyal Yankee fans. I want to congratulate the Detroit Tigers organization and wish them well. Rest assured, we will go back to work immediately and try to right this sad failure and provide a championship for the Yankees, as is our goal every year."

Derek Jeter, who batted .500 in the series, was philosophical: "You've got to play. You don't win games on paper. You've got to come out here and perform. And they pretty much overmatched us in this series."

Alex Rodriguez was frank: "Plain and simple, they dominated us. They absolutely kicked our ass."

The 2007 Yankee season got off to a somber start. On Opening Day, April 2, the wife and son of the late Cory Lidle—who had died in a plane crash the previous October—threw out ceremonial first pitches. Bobby Murcer, battling cancer, was welcomed back. A moment of silence was observed for the recently deceased Hank Bauer and former baseball commissioner Bowie Kuhn.

On Monday, May 7, in a game against Seattle, Bob Sheppard told the 52,553 fans during the seventh-inning stretch to turn their attention to the owner's box on the loge level.

There was Roger Clemens, microphone in hand. "Well, they came and got me out of Texas," he said, "and I can tell you it's a privilege to be back." He went on to describe how "guys had been calling me and e-mailing, and it was pulling at my heartstrings," becoming a touch emotional when he added, "But

in American sports history when all this public money was going into these stadiums.

I've appeared at Old-Timers' games several times since my first return in 1998, but not since the new ballpark was announced because I've been very vocal in my opposition.

Five days after the announcement about the new Yankee Stadium, the Yanks came into Fenway park with just a 1 1/2-game lead. The season had been one of injuries to key players such as Hideki Matsui, Gary Sheffield, and Robinson Cano, but the Yankees were on their game this time around, sweeping all five games, breaking up their American League race with Boston, pushing their lead over the Sox to 6 1/2 games.

A ninth straight division title was clinched on September 20. Torre, acknowledging that his team had not won a World Series in five seasons, said, "We need to make the postseason a lot longer than it's been for us."

It was Yankees–Tigers in the ALDS that began at the Stadium on October 3 with New York heavily favored. Derek Jeter tied a postseason record for hits in a game, going five-for-five with two doubles and a home run. The Yankee won the game 8–4.

The next day's game was rained out. At the afternoon makeup game at the Stadium on October 5th, the Tigers prevailed 4–3.

In Detroit, behind pitcher Kenny Rogers and two relievers, the Tigers defeated New York, 6–0. Torre shook up his lineup for game four. A-Rod,

what was especially influential was when I met with my owner, Mr. Steinbrenner, in spring training and the words he said to me, which I'll keep close to my heart for now."

In center field the scoreboard messaged "Roger Clemens is now a Yankee!" The crowd cheered in approval.

"Make no mistake about it," the returning hero said, "I've come back to do what they only know how to do here with the Yankees, and that's win a championship. Anything else is a failure, and I know that."

The Stadium was lit up again in July as the Yankees racked out 20 hits in back-to-back games for the first time in more than 100 years. They savaged the Devil Rays on the 21st with a 17–5 win and 20 hits. On the 22nd, scoring 10 runs in a fourth inning that featured Alex Rodriguez's 498th career homer, they pounded Tampa Bay for 25 hits in a 21–4 win.

"I've never seen anything like it," Joe Torre said. "Even in batting practice you don't get hits every time you swing the bat. This was certainly pretty incredible—to be able to continue to get hit after hit after hit after hit."

The Stadium was lit up again on August 4 when Alex Rodriguez, 32 years and eight days old, became the youngest player in major league baseball history to hit his 500th home run, joining Yankee Hall of Famers Babe Ruth and Mickey Mantle as a member of the 500-home-run club.

In the bottom of the first inning, A-Rod slammed the first pitch he saw from the Royals' Kyle Davies just inside the left-field foul pole, tarried for a moment at home plate, then threw his hands into the air and ran out the epic clout, pumping his fists, smiling broadly, clapping, blowing kisses into the stands to his wife.

"That felt really good off my bat today," he said later. "I didn't know if it would stay fair or foul. I was so relieved it stayed fair. I acted like a goofball running around the bases but I guess you only do 500 once."

Given a standing ovation from the fans at the Stadium, Rodriguez embraced Derek Jeter and Bobby Abreu waiting for him at home plate after he had driven them in. In front of the Yankee dugout, Rodriguez blew a kiss toward the stands and then exchanged high fives with his teammates.

"It was awesome and then you kind of get that high school reception when you hit a home run and all of the guys are out of the dugout," Rodriguez said.

The curtain call brought roars from the crowd as A-Rod stuck his head out of the dugout. Then, seated next to Jeter in the dugout, he got his head rubbed playfully by the Yankee captain as they both laughed, enjoying the moment.

The marker homer for the 11-time All-Star was his first since July 25. "I haven't hit one in so long," he said after the Yankee 16–8 triumph over Kansas City. "I didn't know if it was going to be foul. Where that ball started, last week that ball would've hooked foul probably about 20 feet."

A Rutgers student who had the ball didn't want to be identified. "I really want it back," Rodriguez said. "But if not, I congratulate him for catching it. Nice catch."

Still flexing their offensive might, the Yanks on the last day of July blasted eight home runs in a 16–3 win over the White Sox. Hideki Matsui homered twice, and Johnny Damon, Jorge Posada, Bobby Abreu, Melky Cabrera, Robinson Cano, and Shelley Duncan hit one each.

A legend passed for the Yankees on August 14, 2007, when "the Scooter," Phil Rizzuto, died at age 89. At Yankee Stadium, his number 10 would be on every Yankee jersey and painted in white on the third- and first-base sides of the infield for the rest of the season. Flags were at half-staff, and the marquee at the ballpark read "Phil Rizzuto, 1917–2007."

The Yankees continued their late-season charge with their 12th win in their last 14 games. On September 20 they completed a three-game sweep

of the Red Sox and pulled to within 1 1/2 games of their first-place Beantown rivals.

The Yankees drew 4,271,083. They had sellouts at more than half of their home games, an average of 42,785 per game.

George Steinbrenner was not at the final game of 2007 nor the previous 79 games. The home opener on April 2 had been the only regular-season game he attended. But fun and games were on display after the final home game of 2007, with Joba Chamberlain taking on the starring role in the tradition of rookies wearing silly garb to end the home part of the season. With *The Wizard of Oz* as the theme for 2007, Chamberlain, in his Cowardly Lion suit, jumped about in the clubhouse in his best Bert Lahr impersonation, telling all he got close to, "Put 'em up! Put 'em up!"

Chase Wright wore the pink dress of the Good Witch of the North. Edwar Ramirez sported the Wicked Witch of the West's outfit, while Phil Hughes clanked around in the Tin Man suit. Kei Igawa was

OPPOSITE: Joe Torre would be out as manager after the 2007 season
ABOVE: Joe Girardi takes the helm for the 2008 season

a Flying Monkey. Shelley Duncan was dressed as the Scarecrow. But it was Ian Kennedy who stole everyone's heart as Dorothy, the brave little girl who only wanted to go home.

Departing the Stadium, the rookies walked on a "Yellow Brick Road" made of yellow cardboard, signed autographs, and boarded the team bus, heading to the airport for a flight to Tampa. There, rumor has it, they went out to dinner in costume.

The Yankees made it to postseason play once again, a wild-card berth against Cleveland. The matchup seemed to push the man some were calling "Silent George" back to his old-time form. Steinbrenner, the elder, went public for *The Record* of New Jersey about Joe Torre: "His job is on the line. I think we're paying him a lot of money. He's the highest-paid manager in baseball, so I don't think we'd take him back if we don't win this series."

Joe Torre did not win the series. His Yankees were defeated in the first round of the playoffs for the third year in a row. Cleveland took three of the four games played. The killer loss, 6–4, before a crowd of 56,315 at Yankee Stadium, was played on October 8, a night the temperature soared to a record 87 degrees. The Yankees batted a puny .228 in the series and pitched for an earned run average of 5.89.

The victors celebrated. The losers stared from their dugout. Paul Byrd, the starting and winning pitcher for Cleveland in the final game, said, "Nothing is tougher than coming into Yankee Stadium and pulling this off."

Yankee general manager Brian Cashman apologized to the team's 77-year-old owner. "All I told him was, 'Sorry, Boss.' That was it."

Shortly after midnight, George Steinbrenner exited the Stadium. Silently, he walked down the steps, avoiding eye contact with the milling mob of media.

Joe Torre would no longer be part of the scene in the Bronx. After a dozen seasons—in which he had gone 1,173–767, trailing only Joe McCarthy for wins among Yankee pilots (1,460)—he rejected a one-year offer that trimmed his base pay and offered performance-based incentives.

Don Mattingly would also no longer be part of the Yankee Stadium scene. He was passed over for Joe Girardi, whose name and image were displayed November 1 on the scoreboard as the new manager of the Yankees. Joe Torre would be in place as the new manager for the Los Angeles Dodgers in 2008.

Also in 2008, the finishing touches will be applied to the new stadium. It will have fewer seats than the old ballpark, 51,800. There will be more luxury boxes and also standing room for a thousand fans.

The cost is estimated at $1.02 billion with the Yankees paying some $800 million for construction, and the city and state contributing $220 million for parkland, improvements in infrastructure, and parking.

The same field dimensions and bullpen placements will exist in the new stadium as were in the old one. The center field video screen will be six times larger than the current stadium's screen. Recreation of original Yankee Stadium features will include: tall cathedral windows, a right-field Yankees bullpen, auxiliary outfield scoreboards, a frieze (facade) on the roof. The exterior facade will emulate what had existed in the original Yankee Stadium. A separate structure, the interior will rise above the top of the exterior. A "great hall" between the exterior wall and the interior structure will feature five to six times more retail space than the current Stadium. Lattice work which rimmed the roof of the original stadium will be in the original copper, affixed to the new park's roof.

Four levels in the main grandstand will stretch from foul pole to foul pole. Almost 30,000 seats will occupy the first two levels while the third level will have 51 luxury suites, eight party suites, and two large outdoor suites. The fourth level will house the upper deck. Monument Park will exist in a different location beyond the fence in center field and below a restaurant in the batter's sight line.

Other features of the new Yankee Stadium complex will include several restaurants (including a members-only restaurant), a martini bar, larger concourses, entertainment areas, a hotel conference center, a high school for sports-focused careers, and four parking garages for almost 10,000 cars. Lonn Trost, the Yankees' chief operating officer, says they "tried to reflect a five-star hotel and put a ballpark in the middle."

The above-ground portion of the old stadium will be demolished and three baseball fields will be constructed in its place. Existing underground clubhouses will remain for replacement park facilities.

One more season, 2008, would still remain for "The House That Ruth Built." One more time it would play host to an All-Star Game, see its seats and aisles swell with millions of fans cheering on the Yankees of New York.

Meanwhile the new stadium would be rising across the street from the old. By the spring of 2009, the cry of "play ball" would be heard. And a new Yankee Stadium era would begin.

OPPOSITE: Mayor Michael Bloomberg, George Steinbrenner, and others break ground on the new stadium, August 16, 2006; The new Yankee Stadium under construction
RIGHT: The Yankee Stadiums, side by side

STADIUMOLOGY

YANKEE STADIUM ALL-TIME ATTENDANCE CHART

1923–2007

MONUMENT PARK

YEAR	GAME AVERAGE	SEASON TOTAL	A. L. AVERAGE
1923	13,251	1,007,066	575,324
1924	13,772	1,053,533	656,930
1925	8,939	697,267	648,356
1926	13,260	1,027,675	614,073
1927	15,020	1,164,015	576,619
1928	13,924	1,072,132	527,649
1929	12,470	960,148	582,809
1930	15,185	1,169,230	585,716
1931	11,773	912,437	485,412
1932	12,337	962,320	391,654
1933	9,579	728,014	365,776
1934	11,100	854,682	470,451
1935	8,826	657,508	461,001
1936	12,605	976,913	522,365
1937	12,715	998,148	591,979
1938	12,368	970,916	555,711
1939	11,313	859,785	533,825
1940	12,761	988,975	679,224
1941	12,368	964,722	613,995
1942	11,974	922,011	525027
1943	7,979	618,330	462,071
1944	10,260	789,995	599,770
1945	11,603	881,845	697,553
1946	29,422	2,265,512	1,202,648
1947	28,115	2,178,937	1,185,759
1948	30,830	2,373,901	1,393,762
1949	29,467	2,283,676	1,341,331
1950	26,857	2,081,380	1,142,795
1951	25,326	1,950,107	1,110,334
1952	21,165	1,629,665	1,036,737
1953	20,368	1,537,811	870,510
1954	19,034	1,475,171	990,296
1955	19,352	1,490,138	1,117,871
1956	19,374	1,491,784	986,710
1957	19,443	1,497,134	1,024,527
1958	18,431	1,428,438	912,004
1959	20,026	1,552,030	1,143,682
1960	20,998	1,627,349	1,153,316
1961	21,444	1,747,725	1,016,302
1962	18,439	1,493,574	1,001,506
1963	16,260	1,308,920	909,485
1964	15,922	1,305,638	923,515
1965	14,982	1,213,552	886,076
1966	14,058	1,12,4648	1,016,674
1967	15,454	1,259,514	1,133,692
1968	14,459	1,185,666	1,131,739
1969	13,185	1,067,996	1,011,227
1970	13,949	1,136,879	1,007,095
1971	13,219	1,070,771	989,047
1972	12,469	966,328	953,211
1973	15,581	1,262,103	1,119,467
1974*	15,717	1,273,075	1,087,275
1975*	16,101	1,288,048	1,099,119
1976	25,314	2,012,434	1,221,484
1977	25,964	2,103,092	1,402,825
1978	28,661	2,335,871	1,466,426
1979	31,722	2,537,765	1,597,999
1980	32,437	2,627,417	1,563,575
1981	30,175	1,614,353	1,004,713
1982	25,200	2,041,219	1,648,604
1983	27,876	2,257,976	1,713,647
1984	22,492	1,821,815	1,711,531
1985	27,510	2,214,587	1,752,302
1986	28,000	2,268,030	1,798,052
1987	29,971	2,427,672	1,948,382
1988	32,717	2,633,701	2,035,688
1989	26,963	2,170,485	2,132,090
1990	24,771	2,006,436	2,166,590
1991	23,009	1,863,733	2,294,113
1992	21,589	1,748,737	2,268,524
1993	29,839	2,416,942	2,380,955
1994	29,656	1,675,556	1,728,728
1995	23,521	1,705,263	1,811,356
1996	27,789	2,250,877	2,122,721
1997	31,856	2,580,325	2,234,523
1998	36,484	2,955,193	2,298,169
1999	40,662	3,293,659	2,286,874
2000	37,956	3,227,657	2,262,557
2001	40,807	3,264,552	2,346,071
2002	42,736	3,461,644	2,207,891
2003	42,785	3,465,600	2,191,745
2004	47,788	3,775,292	2,340,422
2005	50,499	4,090,440	2,360,452
2006	51,858	4,200,518	2,458,741
2007	52,739	4,271,867	2,527,968

*PLAYED AT SHEA STADIUM

NAME	PLAQUE AND MONUMENT DEDICATION
MILLER HUGGINS	MAY 30, 1932
JACOB RUPPERT	APRIL 19, 1940
LOU GEHRIG	JULY 6, 1941
BABE RUTH	APRIL 19, 1949
ED BARROW	APRIL 15, 1954
POPE PAUL VI	OCTOBER 4, 1965
JOE DIMAGGIO	JUNE 18, 1969
MICKEY MANTLE	JUNE 18, 1969
JOE MCCARTHY	APRIL 29, 1976
CASEY STENGEL	APRIL 30, 1976
POPE JOHN PAUL II	OCTOBER 2, 1979
THURMAN MUNSON	SEPTEMBER 20, 1980
ELSTON HOWARD	JULY 21, 1984
ROGER MARIS	JULY 21, 1984
PHIL RIZZUTO	AUGUST 4, 1985
BILLY MARTIN	AUGUST 10, 1986
LEFTY GOMEZ	AUGUST 1, 1987
WHITEY FORD	AUGUST 1, 1987
BILL DICKEY	AUGUST 21, 1988
YOGI BERRA	AUGUST 21, 1988
ALLIE REYNOLDS	AUGUST 27, 1989
DON MATTINGLY	AUGUST 31, 1997
MEL ALLEN	JULY 25, 1998
BOB SHEPPARD	MAY 7, 2000
REGGIE JACKSON	JULY 6, 2002
9/11 VICTIMS	SEPTEMBER 11, 2002
RON GUIDRY	AUGUST 23, 2003
RED RUFFING	JULY 10, 2004
JACKIE ROBINSON	AUGUST 17, 2007

ALL-TIME YANKEE BROADCASTERS

Year	Network	Broadcasters
2007	**WCBS RADIO**	JOHN STERLING, SUZYN WALDMAN; (YES NETWORK): MICHAEL KAY, JOE GIRARDI, KEN SINGLETON, BOBBY MURCER, PAUL O'NEILL, DAVID JUSTICE
2005-06	**WCBS RADIO**	JOHN STERLING, SUZYN WALDMAN; (YES NETWORK): MICHAEL KAY, JIM KAAT, KEN SINGLETON, BOBBY MURCER, PAUL O'NEILL, JOHN FLAHERTY, AL LEITER, DAVID JUSTICE
2004	**WCBS RADIO**	JOHN STERLING, CHARLEY STEINER; (YES NETWORK): MICHAEL KAY, JIM KAAT, KEN SINGLETON, BOBBY MURCER, PAUL O'NEILL
2003	**WCBS RADIO, WCBS-TV, YES NETWORK**	FRED HICKMAN, JIM KAAT, MICHAEL KAY, BOBBY MURCER, PAUL O'NEILL, KEN SINGLETON, SUZYN WALDMAN, CHARLEY STEINER, JOHN STERLING
2002	**WABC RADIO, WNYW-TV, YES NETWORK**	FRED HICKMAN, JIM KAAT, MICHAEL KAY, BOBBY MURCER, PAUL O'NEILL, KEN SINGLETON, SUZYN WALDMAN, CHARLEY STEINER, JOHN STERLING
2001	**WABC RADIO, WNYW-TV, MSG NETWORK**	TIM MCCARVER, BOBBY MURCER, JIM KAAT, KEN SINGLETON, AL TRAUTWIG, SUZYN WALDMAN, JOHN STERLING, MICHAEL KAY
2000	**WABC RADIO, WNYW-TV**	TIM MCCARVER, BOBBY MURCER, JIM KAAT, KEN SINGLETON, AL TRAUTWIG, SUZYN WALDMAN, JOHN STERLING, MICHAEL KAY
1999	**WABC RADIO, WNYW-TV, MSG NETWORK**	TIM MCCARVER, BOBBY MURCER, JIM KAAT, KEN SINGLETON, AL TRAUTWIG, SUZYN WALDMAN, JOHN STERLING, MICHAEL KAY
1998	**WABC RADIO, WPIX-TV, MSG NETWORK**	JIM KAAT, KEN SINGLETON, BOBBY MURCER, AL TRAUTWIG, SUZYN WALDMAN, JOHN STERLING, MICHAEL KAY
1997	**WABC RADIO, WPIX-TV, MSG NETWORK**	JIM KAAT, KEN SINGLETON, BOBBY MURCER, AL TRAUTWIG, RICK CERONE, STEVE PALERMO, SUZYN WALDMAN, JOHN STERLING, MICHAEL KAY
1996	**WABC RADIO, WPIX-TV, MSG NETWORK**	PHIL RIZZUTO, BOBBY MURCER, RICK CERONE, PAUL OLDEN, DAVE COHEN, JIM KAAT, AL TRAUTWIG, STEVE PALERMO, JOHN STERLING, MICHAEL KAY
1995	**WABC RADIO, WPIX-TV, MSG NETWORK**	PHIL RIZZUTO, BOBBY MURCER, PAUL OLDEN, DAVE COHEN, JIM KAAT, AL TRAUTWIG, STEVE PALERMO, JOHN STERLING, MICHAEL KAY
1994	**WABC RADIO, WPIX-TV, MSG NETWORK**	PHIL RIZZUTO, DEWAYNE STAATS, TONY KUBEK, AL TRAUTWIG, JOHN STERLING, MICHAEL KAY
1992-93	**WABC RADIO, WPIX-TV, MSG NETWORK**	PHIL RIZZUTO, BOBBY MURCER, TOM SEAVER, DEWAYNE STAATS, TONY KUBEK, AL TRAUTWIG, JOHN STERLING, MICHAEL KAY
1991	**WABC RADIO, WPIX-TV, MSG NETWORK**	PHIL RIZZUTO, BOBBY MURCER, TOM SEAVER, DEWAYNE STAATS, TONY KUBEK, AL TRAUTWIG, MICHAEL KAY, JOHN STERLING, JOE ANGEL
1990	**WABC RADIO, WPIX-TV, MSG NETWORK**	PHIL RIZZUTO, GEORGE GRANDE, TOM SEAVER, DEWAYNE STAATS, TONY KUBEK, AL TRAUTWIG, MICHAEL KAY, JOHN STERLING, JAY JOHNSTONE
1989	**WABC RADIO, WPIX-TV, MSG NETWORK**	PHIL RIZZUTO, GEORGE GRANDE, TOM SEAVER, TOMMY HUTTON, BOBBY MURCER, LOU PINIELLA, GREG GUMBEL, MICHAEL KAY, JOHN STERLING, JAY JOHNSTONE
1988	**WABC RADIO, WPIX-TV, SPORTS CHANNEL**	PHIL RIZZUTO, BILL WHITE, KEN "HAWK" HARRELSON, HANK GREENWALD, TOMMY HUTTON
1987	**WABC RADIO, WPIX-TV, SPORTS CHANNEL**	PHIL RIZZUTO, BILL WHITE, BILLY MARTIN, HANK GREENWALD, TOMMY HUTTON
1986	**WABC RADIO, WPIX-TV, SPORTS CHANNEL**	PHIL RIZZUTO, BILL WHITE, JIM KAAT, BILLY MARTIN, MEL ALLEN, MICKEY MANTLE, JOHN GORDON, SPENCER ROSS, BOBBY MURCER
1985	**WABC RADIO, WPIX-TV, SPORTS CHANNEL**	PHIL RIZZUTO, BILL WHITE, MEL ALLEN, MICKEY MANTLE
1982-84	**WABC RADIO, WPIX-TV, SPORTS CHANNEL**	PHIL RIZZUTO, FRANK MESSER, BILL WHITE, JOHN GORDON
1981	**WABC RADIO, WPIX-TV, SPORTS CHANNEL**	PHIL RIZZUTO, FRANK MESSER, BILL WHITE, FRAN HEALY
1979-80	**WINS RADIO, WPIX-TV, SPORTS CHANNEL**	PHIL RIZZUTO, FRANK MESSER, BILL WHITE, FRAN HEALY
1978	**WINS RADIO, WPIX-TV**	PHIL RIZZUTO, FRANK MESSER, BILL WHITE, FRAN HEALY
1975	**WMCA RADIO, WPIX-TV**	PHIL RIZZUTO, FRANK MESSER, BILL WHITE, DOM VALENTINO
1976-77	**WMCA RADIO, WPIX-TV**	PHIL RIZZUTO, FRANK MESSER, BILL WHITE
1972-74	**WMCA RADIO, WPIX-TV**	PHIL RIZZUTO, FRANK MESSER, BILL WHITE
1971	**WMCA RADIO, WPIX-TV**	PHIL RIZZUTO, FRANK MESSER, BILL WHITE, WHITEY FORD
1970	**WHN RADIO, WPIX-TV**	PHIL RIZZUTO, FRANK MESSER, WHITEY FORD, BOB GAMERE
1969	**WHN RADIO, WPIX-TV**	PHIL RIZZUTO, JERRY COLEMAN, FRANK MESSER, WHITEY FORD
1968	**WHN RADIO, WPIX-TV**	PHIL RIZZUTO, JERRY COLEMAN, FRANK MESSER
1967	**WHN RADIO, WPIX-TV**	PHIL RIZZUTO, JERRY COLEMAN, JOE GARAGIOLA
1965-66	**WCBS RADIO, WPIX-TV**	RED BARBER, PHIL RIZZUTO, JERRY COLEMAN, JOE GARAGIOLA
1963-64	**WCBS RADIO, WPIX-TV**	MEL ALLEN, RED BARBER, PHIL RIZZUTO, JERRY COLEMAN
1961-62	**WCBS RADIO, WPIX-TV**	MEL ALLEN, RED BARBER, PHIL RIZZUTO
1958-60	**WMGM RADIO, WPIX-TV**	MEL ALLEN, RED BARBER, PHIL RIZZUTO
1957	**WINS RADIO, WPIX-TV**	MEL ALLEN, RED BARBER, PHIL RIZZUTO
1954-56	**WINS RADIO, WPIX-TV**	MEL ALLEN, JIM WOODS, RED BARBER
1953	**WINS RADIO, WPIX-TV**	MEL ALLEN, JIM WOODS, JOE E. BROWN
1952	**WINS RADIO, WPIX-TV**	MEL ALLEN, ART GLEESON, BILL CROWLEY
1951	**WINS RADIO, WPIX-TV**	MEL ALLEN, ART GLEESON
1949-50	**WINS RADIO, DUMONT TV**	MEL ALLEN, CURT GOWDY
1946-48	**WINS**	MEL ALLEN, RUSS HODGES
1945	**WINS**	BILL SLATER, AL HELFER
1944	**WINS**	DON DUNPHY, BILL SLATER
1942	**WOR**	MEL ALLEN, CONNIE DESMOND
1940	**WABC**	MEL ALLEN, J.C. FLIPPEN
1939	**WABC**	ARCH MCDONALD, GARNETT MARKS, MEL ALLEN

SOURCE : BRADFORD H. TURNOW, THE SPORTS PALACE; WWW.HISTORYOFTHEYANKEES.COM

STADIUM FIRSTS

FIRST REGULAR-SEASON GAME AT YANKEE STADIUM, APRIL 18, 1923, A 4–1 WIN OVER BOSTON.
FIRST PITCH THROWN IN YANKEE STADIUM, BOB SHAWKEY, YANKEES, APRIL 18, 1923.
FIRST BATTER AT YANKEE STADIUM, CHICK FEWSTER, RED SOX, APRIL 18, 1923.
FIRST HIT AT YANKEE STADIUM, GEORGE BURNS, RED SOX, APRIL 18, 1923, SECOND-INNING SINGLE.
FIRST YANKEE HIT AT YANKEE STADIUM, AARON WARD, APRIL 18, THIRD-INNING SINGLE.
FIRST ERROR, BABE RUTH, APRIL 18, DROPPED FLY BALL IN FIFTH INNING.
FIRST HOME RUN IN YANKEE STADIUM, BABE RUTH, A TWO-RUN SHOT IN THIRD INNING OFF BOSTON'S HOWARD EHMKE IN A 4–1
    YANKEE VICTORY, APRIL 18, 1923.
FIRST YANKEE WINNING PITCHER IN WORLD SERIES, JOE BUSH, OCTOBER 14, 1923.
FIRST LOSS AT YANKEE STADIUM, 4–3 TO WASHINGTON, APRIL 22, 1923.
FIRST WORLD SERIES GAME IN YANKEE STADIUM, FIRST ONE HEARD ON A NATIONWIDE RADIO NETWORK, OCTOBER 10, 1923.
FIRST WORLD SERIES HOME RUN AT YANKEE STADIUM, CASEY STENGEL OF THE NEW YORK GIANTS HIT AN INSIDE-THE-PARK SHOT IN
    GAME ONE OF THE 1923 WORLD SERIES.
FIRST PLAYER TO HAVE HIS NUMBER RETIRED, LOU GEHRIG, NUMBER 4, ON LOU GEHRIG APPRECIATION DAY, JULY 4, 1939.
FIRST NIGHT GAME AT YANKEE STADIUM, MAY 28, 1946, A 2–1 LOSS TO WASHINGTON.
FIRST WORLD SERIES PINCH-HIT HOME RUN, YOGI BERRA AGAINST THE BROOKLYN DODGERS, GAME THREE OF THE 1947 WORLD SERIES.
FIRST YANKEE STADIUM DAY GAME COMPLETED WITH LIGHTS, AUGUST 29, 1950.
FIRST YANKEE GAME BEHIND THE MICROPHONE FOR BOB SHEPPARD, APRIL 17, 1951, VS. BOSTON.
FIRST HOME GAME OUTSIDE OF YANKEE STADIUM SINCE 1922, APRIL 6, 1974, AS THE YANKS BEGIN PLAYING THE FIRST OF
    TWO SEASONS AT SHEA STADIUM.
FIRST HOME RUN AT REFURBISHED YANKEE STADIUM, DAN FORD OF MINNESOTA, APRIL 15, 1976.
FIRST YANKEE WINNING PITCHER AT REFURBISHED YANKEE STADIUM, DICK TIDROW, APRIL 15, 1976.
FIRST HOME RUN BY A YANKEE AT REFURBISHED STADIUM, THURMAN MUNSON, APRIL 17, 1976.
FIRST CHAMPIONSHIP SERIES GAME AT REFURBISHED YANKEE STADIUM, OCTOBER 12, 1976, A 5–3 WIN OVER KANSAS CITY.
FIRST WORLD SERIES GAME PLAYED BY YANKEES AT NIGHT, OCTOBER 17, 1976, AT CINCINNATI, A 4–3 LOSS TO REDS.
FIRST NIGHT WORLD SERIES GAME AT YANKEE STADIUM, OCTOBER 19, 1976, A 6–2 LOSS TO CINCINNATI.
FIRST TEAM TO HOST BOTH THE ALL-STAR GAME AND THE WORLD SERIES IN THE SAME SEASON, THE YANKEES IN 1977.
FIRST PITCHER TO THROW A REGULAR-SEASON PERFECT GAME AT YANKEE STADIUM, DAVID WELLS, MAY 17, 1998.
FIRST TIME A U.S. PRESIDENT VISITED YANKEE STADIUM DURING THE WORLD SERIES, GEORGE W. BUSH, WHO THREW OUT THE
    FIRST BALL, GAME THREE, OCTOBER 30, 2001.
FIRST NOVEMBER WORLD SERIES GAME, NOVEMBER 1, 2001, YANKEES BEAT ARIZONA DIAMONDBACKS, 3–2, AT THE STADIUM.
FIRST TEAM IN POSTSEASON HISTORY TO WIN TWO STRAIGHT GAMES WHEN TRAILING AFTER EIGHT INNINGS, 2001
    WORLD SERIES, GAMES FOUR AND FIVE AT YANKEE STADIUM.

STADIUM LASTS

LAST GAME AT ORIGINAL YANKEE STADIUM, SEPTEMBER 30, 1973, AN 8–5 LOSS TO DETROIT BEFORE 32,869.
LAST BATTER AT ORIGINAL YANKEE STADIUM, SEPTEMBER 30, 1973, MIKE HEGAN, WHO FLEW OUT TO CENTER FIELD.
LAST HOME RUN AT ORIGINAL YANKEE STADIUM, SEPTEMBER 30, 1973, DUKE SIMS OFF FRED HOLDSWORTH.
LAST PITCH AT ORIGINAL YANKEE STADIUM, SEPTEMBER 30, 1973, JOHN HILLER.
LAST YANKEE VICTORY AT ORIGINAL YANKEE STADIUM, SEPTEMBER 29, 1973, 3–0 OVER DETROIT.
LAST YANKEE WINNING PITCHER AT ORIGINAL YANKEE STADIUM, DOC MEDICH, SEPTEMBER 29, 1973, A 3–0 COMPLETE-GAME
    WIN OVER DETROIT.

OLDEST

DAVID CONE, 36, BECAME THE OLDEST PITCHER TO THROW A PERFECT GAME SINCE CY YOUNG IN 1904, JULY 18, 1999.
YANKEE STADIUM, WHICH OPENED IN 1923, IS THE THIRD-OLDEST MAJOR LEAGUE BALLPARK, BEHIND FENWAY PARK AND WRIGLEY FIELD.

LARGEST

THE YANKEES SET A TEAM RECORD FOR ATTENDANCE FOR AN OPENING DAY GAME WITH 56,717 ON APRIL 10, 1998.

FACTOIDS

- RON GUIDRY WAS A GOOD DRUMMER AND ONCE KEPT A TRAP SET AT YANKEE STADIUM. HE PLAYED IN A POSTGAME CONCERT WITH THE BEACH BOYS.

- BABE RUTH NEVER HOMERED INTO THE RIGHT-FIELD UPPER DECK. THE GRANDSTAND IN RIGHT FIELD ENDED AT THE FOUL POLE AND WAS NOT EXTENDED UNTIL 1937, THREE YEARS AFTER THE SULTAN OF SWAT WAS GONE FROM THE YANKEES.

- ADVERTISING SIGNS THROUGH DECADES HAVE REFLECTED CULTURE:
  "ASK THE MAN FOR BALLANTINE"
  "BRONX SAVINGS BANK, TREMONT AND PARK AVES"
  "BURMA-SHAVE"
  "AVOID 5 O'CLOCK SHADOW, GEM SINGLEDGE BLADES"
  "THE YANKEES USE LIFEBUOY"
  "HORTON'S ICE CREAM"
  "'CALL FOR PHILIP MORRIS'"
  "OFFICIAL TIME LONGINES"
  "STADIUM FAVORITE BALLANTINE ALE BEER"

- IN 1988, BEHIND A WALL THAT WAS CLOSED OFF FOR DECADES, A SCORECARD, A PROGRAM, AND WHAT WAS SUPPOSEDLY THE BASES FOR THE 1936 STADIUM, WERE UNEARTHED.

- BOB WILKINSON, YANKEE STADIUM SUPERINTENDENT, EXPLAINED THAT IN THE WINTER OF 1997, A NEW SEWER LINE WAS PUT IN AND DIGGING WENT DOWN THREE FEET. "WE CAME UPON FLAGSTONES," THE SUPER SAID. "THEY WERE THE FLAGSTONES FROM THE 1923 WALKWAY THAT HAD LED FANS FROM THE FIELD AT THE STADIUM OUT INTO THE STREET."

- OWNER'S BOX: A PERSONAL SUITE BELONGING TO OWNER GEORGE STEINBRENNER IS LOCATED BEHIND HOME PLATE ON THE SECOND DECK, ALONG WITH THE BROADCASTING BOOTHS OF THE YES NETWORK AND THE WCBS RADIO 880/YANKEES RADIO NETWORK, THE PRESS BOX, AND SOME OTHER LUXURY SUITES. THE OWNER (OR PEOPLE HE PERMITS) SITS IN THE BOX ALONG WITH GUESTS. FROM TIME TO TIME YANKEE GENERAL MANAGER BRIAN CASHMAN AND YOGI BERRA WATCH GAMES FROM THERE.

- MOVIES: THE BILLY CRYSTAL FILM 61* WAS ACTUALLY FILMED IN DETROIT'S TIGER STADIUM, NOT YANKEE STADIUM.

STADIUM NO-HITTERS PITCHED BY YANKEES

PITCHER	VS.	DATE
MONTE PEARSON	CLEVELAND	08-27-1938
ALLIE REYNOLDS	CLEVELAND	07-12-1951
ALLIE REYNOLDS	BOSTON	09-28-1951
DON LARSEN	BROOKLYN	10-08-1956**
DAVE RIGHETTI	BOSTON	07-04-1983
JIM ABBOTT	CLEVELAND	09-04-1993
DWIGHT GOODEN	SEATTLE	05-14-1996
DAVID WELLS	MINNESOTA	05-17-1998*
DAVID CONE	MONTREAL	07-18-1999*

*PERFECT GAME
**PERFECT GAME—WORLD SERIES

YANKEE BALLPARKS CHRONOLOGY

YEARS	NAME	SEATING
1903–1912	Hilltop Park	15,000
1913–1922	Polo Grounds II	38,000
1923–1973	Yankee Stadium	67,224
1974–1975	Shea Stadium	55,101
1976–2008	Yankee Stadium	57,746
2009–	New Yankee Stadium	51,800

BY THE NUMBERS AT YANKEE STADIUM

In 1929 the New York Yankees introduced identifying numbers sewn on the backs of player jerseys, the first time that uniform numbers were used on a full-time basis. The original ten Yankee uniform numbers were:

1	EARLE COMBS
2	MARK KOENIG
3	BABE RUTH
4	LOU GEHRIG
5	BOB MEUSEL
6	TONY LAZZERI
7	LEO DUROCHER
8	JOHNNY GRABOWSKI
9	BENNY BENGOUGH
10	BILL DICKEY

Beginning with Lou Gehrig's number 4 in 1939, the Yankees have retired 15 uniform numbers to honor 16 players and managers. Two single-digit numbers have yet to be retired: number 2 (worn by Derek Jeter) and number 6 (worn by Joe Torre). Torre had originally requested number 13 but it belonged to utility man Jim Leyritz. Jeter has said, "All I ever wanted to be was a Yankee. When I was a kid I was always hoping there'd be a jersey left for me to wear with a single digit."

RETIRED NUMBERS

1	BILLY MARTIN*
3	BABE RUTH
4	LOU GEHRIG
5	JOE DIMAGGIO
7	MICKEY MANTLE
8	YOGI BERRA
8	BILL DICKEY
9	ROGER MARIS
10	PHIL RIZZUTO
15	THURMAN MUNSON
16	WHITEY FORD
23	DON MATTINGLY
32	ELSTON HOWARD
37	CASEY STENGEL
42	JACKIE ROBINSON**
44	REGGIE JACKSON
49	RON GUIDRY

* (BOBBY RICHARDSON WAS GIVEN NUMBER 1 AFTER BILLY MARTIN WAS TRADED IN 1957, WHICH HE WORE FROM 1958 TO 1966. MARTIN'S NUMBER WAS RETIRED ON AUGUST 10, 1986.)
** (RETIRED BY MAJOR LEAGUE BASEBALL)

After Allie Reynolds pitched his second no-hitter for the Yankees in 1951, the Hotel Edison, where he along with some teammates lived, changed his room number from 2019 to 0002.

1

Joe DiMaggio, the only player to get at least one hit in All-Star Games at Yankee Stadium, the Polo Grounds, and Ebbets Field.

1.10(c)

The major league rule banning a sticky substance such as pine tar on a bat beyond 18 inches from the bottom. That rule led to the "pine tar affair," Yankees against Royals in 1983.

1 1/2

Uniform number worn by opera star Robert Merrill, the man who for many years sang the national anthem at Yankee Stadium.

2

Alex Rodriguez homered twice in the seventh inning at Yankee Stadium on September 5, 2007, against the Mariners, giving him 48 home runs for the season and 512 in his career. He became the first Yankee to homer twice in an inning since Cliff Johnson on June 30, 1977. Joe DiMaggio in 1936 and Joe Pepitone in 1962 also homered twice in an inning.

3

All three perfect games in Yankee Stadium history were seen by Joe Torre: Larsen's beauty as a 16-year-old fan, and the gems spun by David Wells and David Cone from the dugout as Yankee manager. Don Zimmer was Torre's bench coach for the last two, and he played in the first one as a member of the Brooklyn Dodgers in 1956. The Yankees have the most perfect games pitched by one club, all at Yankee Stadium.

Babe Ruth's uniform number, retired on June 13, 1948.

4

Lou Gehrig's number, retired on July 4, 1939, the first for an athlete in any sport. He is the only Yankee to have worn number 4.

5

On October 16th, 2003, Aaron Boone became only the fifth player—and the second Yankee—to end a postseason series with a walk-off home run. His solo shot in the bottom of the eleventh inning capped a 6–5, game seven victory over Boston, giving the Yankees their 39th American League pennant.

Mickey Mantle reached the gothic iron facade that hung from the old stadium's roof five times.

Joe DiMaggio's uniform number, retired in 1952.

6

Stadiums:
Hilltop Park, 1903–1912
Polo Grounds, 1913–1922
Yankee Stadium, 1923–1973
Shea Stadium, 1974–1975
Yankee Stadium, 1976–2008
New Yankee Stadium, 2009–

On June 6, 1934, Yankee outfielder Myril Hoag tied an American League record with six singles in six at-bats at the Stadium.

The number of Yankee starters—Bill Dickey, Joe DiMaggio, Joe Gordon, Red Rolfe, Red Ruffing, and George Selkirk—in the 1939 All-Star Game at Yankee Stadium.

Mickey Mantle's rookie uniform number, changed by equipment manager Pete Sheehy to number 7 after Mantle was recalled from the Yankees' class AAA affiliate Kansas City Blues.

Don Mattingly hit a grand slam off Boston's Bruce Hurst at Yankee Stadium on September 29, 1987, setting a major league record with six grand slams in a season.

Joe Torre's number.

7

Mickey Mantle's number, retired June 8, 1969. He wore it from 1951 on.

8

The only number to be retired twice by the same team is number 8 of the Yankees. It was retired in 1972 for Bill Dickey and Yogi Berra, both catchers. Berra took number 8 in 1948 after Dickey retired but before he was a coach.

Dwight Gooden's no-hitter on May 14, 1996, was the eighth in Stadium history.

9

Joe DiMaggio's rookie number.

Roger Maris's number, retired on July 13, 1985.

Most hits in an inning given up by Roger Clemens, on August 2, 2007.

10

The Yanks used a record 10 pinch hitters on September 6, 1954, in a doubleheader against the Boston Red Sox. They won the opener 6–5; the Bosox took the second game, 8–7.

Phil Rizzuto's number, retired on August 4, 1985.

Aaron Boone's walk-off homer against the Red Sox on October 16, 2003, was the 10th in Yankee postseason history.

In 2007 Alex Rodriguez became the first player in major league history with 10 straight seasons of at least 35 homers, 100 RBIs, and 100 runs scored.

11

On June 3, 2003, the Yankees named Derek Jeter their 11th captain.

12

Billy Martin's rookie uniform number.

13

Home plate was moved 13 feet forward in 1924, to eliminate the "bloody angle" between the right-field foul line and the bleachers.

14

Yogi Berra stayed away from Yankee Stadium for 14 years, unhappy with the treatment he had received from George Steinbrenner.

$15

Bob Sheppard's per-game earning in 1951 when he began working for the Yankees.

15

On July 18, 1999, David Cone pitched a perfect game against the Montreal Expos. It was the 15th regular-season perfect game.

Thurman Munson's number 15 jersey and catching gear remains in his locker as it was the day he was killed in a 1979 airplane crash. His uniform number, 15, is retired. On September 20, 1980, a plaque honoring his memory was placed in Monument Park.

16

Whitey Ford's number, retired in 1974. The slick southpaw wore number 19 in his rookie season. Returning from the army in 1953, he wore number 16 for the rest of his career.

Dallas Green became George Steinbrenner's 16th manager to be fired, on August 16, 1989.

18

Joe DiMaggio's original uniform number, given to him by equipment manager Pete Sheehy and later changed to 5 for historical significance reasons; Ruth wore number 3 and Gehrig 4.

19

Whitey Ford's rookie uniform number.

21

Paul O'Neill's number. Since O'Neill retired after the 2001 World Series, no Yankee has worn that number.

23

Don Mattingly's number, retired on August 31, 1997.

24

In 1927, 24 of Lou Gehrig's 47 home runs were hit at Yankee Stadium.

25

Gene Michael was the 25th Yankee manager in history, replacing Dick Howser, who quit.

Uniform number selected by Jason Giambi upon his signing with New York. The significance: the digits add up to 7, the number worn by Giambi's dad's idol, Mickey Mantle.

Mel Allen was a Yankee broadcaster for 25 seasons.

26

Thirty-seven World Series have been played at Yankee Stadium, with the Yankees winning 26.

28

Thurman Munson's rookie uniform number.

Of the 60 record-setting home runs hit by Babe Ruth in 1927, 28 of them were hit at Yankee Stadium.

29

Earle Combs and Roger Peckinpaugh shared the Yankee record for hitting in the most consecutive games, until Joe DiMaggio broke the major league record in 1941.

30

Lou Gehrig and Roger Maris are tied for the most single-season Yankee Stadium home runs: Gehrig hit 30 of 49 in 1934, and Maris hit 30 of 61 in 1961.

32

Elston Howard's number, retired on July 13, 1985.

Joe Girardi was introduced as the 32nd manager in the team's 103-year history.

35

Yogi Berra's rookie number.

37

Yankee Stadium has hosted 37 World Series.

Of the 37 players who performed for the 1949 Yankees, only Yogi Berra still played for them in 1960. Casey Stengel's number, retired in 1970.

40

Phil Rizzuto spent parts of 40 seasons as a Yankee broadcaster.

42

Mariano Rivera is the last Yankee player to wear number 42, which has been retired from Major League Baseball in honor of Jackie Robinson.

44

Reggie Jackson's number, retired in 1993.

46

Don Mattingly's rookie number.

49

Ron Guidry's number, retired in 2003.

50

On June 1, 1999, at Yankee Stadium, Derek Jeter had reached base in all 50 Yankee games that season.

56

Joe DiMaggio's 56-game hitting streak included 56 singles and runs scored. It covered 53 day games, 3 night games, 29 at Yankee Stadium, and 27 road games.

Dave Righetti's rookie number.

58

Mariano Rivera's original number.

63

The original number of Bernie Williams.

65

Most home wins in a season, 1961.

83

Of 158 home runs hit by the 1927 Yankees, 83 were hit at Yankee Stadium.

88

Number of pitches David Cone tossed in his perfect game on July 19, 1999 — 68 strikes and 20 balls.

89

On September 30, 2001, the Yankees and the Orioles play to a 1–1 tie in 15 innings, the 89th tie in Yankee franchise history. It is Cal Ripken's last game at Yankee Stadium.

97

Don Larsen used this number of pitches to hurl his perfect game against the Dodgers at Yankee Stadium in the 1956 World Series.

100

Babe Ruth on September 24, 1920, hit his 100th home run, off Washington's Jim Shaw.

120

In his perfect game pitched on May 17, 1998, David Wells threw 120 pitches.

126

The number of games that Cal Ripken played at Yankee Stadium—more than any other opposing player (June 18, 1982–September 30, 2001).

148

On May 12, 1959, Yogi Berra's errorless streak of 148 games ended when he made an error on his 34th birthday.

163

During the regular season, Mickey Mantle recorded 163 career home runs batting right-handed.

174

The number of pitches Doc Gooden threw in his no-hitter on May 14, 1996.

185

The number of working days it took for the original Yankee Stadium to be built.

266

Mickey Mantle hit 266 homers at Yankee Stadium from 1951 to 1968, most ever by a single player in the Stadium.

300

Roger Clemens became the 21st pitcher in major league history to win his 300th game, on June 13, 2003. He was the first Yankee to win it in front of the home fans.

373

During the regular season Mickey Mantle recorded 373 career home runs batting left-handed.

400

Mariano Rivera saved his 400th game on July 16, 2006.

413

Smallest home attendance for a game, on September 25, 1966.

500

The number of workers who built the original Yankee Stadium.

Alex Rodriguez hit his 500th home run on August 4, 2007.

536

On September 20, 1968, Mickey Mantle hit his 536th and final home run.

1,245

The "continuation" of the "pine tar game" between the Yankees and the Royals drew just 1,245 fans to witness what could have been just four outs of play. The "continuation" lasted 9 minutes and 41 seconds.

1927

The 1927 Yankees team won 57 games at the Stadium to tie an American League record. They batted .312 there as a team, paced by Ruth's .372. Of their team record 158 home runs, 83 were slugged at the Stadium.

2000

For the first time since 1903, two teams played two games in different stadiums on the same day, July 8, 2000. Game one was at Shea Stadium, and the second game was at Yankee Stadium.

2,385

The number of backless seats spread over 27 rows behind the right-field fence in the bleachers in the original Yankee Stadium.

3,654

The number of home runs Yankees hit at the original Yankee Stadium, 1923–1973.

$5,000

The reward promised to the one who caught the 61st home-run ball of Roger Maris.

$6,000

The amount Don Larsen received for being on Bob Hope's TV show after he pitched his perfect game in 1956.

15,000

The Yankees played their 15,000th regular-season game, defeating Tampa Bay on July 22, 1999. Their all-time record to that point in time was 8,451 won, 6,463 lost, plus 86 tie games.

20,000

Letters that Mickey Mantle never answered and that were not bid on in the original Yankee Stadium fire sale in 1974.

51,800

Seating capacity of the new Yankee Stadium, scheduled to open April 2009.

57,000

Number of people in attendance at Yankee Stadium in 1956 when Don Larsen pitched his perfect game.

83,533

The largest Yankee Stadium crowd, a doubleheader with the Red Sox, on May 30, 1938.

$451,541

The uniform Lou Gehrig wore during his farewell speech in 1939 sold for this amount in 1999.

1,007,066

First-season attendance at Yankee Stadium, 1923.

$2,500,000

Cost of building the original Yankee Stadium.

2,561,123

Shea Stadium attendance for the Yankees, 1974–1975.

4,090,440

Number of fans who attended Yankee games at the Stadium in 2005.

4,248,067

Number of fans who went through the Yankee Stadium turnstiles in 2006.

4,271,083

Number of fans who attended Yankee Stadium games in 2007, an all-time high for the franchise.

64,188,862

Yankee Stadium attendance, 1923–1973.

$1 BILLION

Between 2001 and 2007, the Yankees did not win a World Series, despite spending more than $1 billion on salaries.

$1 BILLION PLUS

The worth of the Yankees according to Forbes magazine.

$1.02 BILLION

Estimated cost of building new Yankee Stadium, slated to open in 2009.

ACKNOWLEDGMENTS

To my wife, Myrna Katz Frommer, who has been there throughout my long writing career in all its ups and downs, its twists of fate, its deals worth doing, its deals that never got done—sometimes as co-author, always as critic, confidant, and chum. Her fingerprints are all over this book, and *Remembering Yankee Stadium* is the better for it. I am, as always, in her debt.

To my son, Fred Frommer, an excellent political journalist and my co-author of several sports books, including *Red Sox vs Yankees: The Great Rivalry.* He was of invaluable assistance, from reading an evolving manuscript to checking facts and offering suggestions that invariably improved this work.

To the other Frommers: Jennifer, Ian, Jeff, Michele, Laura, Arielle, Gabriel, and Alexander, who just by being there make me want to—in the words of the late Al Lewis of Munsters fame—"outwork the horse."

To Paul Doherty, who brings to mind the line of a song from *The Sound of Music:* "Somewhere in my youth or childhood, I must have done something good." Only I don't know what I ever did to deserve Paul Doherty, New York Yankee fan extraordinaire and Yankee encyclopedia personified. He came to me as a guardian angel, looking over my shoulder and informing every page of this book from his own oral history to his exceptional fact-checking, proofreading, conduit to interviews, and repository of audio and visual gems.

To the team at Stewart, Tabori & Chang, particularly Leslie Stoker, whose support and faith in this project got it off the ground, and my young and talented editor Kristen Latta, a wise and steady counsel throughout. Thanks also to Galen Smith and Claire Greenspan.

To John Clifford and Herb Thornby of Think Studio, for the top-flight design job.

To Bill Drennan, copyeditor extraordinaire, you did it again.

To Al Zuckerman, the kind of agent I always dreamed of having and finally have, for believing in the project and getting the deal.

To Bob Sheppard, the touch of class for the Yankees through all the decades, who adds grace and elegance to this project with his introduction and oral history.

For providing truly unique, defining, and evocative images: Paul Doherty; Ron and Howard Mandelbaum of Photofest, New York; Yvette Reyes of AP Images for caring and much appreciated help with images; Marshall Fogel and Jimmy Catanzaro (jimmycatanzaro@yahoo.com), collectors of the highest rank and first-class gentlemen, who allowed the use of photos from their priceless and precious collections, and Dan Wulkan who put me in touch with them; Pat Kelly, photo archivist at the National Baseball Hall of Fame in Cooperstown, New York; Seth Swirsky, Dartmouth alum, sports fan, and collector whose magical website www.seth.com rendered up so many images that made their way into this work; Clay Luraschi of Topps; Paul Veneklasen for Stadium shots, 1967; Jay Schwall for demolition photos in 1973 and 1974.

At Dartmouth College: Susan Bibeau, Wole Ojurongbe, Mike Beahan, the Dartmouth Library, and its helpful and caring staff.

Nick and Patty Anis, Hardy and Joan Astley, and Bill Werber, the oldest living New York Yankee.

Top Yankee fan Mick Ciasco of BMW Manhattan, who keeps me on the go.

The readers of FrommerSportsNet (harveyfrommersports.com) for suggestions.

Search engine ProQuest, an invaluable tool that enabled me to be transported back through time.

Jeff Idelson, president of the National Baseball Hall of Fame, who helped me make contact with the Hall of Famers who grace these pages.

Sean Holtz, founder of the Baseball Almanac, www.baseball-almanac.com. "Where what happened yesterday is being preserved today."

Michael Aubrecht at www.pinstripepress.net.

Phil Speranza at www.BehindtheBombers.com.

Frank Russo at thedeadballera.com and www.findagrave.com.

Bradford H. Turnow at ultimateyankees.com.

Aron Wallad at www.baseballsprideandjoy.com.

Herb Rogoff at One More Inning.

All the voices who gave of their time and energy, insight and memories. They truly enhanced *Remembering Yankee Stadium.*

Finally, a debt is owed to all those talented scribes who wrote books, accounts, and articles about Yankee Stadium. They paved the way for this effort and are listed in the bibliography.

Every effort has been made to trace copyright holders. If any unintentional omissions have been made, Stewart, Tabori & Chang would be pleased to add appropriate acknowledgment in future editions.

© Associated Press: pages 6-7, 10-11, 21, 44, 50 (Gehrig), 53, 62, 65, 69, 72, 75 (line to see Ruth), 76-77, 83, 89, 92, 99, 100, 102, 103, 110, 114-15, 116, 126, 139, 143 (fans taking mementos), 147, 151, 153, 156-57, 158, 159, 161, 162, 163, 164, 167, 170 (fans in line), 171, 174-75, 178-79, 180, 182, 185, 187, 188, 189, 190 (Torre and Steinbrenner), 191, 192, 195, 196-97, 198, 200, 202, 203, 204, 205, 206, 207, 209, 210, 215, 216-17, 218, 219, 220, 222, 223, 224, 225

Courtesy of Michael Bolton: page 21

Courtesy of Chris Carter: page 21

Courtesy of Jimmy Catanzaro: pages 12-13, 22, 37, 46, 67, 90, 104, 106, 112, 120

© Corbis/Bettmann: pages 2-3, 15, 20, 29 (exterior), 47, 51, 57, 58, 64, 71, 80, 86, 97, 109, 117, 118, 130-31, 135, 136, 149, 150, 169, 212-13, 221

Courtesy of Paul Doherty: pages 22, 132 (blue and white stands), 145, 146

© Getty Images: page 186

Courtesy of Rich Marazzi: page 23

Courtesy of Marshall Fogel Collection: pages 26, 29 (top two, bottom left), 31 (left), 32, 38, 41, 75 (laying wreath), 119

Courtesy of Dan McCourt: page 24

Courtesy of the National Baseball Hall of Fame Library, Cooperstown, NY: pages 31 (right), 34 (1923 Yankees), 36, 39, 42, 50 (ticket), 52, 59, 60 (programs), 68, 82, 87, 88, 91, 108, 125, 127, 128, 152, 155, 170 (ticket and program), 190 (ticket), 199, 208

Courtesy of Tracy Nieporent: page 24

Courtesy of Chris Pavia: page 24

© Photofest: pages 4-5, 8-9, 28, 30, 48, 60 (arm patch), 61, 84, 95, 111, 121, 166, 168, 183

Courtesy of Seth Swirsky: pages 1, 25, 34 (baseballs), 40, 56, 93, 132 (baseball), 143 (chair)

© Topps: pages 134, 155

© Topps, courtesy of Fred Frommer: pages 96, 172

Courtesy of Brad Turnow: page 25

© Veneklasen Associates, courtesy of Paul Doherty and Jim Good: pages 18, 129, 132 (green stands)

Courtesy of Daniel Wulkan: page 45

INDEX

INDEX

INDEX

INDEX

ALSO BY HARVEY FROMMER

Five O'Clock Lightning
Old Time Baseball
Where Have All Our Red Sox Gone?
The Sports Junkie's Book of Trivia, Terms, and Lingo
Red Sox vs Yankees: The Great Rivalry (with Frederic J. Frommer)
A Yankee Century
Shoeless Joe and Ragtime Baseball
Rickey and Robinson: The Men Who Broke Baseball's Color Line
New York City Baseball: The Last Golden Age, 1947-1957

It Happened in the Catskills (with Myrna Katz Frommer)
It Happened in Brooklyn (with Myrna Katz Frommer)
It Happened on Broadway (with Myrna Katz Frommer)
It Happened in Manhattan (with Myrna Katz Frommer)
Growing Up Jewish in America (with Myrna Katz Frommer)

INDEX

1928

YANKEE STADIUM

World's Championship Games

Important
Read notice and warning on reverse side of this ticket.

GAME

1

DO NOT DETACH
this coupon from

RAIN CHECK

WORLD'S 1928 SERIES

NATIONAL LEAGUE

READ the notice printed on reverse side of attached coupon.

Jacob Ruppert
President

M.B. BROWN PTG & BDG CO., N.Y.

D SERIES

National League

YANKEE STADIUM

YORK YANKEES
Agent

SECTION

3

ROW

M

SEAT

16

UPPER STAND

RESERVED SEAT

ENTER AT GATE 6